TESI GREGORIANA

Serie Teologia

— 5 —

ISAAC KIZHAKKEPARAMPIL

The Invocation of the Holy Spirit as Constitutive of the Sacraments according to Cardinal Yves Congar

EDITRICE PONTIFICIA UNIVERSITÀ GREGORIANA
Roma 1995

Vidimus et approbamus ad normam Statutorum Universitatis

Romae, ex Pontificia Universitate Gregoriana
die 25 mensis maii anni 1995

R.P. Prof. PHILIP J. ROSATO, S.J.
R.P. Prof. CHARLES POTTIE, S.J.

ISBN 88-7652-692-7

GREGORIAN UNIVERSITY PRESS
Piazza della Pilotta, 35 – 00187 Rome, Italy

ACKNOWLEDGEMENT

No endeavor of this kind is purely an individual effort. It is with the recognition of those lasting bonds of friendship and faith and with a heart overflowing with thanksgiving that I should like to gratefully acknowledge those many people who have helped me in countless ways in the research and publishing of this dissertation. Realizing that I can not particularly acknowledge all those who have been of assistance and encouragement to me and also taking the risk of perhaps forgetting someone to whom I should formally express my gratitude, I would like to mention those individuals whose help has proven invaluable in the long arduous process of researching, compailing, editing and publishing this dissertation.

To begin with I bow my head before our God, who has called, anointed and sustained me to *con-celebrate* with his Spirit to build up his Mystical Body.

I thank Prof. Philip Rosato S.J., who accompanied my research with expert guidance, friendly support and above all with marvelous understanding and constant encouragement. May I place on record how much I was inspired by his own academic discipline and profound scholarship. My sincere gratitude is due to Prof. Charles Pottie S.J., other Professors and staff of the Pontifical Gregorian University.

I am deeply indebted to my Bishop Rt. Rev. Geevarghese Mar Timotheos who sent me to Rome and to my fellow priests of the diocese of Tiruvalla for their constant encouragement and support. To the Congregation for the Oriental churches I owe deep thanks for the scholarship which made possible my stay and studies in Rome. Instituto Maria Immacolata deserves thanks for giving me accommodation. My heart-felt thanks are also due to my friends and well wishers here in Rome and elsewhere.

Finally, I am indebted to my Parents, brothers and sisters, who were always ready to stay at my side in all my needs and were sincerely interested in the progress of my studies. Without the love and support of them, I would not have been able to bring this thesis to completion.

«I thank my God in all my remembrance of you» (Phi 1,3)

Catholic Bishop's House,   Isaac KIZHAKKEPARAMPIL
Thiruvalla, India, October 19, 1995

PRESENTATION

In 1981, soon after I published my doctoral thesis on the pneumatology of Karl Barth, I received a quite unexpected note from the late Yves Cardinal Congar who was then an insatiably productive Dominican friar residing at the Couvent Saint-Jacques in Paris. He had seen an announcement that my work had appeared in print, and asked me to send him a copy of it for his perusal. On the one hand, I was not unduly surprised by his keen interest in any book which treated the theology of the Holy Spirit, since his unabated intellectual curiosity regarding this theme was indeed well known to all who are familiar with his writings. On the other hand, I was intrigued that he, the renown Catholic advocate of a balanced christological and pneumatological explication of Christian revelation, deemed it important, by means of his modest and sincere request, indirectly to encourage a fledgling theology professor at the Jesuit University of St. Joseph in Philadelphia to further his initial research, and to regard it as most valuable in itself and timely for the Church.

Now fourteen years later, I have the distinctive honor of presenting the published version of the doctoral thesis of my student, Fr. Isaac Kizhakkeparampil, a presbyter of the diocese of Tiruvalla in Kerala, India, on a particular aspect of the pneumatology of Yves Congar, that is, his claim that the solemn invocation of the Holy Spirit is as constitutive of the sacraments of the Church as is the formal recitation of the words of Jesus Christ. I write these remarks with the same intention with which Congar wrote to me years ago, for I too, besides publicly appreciating a fine piece of scholarship by a student at the Pontifical Gregorian University in Rome, would like to inspire him to continue his research in this field in the years ahead. I do so fully aware that, if Congar had not died before this publication appeared, a letter from him most likely would have arrived soon on the desk of Fr. Isaac both as a tribute to his achievement and as an incentive to his further reflection on the topic. Thus, my own experience has taught me that what I say here would be heartily endorsed by the late Dominican theologian.

This publication synthesizes in an admirable way the careful study which its author undertook of the various works of Congar which explicitly treat the theological importance of the sacramental epiclesis. Moreover, while the central part of the text exposes and analyzes the thought of Congar in this regard in a detailed and systematic manner, its opening part provides an illuminating background which depicts the gradual development of Catholic pneumatology in this century, and its closing part offers a well founded and carefully crafted evaluation of the findings. Thus, far from consisting solely of an accurate description of the content of Congar's thought on the epiclesis of the Holy Spirit as it is articulated by the Church especially during the sacramental celebrations of Baptism, Confirmation, Eucharist and Orders, this work situates the topic in its historical context, and foresees some concrete means by which it can be clarified and highlighted further. The author's ardor for scholarship, search for keen perception and sound critique, and desire to forge on enthusiastically are therefore reflected in each of the major parts of this study.

Yet another factor which would surely have gratified Yves Congar is that the author of this study belongs to the Syro-Malankara rite of the Church, and thus is particularly capable, by spiritual tradition and personal disposition, of carrying on the ecumenical dialogue with the Orthodox community in his native land and throughout the world. The appearance of this study would have been for Yves Congar, as it is for all of us who know Fr. Isaac, a harbinger of the theological maturity of the Catholic Church in the Indian sub-continent. That this study, being the sign of hope that it is, is so well conceived, researched and written is a patent tribute to the talent and zeal of Fr. Isaac. It is my sincere hope that the publication of this research project in the series «Tesi Gregoriana» might spur its author on to teach well, to deepen through subsequent reflection and to formulate in print the insights which he has grasped so thoroughly during the culminating period of his theological formation in Rome.

Pontifical Gregorian University   Philip J. ROSATO, S.J.
Rome, October 19, 1995

GENERAL INTRODUCTION

This study comprises a systematic investigation of the recently rediscovered epicletic dimension of the sacraments of the Church, as it is explicated in the writings of Cardinal Yves Congar who has been a renown spokesman of this development in the Western Catholic tradition. In the beginning of the present century, the theology of the Latin Church did not explicitly connect the treatise on the Holy Spirit with that on the sacraments. This does not mean that the Latin Church denied the pneumatological aspect of sacramental theology; instead, the emphasis in this field of theology was predominantly christological. This one-sided approach failed to do justice to the early Christian tradition which rested on a trinitarian understanding of the efficacy of the sacraments. In fact, objections were raised by Orthodox theologians who claimed that their Catholic counterparts seemed to annex some reflections on the activity of the Holy Spirit in the sacraments to a matrix already determined by christological ones alone. To explain and counter such objections, even before the Second Vatican Council, Congar urged Western theologians to re-evaluate the indispensable role played by the Holy Spirit in the liturgy of the Church, and thus to grant pneumatology its proper place in sacramental theology.

As early as 1937, Congar advocated the introduction of pneumatological considerations into sacramental theology, although he was to develop a systematic presentation of them only many years later. In all his subsequent books, articles and interviews, he sought both to be faithful to the Christian sources regarding the work of the Holy Spirit in the sacraments, and to be attentive to the thought-pattern and experience of twentieth-century believers. Drawing inspiration from the Fathers of the Church, he affirmed that in the sacraments, which actualize the existential salvation of the faithful, there are involved not only the mission of the Son but also that of the Holy Spirit. Therefore, in sacramental celebrations one should recognize the co-ordination between the *anamnesis* and the *epiclesis*, their constitutive aspects. Since Congar considered the sacraments as the mystical and historical prolongations not only of the incarnation and of the paschal mystery of Christ but also of the outpouring of the Holy Spirit on Pentecost, he stressed the inherent connection between the solemn invocation of the divine *Pneuma* and the formal memorial of the words and actions of the divine *Logos*. This study offers a detailed investigation on how Congar understands the invocation of the Holy Spirit to effect the sacraments of the Church. What led Congar to do this, how he argued his point, and what he achieved in the process are the questions which this study sets out to answer.

In order to maintain a precise focus, this study concentrates on the thought of Congar regarding the epicletic dimensions of four of the sacraments of the Church: Baptism, Confirmation, Eucharist and Order. Without entering into a detailed inquiry either the christology or the ecclesiology of Congar, it offers an accurate exposition only of those works which relate to these specific rites. Recourse is had to his other writings only insofar as they offer a more adequate understanding of the topic. Thus, his reflections on the relationship of the Holy Spirit to all the sacraments receive some consideration. The novelty of the theme of this study consists in its examination of the intrinsic function of the invocation of the Holy Spirit in the sacraments, since there has been until now no extensive elaboration of Congar's thought on this subject. In view of the monographic nature of this study and its principal goal of comprehending the insights of Congar concerning the invocation of the Holy Spirit as a constitutive aspect of the sacraments, a select writings of him is being examined.

The study is arranged in such a way as to present the four major chapters of Part II, which expose the theological insights of Congar on the topic, in between one preparatory chapter [Part I] and one concluding chapter [Part III]. The first chapter treats the problematic in an historical way by tracing the gradual progress of Congar in formulating a christic-pneumatic approach to sacramental theology; here his search for balance between christocentrism and pneumatocentrism is viewed as a response to such phenomena as the revitalization of Thomism, the return to biblical, patristic and liturgical sources and the emergence of ecumenical dialogue with other Churches, especially with the Orthodox. The four chapters of Part II provide an objective exposition of the manner in which Congar perceives the constitutive role of the Holy Spirit in effecting the sacraments. Finally, the concluding chapter puts forward a critical appraisal of the achievement of Congar regarding an appreciation of the invocation of the Holy Spirit at sacramental celebrations. Then a few aspects of his thoughts that call for further clarifications are indicated. The thesis closes by proposing some prognostic reflections concerning how certain limitations of his argumentation might be rectified in the future, and thus might reinforce the indisputable value of his contribution to renewed understanding of the sacramental epiclesis.

The actuality of the present study rests in the widely recognized need of Catholic theology to balance its predominant christological conception of the sacraments with a more fully developed pneumatological one. The contribution to attaining such balance offered by this study consists in investigating precisely how pneumatology was integrated by Congar into his sacramental theology. Besides elucidating his anamnetic and epicletic understanding of the sacraments, a blue-print is sketched which could serve as a basis for further contemporary research regarding the invocation of the Holy Spirit as constitutive of the saving signs of the Church.

The theme of this study has to include in a decidedly trinitarian perception of sacramental efficacy. The question of the constitutive epicletic dimension of the sacraments is first and foremost a corrective of the binitarian nature of many treatments of Catholic doctrine on the sacraments. The entire panorama of Christian revelation cannot in any way be limited to the sole truth that the Father has sent his only Son, Jesus, and that he in turn has instituted many effective signs of salvation. For it leaves out the complementary truth that the signs of Jesus are re-actualized and interiorized in each age through the activity of the Holy Spirit. Although the Father-Creator is the origin of the sacraments and the Son-Redeemer gave them their substance, it is the Spirit-Sanctifier who grants them their efficacy. During the messianic time, the Holy Spirit acts in and through the various sacraments of the community, so as to lead it forward to the Son who is to come again and to the heavenly Father. Therefore, the invocation of the divine *Pneuma* in the sacraments not only guarantees the validity of the original movement «Father - Son - Spirit» towards the believing community, but also spearheads the eschatological movement «Spirit – Son – Father» so that it can contribute in a mysterious way to the glory of the Trinity at the end-time.

Furthermore, since this study fosters a retrieval of the charismatic nature of the Christian community which stresses that both the ordained and the baptized form the Church as the living Temple of the Holy Spirit, it helps to overcome the distorted view that the sacraments of the Church are enacted only by the ordained ministers acting *in persona Christi*. Such an hierarchical conception of the sacraments of the Church fails to admit that the ordained also act *in persona ecclesiae*, so that the gifts and charisms of the Spirit which are given to the baptized are included. Consequently, this study views the Church as a communion of persons who enjoy differing gifts and charisms of the Spirit, so that their unity might be strong in itself and credible to others. Congar understood the hierarchical ministry as a special gift intended to stimulate the ordained to concelebrate with the Spirit at the sacraments, so that the communion of the baptized be built up. This study urges that a charismatic understanding of the Church leads to further reflection on the integrated functions exercised by the common and ministerial forms of priesthood in enacting the sacraments.

Finally, the timeliness of this study arises from its ecumenical implications. Catholics research on the constitutive dimension of the invocation of the Holy Spirit in the sacramental rites will at least help to bridge the gap created between the Churches of East and West. The attempt to arrive at a proper and adequate understanding of the conjunction between the anamnesis and the epiclesis as the constitutive elements of the sacraments can further Christian ecumenism, and lead the Churches towards the desired reunion based on common theology and mutual reception of the sacraments without any conditions. This study is also related to the problem concerning the proper adaptation of sacramental theology and practice to the contemporary situation of Christians living in quite different cultures. It proposes that presenting and emphasizing the epicletic understanding of the sacraments might help the Christian communities existing in lands in which the majority of the population is non-Christian to enter into dialogues and to take note of the presence of the Holy Spirit within other religions. The Spirit certainly comes from and leads to the Father through the Son, but he never stops to use also the anthropological and sociological factors of world religions and their rituals to manifest in some measure this trinitarian mystery.

PART ONE

THE GENESIS OF THE EPICLETIC DIMENSION OF THE SACRAMENTAL THEOLOGY OF CARDINAL YVES CONGAR

CHAPTER ONE

From a Nascent to a Developed Understanding
of the Church and the Sacraments as Epicletic

In recent times, Western Christianity has attained a remarkably vivid awareness that the nature of the Church and the sacraments is epicletic. The opening part of this study employs the historical method, in order to situate in its proper context the thought of Congar concerning the invocation of the Holy Spirit as constitutive of the sacraments of the Church. This introductory part, therefore, accumulates and examines diverse historical data in a rather concise fashion. This procedure obviously necessitates a certain selectivity, since its aim is simply to prepare the reader to comprehend the nucleus of the thesis to be presented in the expository chapters of the second part. Here concentration is placed on three factors which influenced Congar's thought: historical, ecumenical and conciliar. These considerations led him to the insight that the Church and the sacraments are epicletic, since they depend on the activity of the Holy Spirit in the baptized and ordained members of the Church. In this introductory part it suffices to delineate the historico-theological horizon against which Congar's writings on the invocation of the Holy Spirit as constitutive of the sacraments of the Church can be properly understood.

Congar came to this awareness very early in his theological studies. He stressed the indispensable role of the Holy Spirit in the divine economy of salvation, especially as it relates to the symbolic activities of the Church of Jesus Christ. Already in 1940's, Congar's writings advocated the introduction of both christic and pneumatic considerations into ecclesiology and sacramental theology, although he was to develop a systematic treatment of the Holy Spirit only many years later. By granting a proper place to pneumatology as well as to christology he began to perceive that the Church is a living organism instituted by Christ and animated by the Spirit. Scriptural, liturgical and patristic studies led him to understand that the cultic actions of the Church are carried out not only by the ordained ministers but also by the baptized, since both the common and the ministerial forms of Christian priesthood are the *loci* of the presence of the Holy Spirit and of his divine power. Thus, all members of the Church have a part to fulfill in invoking the Holy Spirit, so that the liturgical symbols become efficacious for the salvation of the world. Therefore, the first sub-section of this chapter concerns the theological developments which aided Congar to formulate this position.

Apart from the biblical, liturgical and patristic studies another factor which induced Congar to restate the epicletic aspect of ecclesiology and of sacramental theology was his participation in the theological conferences conducted by the Russian Orthodox emigrants living in Paris. From this contact he began to understand that in the divine economy of salvation the work of Christ can never be separated from that of the Holy Spirit. Both divine Persons exist in union with the Father, and both render the Church and the sacraments channels of sanctifying grace for humanity. The influence of Eastern theology can be noted in Congar already in 1928, when he chose *L'unité de l'Église* as the topic of his doctoral thesis. Then in 1937, his first book, *Chrétiens désunis*, intended to bring to light the unity that should exist among Christians who have been called by God on the basis not only of the sending of the Word at the Incarnation but also of the sending of the Holy Spirit at Pentecost. Although Congar appreciated the invaluable insights of Eastern theology, he was also able to state frankly his critical observations concerning some of its dimensions. Yet, his efforts to contribute to a more balanced christic-pneumatic understanding of the Church and the sacraments can without doubt be viewed as the fruit of the serious dialogue he undertook with theologians of the Eastern Churches. This is the theme of the second sub-section of this chapter.

Furthermore, it is no secret that Congar played a considerable role not only at the sessions of Vatican II, but also in its preparatory phase. His influence was exerted chiefly in five of the Council's theological commissions in which he acted as drafter and editor of various documents on the basis of his recognized scholarly competence. By adopting a position which was thoroughly trinitarian Congar urged that the Church be presented as the continuation of the missions of the Son and of the Holy Spirit. As is explicitly put forward in *Ad Gentes*, the *Decree on the Church's Missionary Activity*, the fact that the Church is the continuation of two divine salvific missions means that the Christ-event alone cannot explain the *ecclesia* fully. The members of the community that Jesus founded during his public life did not fully understand what he had said and done, until it became clear to them through the Spirit-event, the outpouring of divine love and power upon them at Pentecost. In fact, the passion, death and resurrection of Jesus were accompanied by the Holy Spirit, and were the conditions of possibility for this outpouring. Therefore, the work of the Holy Spirit cannot be separated from that of the incarnate Son, for the divine *Pneuma* has a mission which both penetrates and fulfills the mission of the divine *Logos*. For Congar, the Spirit acts in the Church and in the sacraments so that the christological moment of salvation is made accessible and efficative through his epicletic power. The third and final sub-section of this chapter therefore provides a succinct survey of Congar's attempt at the Council to reaffirm the Church as the privileged continuation of the divine salvific missions of the Son and of the Spirit.

1. The Historical Research of Congar: Rediscovery of the Spirit as the Animator of the Cultic Actions of the Baptized and Ordained Members of the Church

Since other published studies of a particular dimension of the theology of Congar have already examined the historico-intellectual influences which constitute the panorama necessary to appreciate his contribution properly[1], this study of his epicletic understanding of the sacraments should not repeat what has been analyzed elsewhere, but should center precisely on what led Congar to pursue its development. How did he pass from a conception of the sacraments which was christological, and thus tended to be anamnetic and juridical, to one which was pneumatological, and thus epicletic and charismatic? In order to answer this question, this sub-section proposes the thesis that his return to the scriptural, patristic and liturgical sources by which to articulate a modern theology of the laity induced him to envision an approach to the sacraments of Baptism and Confirmation that was decidedly different from that normally presented in Neo-thomistic manuals.

---

[1] Cf. J.P. JOSSUA, *Yves Congar.* Theology in the Service of God's People, Chicago 1968, 13-86; see also C. MCDONALD, *Church and World in the Plan of God.* Aspects of History and Eschatology in the Thought of Père Congar O. P., Bern 1982, 7-21; T.I. MCDONALD, *The Ecclesiology of Yves Congar.* Foundational Themes, Milwaukee 1984, 27-40; A. NICHOLAS, *Yves Congar,* London 1989, 1-12; J. AREEPLACKAL, *Spirit and Ministries.* Perspectives of East and West, Bangalore 1990, 55-70.

Because the baptized and confirmed receive the Holy Spirit in order to express their participation in the common priesthood of the Church by using their own charisms, Congar realized that these sacraments could best be expounded in pneumatological terms on the basis of the unction with which the divine *Pneuma* is entailed. This could also be understood in epicletic terms on the basis of the invocation pronounced on the catechumens, and in charismatic terms on the basis of the personal Christian vocation which all members of the Church are to assume. Furthermore, Congar was then able to view Ordination to ecclesial ministry, which is meant to serve the common priesthood of the baptized and the confirmed, in similar pneumatological, epicletic and charismatic terms. In the pages that follow, this emergence of a point of view complementary to the christological, anamnetic and juridical one which was dominant at the time of his theological formation is explained in relation to how Congar conceived the co-ordination of the two forms of Christian priesthood in the cultic acts of the Church.

While many theologians[2] focused on the christological, anamnetic and juridical aspects of the sacraments, it happened that the notion of charism played a minor role in Catholic dogmatics regarding the signs of salvation. The concept reappeared in Catholic ecclesiology and pastoral theology with the two encyclicals of Pius XII: *Mystici Corporis* (1943) and *Mediator Dei* (1947)[3]. Congar notes that the entire Church enjoys the gifts of the Spirit, and therefore it is not merely a juridical entity, an organized society administered by divinely appointed leaders, but also a people of God building itself up through multiple self-communications of the Holy Spirit[4]. Congar came to understand the Church as established structurally by Jesus Christ and as animated continually by the Holy Spirit since the anointing of Jesus Christ became its anointing at Pentecost. Yet,

---

[2] Cf. J. H. CREHAN, «The Theology of Eucharistic Consecration: "Role of the Priest in Celtic Liturgy"», *TS* 40 (1979) 334-343; see also W.P. ROBERTS, *Encouters with Christ.* Introduction to the Sacraments, New York 1985; K.B. OSBORNE, *Sacramental Theology.* A General Introduction, New York 1988.

[3] Cf. Y. CONGAR, *Jalons pour une théologie du laïcat*, Paris 1953, 57-58, 243; Eng. trans. D. Attwater, *Lay People in the Church*, London 1964, 37, 187. This was the first time the Catholic Church spoke officially about the importance of charism with an ecclesiological bearing. Cf. Y. CONGAR, *Théologie du laïcat* 289-290 (*Lay People in the Church*, 219); see also «L'*ecclesia* ou communauté chrétienne, sujet intégral de l'action liturgique», in *La liturgie après Vatican II*: Bilans, Études 66, eds. J.P. JOSSUA –Y. CONGAR, Paris 1966, 268-272.

[4] Cf. Y. CONGAR, *Esquisses du mystère de l'Église*, Paris 1941, 164-165; Eng. trans. A.V. Littledale, *The Mystery of the Church*, Baltimore 1965, 133; see also *Théologie du laïcat* 361-362 (*Lay People in the Church*, 266).

charisms were not given solely to help the Church at its beginning. They are constantly given by the Spirit for the good of all the dimensions of the existence of the Body of Christ, such as its preaching, celebration of sacraments and pastoral service. Through the interminable distribution of various gifts, the Holy Spirit promotes different vocations or ministries in the Christian community: «In the Church each member, each cell of this body is living; [...] all the members do not have the same function in the Body, and so its one single soul, the Spirit of Christ, does not animate all the members for the same purpose and in the same way»[5]. In this passage, Congar states that particular tasks are given to Christians as mandates by which to build up the Church. The power of the Holy Spirit enables these charisms to function in unison, while he respects and guarantees their differences. The sharp distinctions that existed between the institutional and the charismatic dimensions of the Church have to be overcome so as to ensure its unity of life and mission.

When Congar first began writing about the Church, he was influenced chiefly by neo–Thomist authors: Cardinal Charles Journet of Fribourg and his own French Dominican predecessor, Ambrose Gardeil. In their analyses, carried out with the aid of Aristotelian terms, they considered the efficient causality at work in the Church to be solely the act by which Christ forms the community of the faithful through the apostolic hierarchy. According to this analysis, Christ makes the hierarchy, and the hierarchy makes the Church. Although Congar found elements of truth in the thesis they had put forward, he was not convinced that it captured the whole truth[6]. Their concept of the Church did not contain a word about its mystical aspect. They were concerned only with its organization as a society guided by the exercise of hierarchical power. Unfortunately, their thesis left out the Holy Spirit who continually grants charisms, that is, gratuitous gifts, to all members of the community for its proper up-building. This forgetfulness of the indispensable role of the baptized in the Church was one of the causes of clericalism and triumphalism. These negative traits of the Church led to the misconception that the faithful were simply to be submissive to the hierarchy. In the words of Congar: «The community is useful for the affirmation of the Christian function of the Catholic Church, but it is not at all necessary for the existence of that

---

[5] Y. CONGAR, *Si vous êtes mes témoins*. Trois conférences sur laïcat, Église et monde, Paris 1959, 102; Eng. trans. D. Attwater, *Laity, Church and World*, Baltimore 1960, 70; see also *Théologie du laïcat*, 413-414 (*Lay People in the Church*, 297-298).

[6] Cf. Y. CONGAR, «My Path-findings in the Theology of the Laity and Ministries», *TJ* 2 (1972) 175.

Once the mystery of the Church is described in all its dimensions, Congar considers the common priesthood as the essential component within the whole ecclesiological reality. To him, therefore, the theology of the common priesthood is the matrix of a valid ecclesiology. At a time when the faithful were defined as those «who are not clerics or who kneel before the altar or who sit below the pulpit»[15], Congar affirmed that each ecclesial community is constantly being formed by the gifts of the Spirit, so that all the members can exercise their particular priestly status[16]. In order to define the priestly nature of the faithful, Congar first reflects on the priesthood of Christ. By studying the appropriate texts of the Bible and of the apostolic Fathers, he can aver that the uniqueness of Christ's priesthood is shared in, to some extent, by all Christians: «There is only one Christ, there are many Christians. It is precisely God's purpose that many should have part in Christ and that, being persons, they should freely and really co-operate in such participation»[17]. Accordingly, Congar maintains that, since there is only one high priest in heaven for evermore, all the faithful enjoy a real priestly status by being incorporated into Christ by the sacraments of Baptism and Confirmation. Through these rites, the Holy Spirit makes them sharers in Christ's threefold office: a prophetic, priestly and pastoral authority. Congar further states that, since Christ was not born into a priestly class, he became a priest only through being anointed by the Holy Spirit. Therefore, the priesthood of Christ is extended by the Holy Spirit to all those who participate in his words and actions through the confession of faith and the reception of the sacraments[18].

Congar argues that priestly status of the faithful can be defined in terms of mediation, consecration or sacrifice. It is to the latter, however, that Congar grants greater importance, while not disallowing the element

---

[15] Y. CONGAR, *Théologie du laïcat*, 7 (*Lay People in the Church*, xi).

[16] Cf. Y. CONGAR, *Sacerdoce et laïcat devant leurs tâches d'évangélisation et de civilisation*, Paris 1962, 318-319; Eng. trans. A. Hepburne-Scott, *Priest and Layman*, London 1967, 289.

[17] Y. CONGAR, *Théologie du laïcat*, 165 (*Lay People in the Church*, 129); see also «Le diaconat dans la théologie des ministères», 130-131. It is a fact that the New Testament never applies the words *hiereus* or *archiereus* to priests of the hierarchy. It uses them only to denote either Christ or all Christians. Congar's historical study shows that until the end of the second century one cannot find any explicit testimony to the existence of another source of priesthood besides Baptism, namely, Ordination of higher ministers by an episcopal laying-on of hands. Cf. Y. CONGAR, *Théologie du laïcat*, 190 (*Lay People in the Church*, 147).

[18] Cf. Y. CONGAR, *Théologie du laïcat*, 174-175, 195-196 (*Lay People in the Church*, 133, 150-151).

of truth in the other two: «In our opinion, faithfulness to Holy Scripture and sound theology requires that priesthood be defined as the quality which enables a human being to come before God to gain his grace, and therefore fellowship with him, by offering up a sacrifice»[19]. The sacrificial function of the faithful consists in offering to God, through Christ and in the Spirit, a twofold cultus, interior and exterior. Their existential worship comprises acts of faith, hope, charity, and of all those virtues which bind them to God as his friends; acts of devotion and prayer; and furthermore, moral acts of conscience inasmuch as they render them holy in God's presence. The cultic worship of the faithful encompasses their participation in the liturgical life of the Church which has the Eucharist at its center[20]. Thus, Congar notes that, since the Holy Spirit enables the members of the common priesthood to offer true worship with Christ to the Father, the epicletic nature of the Church is rooted in Baptism and Confirmation.

Yet, in order to insert the special role of the apostolic college within the pneumatic understanding of worship, Congar states that the Holy Spirit was given to the Twelve at the foundation of the Church, so that they could be the seeds of the new people of God[21]. The Spirit works through the Apostles not only in the preaching of the Word of God but also in the enactment of the sacraments. Although Jesus Christ instituted the latter through the *acta et passa* of his public life, they become fully effective only when the Holy Spirit is sent to the Church. Therefore, Congar states that the invocation of the Holy Spirit is an inherent aspect of effecting the sacraments. The Spirit enables the sacramental actions of the ordained on behalf of the baptized to be efficacious. In and through the sacraments, the Holy Spirit unites the faithful to the passion, death and resurrection of Jesus Christ (cf. 1 Cor 11, 26)[22]. The unction with the Holy Spirit that ministerial priests receive at the rite of Ordination is not a privilege but a mandate to build up the messianic community into a ever more perfect spiritual reality. The difference between the common and the ministerial forms of Christian priesthood is that the ordained have the authority to act as ecclesial persons in imparting grace through word,

---

[19] Y. CONGAR, *Théologie du laïcat*, 200 (*Lay People in the Church*, 154-155).

[20] Cf. Y. CONGAR, *Théologie du laïcat*, 176-178 (*Lay People in the Church*, 135-137).

[21] Cf. Y. CONGAR, *Les voies du Dieu vivant*. Théologie et vie spirituelle, Paris 1962, 174; Eng. trans. A. Manson – L.C. Sheppard, *The Revelation of God*, New York 1968, 157; see also «Le diaconat dans la théologie des ministères», 130.

[22] Cf. Y. CONGAR, *Théologie du laïcat*, 100 (*Lay People in the Church*, 71); see also *Mystère de l'Église*, 158 (*Mystery of the Church*, 128).

ritual and service. By seeing the pneumatological basis of the prophetic, sanctifying and pastoral office of the ordained in and for the baptized community, Congar tries to restate the understanding of the sacred minister in the early Church: the ordained act not only *in persona Christi* but also *in persona ecclesiae*[23].

According to Congar, the representative role of those ordained to the ministerial priesthood can be said to reach its fullest expression in the Church's liturgico-sacramental celebrations, at which they facilitate a meeting between the community and its head, Jesus Christ. At the worship of the Church, the Holy Spirit enables words and actions of the ordained to effect the greater unity of the Mystical Body. Congar bases this insight on the premise that the ordained act as the representatives both of Christ and of the Church: «Jesus no longer offers his sacrifice on earth except by means not only of the priesthood, but also of the Church's offering: by adding the memorial of his death, in the celebration of which the priest acts as sacramental minister of Christ, to the Church's rite of worship in which the priest acts as minister of the Church»[24]. By emphasizing the pneumatological aspect of the ministerial priesthood, Congar could affirm first and foremost that the baptized and the ordained mutually condition each other. In the early Church the existence of the ordained ministers would have been inconceivable apart from their fundamental relation to a community. Therefore the election of candidates for apostolic ministry was an organic part of the process which led to their ordination, and was regulated by a profound sense of *koinonia*, that is, in a *collegial* manner[25]. Congar asserts that, although the rite of ordination established a permanent bond between the community and those ordained, since they were to serve the believers to whom they had been sent, the relation itself began on the day they adopted this diaconal way of life[26]. Accordingly, ecclesial ministers were understood as possessing pneumatic gifts not for themselves, but for the community they were to build up. Thus, Congar insists that medieval phrases, such as *Sacerdos alter Christus*, are to be understood as describing the spiritual

---

[23] Cf. Y. CONGAR, «Structure du sacerdoce chrétien», *LMD* 27 (1951) 75-76.

[24] Y. CONGAR, *Théologie du laïcat*, 286 (*Lay People in the Church*, 217); see also «L'*ecclesia* ou communauté chrétienne, sujet intégral de l'action liturgique», 263.

[25] Congar even finds instances where the community presented the bishop one of its candidates to be ordained a priest or a bishop without previously consulting him and, in some cases against his own wishes. Cf. Y. CONGAR, «My Path-findings in the Theology of Laity and Ministries», 179.

[26] Cf. Y. CONGAR, *Théologie du laïcat*, 191 (*Lay People in the Church*, 148).

and functional aspects of ministry, but not its ontological and juridical status.

When in the *Dogmatic Constitution on the Church*, the bishops at Vatican II placed the chapter on the People of God before that of the hierarchy, and in the *Decree on the Church's Missionary Activity* stated that the whole Church is missionary, for each Christian has a mandate to build up the Church, Congar's reflections on the Spirit as the animator of the cultic actions of the baptized and ordained members of the Church became recognized authoritatively. At the core of these reflections was his understanding of the dignity of the baptized and of the confirmed on the one hand, and of the ordained on the other. This dignity has nothing to do with organizational power in the secular sense of the term, but with the empowerment for preaching, worshipping and service, so as to build up the Church and the Kingdom of God in the world. This empowerment results from an invocation of the Holy Spirit on all Christians at their Baptism and Confirmation, and on some of them at their Ordination to ecclesial ministry. The unifying and missionary power of the Holy Spirit is called down in and through these sacraments so that various charisms be affirmed and strengthened for the good of the whole life of the Church and for its mission in society.

Thus, by means of complementing previous emphasis on the christological, anamnetic and juridical aspects of the sacraments with those that are explicitly pneumatological, epicletic and charismatic, Congar was able to apply to one branch of theology the many rediscovered insights drawn from the return to the sources of the Christian tradition. Another major influence on these insights of Congar, apart from his acquaintance with biblical, patristic and liturgical sources, was his interest in ecumenical contacts, especially with the Orthodox Churches of the East. Therefore, the following sub-section is devoted to this theme.

2. The Ecumenical Openness of Congar: Comprehension of the Orthodox Insistence on the Pneumatic Nature of the Church and the Sacraments

The rediscovery of biblical, patristic and liturgical sources was enriched mainly by the *ecumenical movement*, which began in the early decades of this century. Congar was exposed to Orthodox thinking through his contact with the Russian emigrants in Paris. His close personal association with them and the conversations that he held with them made him aware of the pronounced role that the Eastern Churches attribute to the Holy Spirit in their understanding of the Church and of the sacraments. Without any hesitation he strongly acknowledged that, rather than depreciating the worth of his own tradition, these encounters greatly enriched his own perception not only about the Church of the East but also of the Church of the West.

> The discovery of another spiritual world does not uproot us from our own, but changes the way we look at many things. For myself, I remain a Latin Catholic, a fact I do not hide from myself or from others, but ecumenism has freed me from a certain narrowness of outlook, characteristics of the Latin and of the Mediterranean man, by bringing me into touch with Eastern Christians, [...][27].

Thus, due to repeated encounters with Orthodox theologians even before Vatican II, Congar was able to propose a christic-pneumatic renewal of Catholic ecclesiology and sacramental theology.

Yet, as one of the current spokesmen of the Orthodox Church, Alexander Schmemann, has remarked, in spite of the dialogue with the West that began half a century before, it is still difficult for Catholic theologians to understand the viewpoint of the Churches of the East. To him, this difficulty can be traced to the lack of perception in the West with regard to the Eastern *world-view*[28]. Western Christian theology, almost from its very beginning, was marked by an intellectual and academic stance closely resembling that taken by science. But in general, one would have to say that the Orthodox Churches have not adopted a scientific approach to theology. Since their thinking resembles art rather than science, it justly could be qualified as anti-academic[29]. While the transcendence of God and the creation of the world out of nothing are central themes in Western theology, the Orthodox emphasize the immanence of God in the world[30]. Due to these different viewpoints, the

---

[27] Y. CONGAR, «Ecumenical Experience and Conversion: A Personal Testimony», in *The Sufficiency of God*. Essays in Honour of W. A. Visser't Hooft, eds.M.C.Robert – W.C. Charles London 1963, 72-73; see also «Rapprochements entre chrétiens: redécouverte catholique», *VUC* 29 (1951) 2-5.

[28] Cf. A. SCHMEMANN, *Church, World, Mission*. Reflections on Orthodoxy in the West, New York 1979, 25; see also J. MEYENDORFF, «Vatican Second and Orthodox Theology in America», in *Vatican Second*: An Interfaith Appraisal. International Conference, ed. J. H. MILLER, Notre Dame 1966, 612.

[29] Cf. P.K. TONY, «A Study of Thematic Differences between Eastern and Western Religious Thought», *JES* 10 (1973) 337.

[30] Cf. L. RICHARD, «The Witness and the Mission of the Eastern Catholic Churches», *Dia* 15 (1980) 160; see also Y. CONGAR, *Chrétiens en dialogue*: Contributions catholiques à l'oecuménisme, Paris 1964, 274-275; Eng.trans.

tenets of Orthodox theology lose their original meaning when Western theologians attempt to understand them in terms of their own categories. On the other hand, the dogmatic issues of the Western Church can be comprehended by the Orthodox only when they are related to the concrete realm of *experience*[31].

The understanding of the Church and the sacraments which Congar acquired through contact with the Orthodox Church is chiefly characterized by the pronounced Trinitarian theology which is considered the unshakable foundation and object of all religious thought, of all piety, of all spiritual life, and of all experience[32]. In the Orthodox Church this is basically founded on the insights of the Cappadocian Fathers[33]. They first treat the triplicity of equal *hypostases* [persons], and only thereafter the identity of the divine *ousia* [substance]. The term *hypostasis* means a concrete individual with definite characteristics, as opposed to the term *substratum* or *ousia* which denotes a reality which can be participated in by many individuals[34]. Thus, the Cappadocians emphasize that each of the three Persons is God acting for humanity in a different way. They account for the unity of the Persons by means of their theory of relations. The coherence or oneness of God does not exclude the multiplicity or distinct actions of the three Persons. Hence, the oneness of the Trinity entails a coherence of distinct actions undertaken in the history of creatures, and is considered to be dynamic rather than static. In short, the concept of communion occupies a central place in the Cappadocian trinitarian theology, but without devaluing the monarchy of the Father[35].

P. Loretz,*Dialogue between Christians*: Catholic Contributions to Ecumenism, London 1966, 233.

[31] Cf. A. SCHMEMANN, *Church, World, Mission. Reflections on Orthodoxy in the West*, 20.

[32] He clearly recognized this in many of his writings. Cf. Y. CONGAR, «Pneumatologie ou christomonisme dans la tradition latine?» *ETL* 45 (1969) 406; see also *La Parole et le Souffle*, Paris 1984, 167-168; Eng. trans. D. Smith, *The Word and the Spirit*, London 1986, 105.

[33] «The chief Cappadocian doctors are St. Basil; his longtime friend and co-defender of the faith, St Gregory Nazianzus, venerated as "the theologian"; and Basil's younger brother, St. Gregory of Nyssa». B. BOBRINSKOY, «The Indwelling of the Spirit in Christ; Pneumatic Christology in the Cappadocian Fathers», *VTQ* 28 (1984) 50.

[34] Cf. V. LOSSKY, *Orthodox Theology*. An Introduction, New York 1989, 38; see also J. MEYENDORFF, *The Byzantine Legacy in the Orthodox Church*, New York 1982, 154; C.M. LACUGNA, *God for Us: The Trinity and Christian Life*, New York 1992, 66-68.

[35] Cf. T. PARKER, «The Political Meaning of the Doctrine of the Trinity», *JR* 60 (1983) 173.

Since the Orthodox Church regards the Holy Spirit as the divine Person co-equal and co-eternal with the other two, it insists that, within the divine plan of salvation, the actions of the Son and of the Spirit are complementary rather than antithetic. Relying on the insights of St. Irenaeus, Orthodox theologians assert that the Word and the Spirit are the two hands of the Father, so that together they realize every aspect of the salvific economy of the Holy Trinity[36]. Accordingly, they state that the Holy Spirit is present at the eternal birth of the Son, at his historical conception in the virgin Mary, and at his birth in the hearts of believers. There is, therefore, a total reciprocity between the actions of the Word and those of the Spirit. It can be said that the Holy Spirit precedes the Son in the incarnation, whereas the incarnate Word is the precursor of the full gift of the Spirit at the event of Pentecost: «For the Cappadocian Fathers as well as for St. John Chrysostom, to speak of the presence of the Spirit in Jesus at the various stages of his human life is above all to remember that the very name of "Christ" is supremely trinitarian and "Pneumato-phoric"»[37]. Jesus of Nazareth was submissive to the Spirit during his earthly life, so that his forgiving of sins, casting out of devils, self-sacrifice on the cross and glorification were the result of the sanctifying operation of the divine *Pneuma* within him[38]. The co-ordination between Word and the Spirit in the events of redemption is referred to by Orthodox theologians as the *co-service*, or the *reciprocity of service*[39]. Their operations are distinct, and at the same time complementary, since they seek the one goal of serving the salvation of humanity and the glory of the Father.

In the Eastern Churches, Pentecost is viewed as the supreme goal of the saving self-revelation of the Word, the ultimate manifestation of the *co-service* of the second and the third divine Persons: «It is not a continuation of the Incarnation. It is its sequel, its result»[40]. For Eastern theologians, Incarnation, Redemption and Pentecost are inseparable

---

[36] Cf. ST. IRENAEUS, *Contra Haereses* IV, *Praefation*; PG 7, 975B.

[37] B. BOBRINSKOY, «The Indwelling of the Spirit in Christ; "Pneumatic Christology in the Cappadocian Fathers"», 61.

[38] Cf. N. NISSIOTIS, *Die Theologie der Östkirche in ökumenischen Dialog*: Kirche und Welt in Orthodoxer Sicht, Stuttgart 1968, 72; see also J. MEYENDORFF, *The Orthodox Church*, London 1962, 192.

[39] Cf. V. LOSSKY, *In the Image and Likeness of God*, New York 1985, 109-110; see also N. NISSIOTIS, «Pneumatological Christology as a Presupposition of Ecclesiology», *Oec* 2 (1967) 240-243.

[40] V. LOSSKY, *The Mystical Theology of the Eastern Church*, Cambridge 1991, 159; see also ID., *In the Image and Likeness of God*, 109.

mysteries since they entail the divinely ordained co-operation of the Word and the Spirit for the sanctification of human beings. Furthermore, Pentecost is the beginning of the personal, immediate and permanent presence of the Holy Spirit in the Church, so that his fruits and gifts are bestowed and experienced in time and space[41]. Within the life of the Church, the *kenosis* of the Holy Spirit unites human beings to Christ the risen Lord, who in turn leads them to the Father. Therefore, Orthodox theologians state that there is no christology without pneumatology, and no pneumatology without christology for in the economy of salvation the personal mission of the Son is complemented by that of the Spirit:

> To speak of Orthodox pneumatology does not mean exposing a doctrine of the Holy Spirit. The Holy Spirit cannot become a formula, a dogma apart. Pneumatology is the heart of Christian theology, it touches all aspects of faith in Christ. It is a commentary on the acts of the revealed triune God, the life of the Church, and of the man who prays and is regenerated [...]. Orthodox pneumatology does not allow the doctrine of the Holy Spirit to become a separate chapter of dogmatic theology[42].

Through the work of the Spirit in the Church, Christians pass «from the bondage of corruption unto the glorious liberty of the children of God» (Rom 8, 21). The Church is the «household of God» (Eph 2, 19), in which believers have the opportunity to cultivate a bond of personal love not only with their fellow human beings in the Holy Spirit, but also with each Person of the Holy Trinity.

In order to affirm the divine as well as the human dimension of the Church, Orthodox theologians view it as a theandric reality which can never be fully expressed in rational concepts. While not denying the significance either of its human dimension or of its historical character, they recognize that Church is an embodied mystery which transcends time and space[43]. It has its beginning and end in the gratuitous actions of the triune God who seeks the free and the personal participation of human persons in the divine glory of the Kingdom:

> It is because of this reference that the priorities given in ecclesiology are expressed by subjects like the body of Christ, or the bride of Christ, the insistence on the Trinitarian basis for the communion of the Church, the interpretation of the Church as a continuous Pentecost, or as the celestial

---

41 Cf. N. NISSIOTIS, «Pneumatologie Orthodoxe», in *Le Saint Esprit*, ed.F.J. Leenhardt, Geneva 1963, 93.

42 N. NISSIOTIS, «Pneumatologie Orthodoxe», 86; see also J. ZIZIOULAS, *Being as Communion*: Studies in Personhood and the Church, New York 1985, 132.

43 Cf. V. LOSSKY, *The Mystical Theology of the Eastern Church*, 175; see also P. EVDOKIMOV, *L'Esprit saint dans la tradition orthodoxe*, Paris 1969, 12-13.

Jerusalem established in history, reflecting in it the permanent divino-human intercourse as the image of the incarnate Word[44].

In this text, the Church is regarded primarily not as a juridical entity but as a sacramental organism whose main purpose is to manifest and communicate the in-breaking of the Kingdom of God into history through the missions of the *Logos* and the *Pneuma*. Thus, the Church as the Body of Christ and the Temple of the Holy Spirit reflects its communion with the triune God. It is neither a collection of individuals unrelated to each other, nor a system of regulations to which individual persons are sub-ordinated in importance. The Church is a community of persons, up-holding each in their life in Jesus Christ, and sustained by the Holy Spirit through its various forms of gifts[45].

One of these forms most central in Orthodox thinking is the presence of the Holy Spirit in the liturgy of the Church. The Orthodox approach to the truth and practice of religion is fundamentally a liturgical one, since proper doctrine and behaviour are acquired in the context of divine worship. It is no coincidence therefore, that the word *Orthodoxy* should signify both right belief and right worship, for the two realities are understood to be inseparable. According to His Holiness Alexij (+1970), the Patriarch of Moscow, the Church is chiefly to be defined as the community which celebrates the divine liturgy throughout history. Worship and doctrine come first, and discipline only second[46]. Moreover, liturgy is presented as an eschatological event, in the sense that what is accomplished on earth is a true manifestation of what takes place in heaven. Therefore, with regard to the liturgy, Orthodox theologians do not find any separation between the *sacred* and the *secular*, but affirm that all of life forms a continuum, since the Holy Spirit both transplants believers into the eschatological world, and enables the world to come to be present here and now[47]. Thus, the liturgy is the *locus* where the Holy Spirit brings about the *transformation* of the cosmos[48].

---

[44] N. NISSIOTIS, «The Church as a Sacramental Vision and the Challenge of Christian Witness», in *Church, Kingdom, World*, ed. L. Gennadios, Geneva 1986, 101.

[45] Cf. B. BOBRINSKOY, «Le Saint-Esprit dans la liturgie», *SL* 1 (1962) 49; see also H. WYBREW, *The Orthodox Liturgy*: The Development of the Eucharistic Liturgy in the Byzantine Rite, London 1990, 178.

[46] Cf. R. TAFT, «The Spirit of Eastern Christian Worship», *Dia* 12 (1977) 103.

[47] Cf. N. NISSIOTIS, «Worship, Eucharist and Intercommunion: "An Orthodox Reflection"», *SL* 2 (1963) 195; see also P. EVDOKIMOV, *La preghiera della Chiesa orientale*, Brescia 1970, 39.

[48] Orthodox liturgy and spirituality stress the cosmic dimension of salvation. The coming of the Spirit transfigures the material world, permitting the grace of God to shine

The chief place in Orthodox worship belongs to the sacraments or, as they are called in Greek, the *mysteria*[49]. As mysteries the sacraments unite things visible and invisible, exterior form and interior content. This is possible because in the sacraments the Holy Spirit conjoins the terrestrial and the eternal: water and justification, oil and sanctification, bread and wine and communion. Thus, the Church must primarily invoke the Holy Spirit if the sacraments are to be divine channels of human salvation:

> In response to the Church's invocation, the Spirit makes the blood shed by Christ on the cross circulate in His body, the Church, to call the Church to a charismatic life, to up-build it, to fill it with life, and to guide it into the fullness of truth. The Spirit invoked by the Church makes the salvation accomplished once and for all by Christ a permanent reality within history[50].

In fact, there exists no liturgical service in the Orthodox Church which does not contain an invocation that the Father send the Holy Spirit to the assembly. The reason is that «there is no access to the Father except by the Son, and there is no access to the Son save by the Holy Spirit»[51]. For Orthodoxy, therefore, the epiclesis embodies the essence of the Church's faith, liturgy, and life. The Pentecost-event, which happened once in the past, is always happening again in the sacraments of the Church.

At the very beginning of their lives as Christians, Baptism, Confirmation and Eucharist engraft the catechumens into the mysteries of Easter and Pentecost[52]. The unique rite of Christian initiation is constantly renewed by the Holy Spirit through the Eucharist celebrated in

---

through it, freeing it from the servitude which sin brought to the whole cosmos. Through the Spirit the material world is made capable of being used for man's salvation. Cf. B. BOBRINSKOY, «Présence réelle et communion eucharistique», *RSPT* 53 (1969) 408; see also A. SCHMEMANN, *The Eucharist*, New York 1990, 222.

[49] Cf. P. EVDOKIMOV, *The Sacrament of Love*, New York 1985, 124. Alexander Schmemann is of the opinion that the authentic position of the Orthodox Church was to explain the sacraments in the context of the liturgy. But the fatal error of post-patristic rationalism was the isolation of the sacraments from the liturgy as the total expression of the Church's life and faith. Here liturgy was reduced into the category of *piety*. Cf. A. SCHMEMANN, *For the Life of the World*, New York 1988, 150.

[50] N. NISSIOTIS, «Called to Unity: "The Significance of the Invocation of the Spirit for Church Unity"», *Lausanne 77 Fifty Years of Faith and Order, Faith and Order Paper* no: 82, Geneva 1977, 53; see also ID., «La pneumatologie ecclésiologique au service de l'unité l'Église», *Ist* 12 (1967) 335.

[51] P. EVDOKIMOV, *L'Esprit saint dans la tradition orthodoxe*, 102.

[52] Cf. V. LOSSKY, *The Mystical Theology of the Eastern Church*, 170; see also ID., *In the Image and Likeness of God*, 108; B. BOBRINSKOY, «Le Saint-Esprit dans la liturgie», 56.

the assembly of the Church. Nonetheless, Baptism and Eucharist are considered as instituted directly by Jesus of Nazareth, and are called *evangelical sacraments*, whereas the other sacraments are viewed as indirectly founded by the historical Jesus. Furthermore, it is impossible for the Orthodox to say that the real presence of Christ in the Eucharist is effected only by the sacrament of Order. The real presence is also grounded on the truth and catholicity of the traditions of the Church[53]. Due to Western influence, most Orthodox theologians admit that there are seven official sacraments, although some question the wisdom of limiting the *holy mysteries* to seven[54].

Since everything pertaining to the Eucharist nourishes the life of Church, Orthodox theologians grant prominence to it among the sacraments. At the Eucharist, the Church re-enacts the entire history of human redemption, as is quite explicit in its *anaphora* [eucharistic prayer]. There are recounted the saving acts of the Father who finally sent his Son; of the Son who offered himself for the sins of the world and has been taken up in glory; and of the Holy Spirit who now completes the redemptive mission of the Son by dwelling in the Church[55]. The Orthodox adamantly maintain that, in the course of the Eucharistic prayer, an actual transformation of the elements of bread and wine takes place. This transformation does not occur simply during the recitation of the words of institution, but in conjunction with the epiclesis, the liturgical act of invoking the Holy Spirit[56]. Even if by the fifth century

---

[53] Cf. J. MEYENDORFF, «Notes on the Orthodox Understanding of the Eucharist», *Con* 3 (1967) 28.

[54] The word *sacrament* was never restricted by its identification with our current seven sacraments. This word embraced the entire mystery of the salvation of the world and humankind by Christ and in essence the entire content of the Christian faith. Accordingly there are, for example, special forms of many blessings (of a Church, of holy water, especially at Epiphany, then of bread, fruit, all objects); even funerals and monastic vows were once formally called sacraments. All these rites as well as many others, such as the consecration of crosses and icons, do not differ from the "seven sacraments" in what concerns their active force, for they also confer the grace of the Holy Spirit when certain exterior forms are observed. Cf. J. MEYENDORFF, *The Orthodox Church*, 72-73; see also A. SCHMEMANN, *The Eucharist*, 217.

[55] Cf. J. J. von ALLMEN, *Worship*: Its Theology and Practice, New York 1965, 28-29.

[56] Cf. P. EVDOKIMOV, *L'Orthodoxe*, Paris 1959, 356; see also ID., *La preghiera della Chiesa Orientale*, 108. Just as the Orthodox liturgy is always eucharistic, involving the expression of thanksgiving implying anamnesis, so it is always epicletic, calling on the Father to make Christ present here and now. Therefore, there is no community which places the same emphasis on the epiclesis as does the Orthodox Church.Cf.

all the major writers in the East attributed a consecratory significance to the epiclesis, they were at the same time unanimous in insisting that the words of institution also have such a significance: «Eastern theologians never considered the epiclesis as a consecratory formula by itself. The priest pronounces the prayer *in persona ecclesiae* and asks that the Father send the Spirit and sanctify the gifts. The words of Christ are an historical or narrative statement which is part of the narrative of the saving acts of Christ»[57]. The invocation of the Holy Spirit at the Eucharist is based on the conviction that the same divine power which rendered the ministry of Jesus effective is now sent by the Father upon the ecclesial offerings, in order that they be changed into the body and blood of the Lord as a sign that the prayer of the community has been heard[58].

The solemn invocation of the Holy Spirit is emphasized in Orthodox sacramental theology precisely in order to affirm the biblical and patristic insight that the divine *Pneuma* permeates the entirety of the Church's life. This insight frees the Church from all forms of self-sufficiency, triumphalism and institutional stagnation: «It is not the Church which, through the medium of its institutions, bestows the Spirit, but it is the Spirit, which validates every aspect of Church life, including the institutions»[59]. The ecclesial institution, as a charismatic communion created by the Spirit, exists only epicletically. By invoking the Spirit, therefore, the Church implores divine judgement on its own ecclesiastical structures, with a view that they be constantly purified and renewed. It follows that Eastern theologians regard the absence of the epiclesis in the Western tradition as the cause of its christocentric, hierarchical and juridical thinking: «In consequence, the charisms, instead of being the driving force of a dynamic unity, as they were meant to be, become occasions of separation and division. Pneumatology then runs the risk of

---

B. BOBRINSKOY, «Le Saint-Esprit dans la liturgie», 52, 55; see also L. VISCHER, «The Epiclesis, Sign of Unity and Renewal», *SL* 6 (1969) 30.

[57] R.A. ADAMS, «The Holy Spirit and the Real Presence», *TS* 29 (1968) 50; see also N. NISSIOTIS, «La pneumatologie ecclésiologique au service de l'unité l'Église», 335; ID., «Called to Unity: The Significance of the Invocation of the Spirit for Church Unity», 54; J. ZIZIOULAS, «The Pneumatological dimension of the Church», *ICR* 1 (1974) 148-149; M. RYK, «The Holy Spirit's Role in the Deification of Man according to Contemporary Orthodox Theology (1925-1975)», *Dia* 10 (1975) 114-115.

[58] Cf. N. NISSIOTIS, «Called to Unity: The Significance of the Invocation of the Spirit for Church Unity», 54; see also E. TIMIADIS, «The centrality of the Holy Spirit in Orthodox Worship», *EF* 60 (1978) 318-319; B. BOBRINSKOY, «Le Saint-Esprit dans la liturgie», 56.

[59] J. MEYENDORFF, *Catholicity and the Church*, New York 1983, 28.

becoming one more ideological element in the contemporary theology of sharpening divisions»[60].

In his effort to engage in ecumenical dialogue with the Orthodox, Congar was convinced that the return to biblical, patristic and liturgical sources had already prepared Catholicism to adopt a christic-pneumatic approach to the sacraments. The pneumatological themes evident in these sources, long overlooked because of the apologetic concerns of the post-Tridentine period, could bring twentieth-century Catholic sacramental theologians to rediscover the Orthodox tradition in this regard, and conjoin its insights to their own[61]. In this way they could complement their own preferred emphasis on the liturgical anamnesis as the basis of sacramental efficacy with that of the East on the liturgical epiclesis; they could also profit from Orthodox reflections on the ecclesial rather than individual understanding of sacramental grace, and on the creative power of the Holy Spirit in all dimensions of the life of the Church rather than on the juridical and ritualistic legislation of the Church to which the divine *Pneuma* appeared to be bound. Because of this influence, Congar could make the following statement in one of his final works:

> I find myself quite at home with the writings of St. Basil, St. Gregory Nazianzen, Simeon the New Theologian, St. Sergius and many others. And there are also others of more recent date like Paul Evdokimov and O. Clément. Without wishing to appear possessive, we may think of them as ours. They express and nurture our experience of the Spirit and what we believe about him[62].

In short, Congar was induced by his Orthodox dialogue-partners further to champion, through his studies and writings, the shift from a

---

[60] N. NISSIOTIS, «Called Unity: The Significance of the Invocation of the Spirit for Church Unity», 58; see also ID., «The Importance of the Doctrine of the Trinity for Church Life and Theology», in *The Orthodox Ethos*, ed. J. Philippou, Oxford 1964, 38.

[61] However, it is to be remarked in this context that Congar's enthusiasm for Eastern theology is not without a critical dimension. In particular, he finds the ecclesiology of Serge Boulgakov to be inadequate, since it stresses the transcendent elements of the Church, without giving sufficient attention to her visible structure. Cf. Y. CONGAR, «Pensée Orthodoxe sur l'unité de l'Église», *LVI* 13 (1934) 294-314.

[62] Y. CONGAR, *Appelés à la vie*, Paris 1985, 93; Eng. trans. W. Burridge, *Called to Life*, London 1986, 86; see also ID., *La Parole et le Souffle*, 184 (*The Word and the Spirit*, 115). This is very evident in his comprehensive work on the Holy Spirit, *I Believe in the Holy Spirit* 3 vols. Relying on the Orthodox understanding of Church, Congar includes one chapter on the Holy Spirit and another on anthropology, and tries to integrate the work of the Holy Spirit in all aspects of theology. Cf. Y. CONGAR, *Je crois en l'Esprit Saint, II*: Il est Seigneur et Il donne la vie, Paris 1979, 90; Eng. trans. D. Smith, *I Believe in the Holy Spirit*: Lord and Giver of Life: vol. 2, London 1983, 66.

christocentric to a christic-pneumatic understanding of the sacraments on the part of his Catholic colleagues. This shift was in fact advocated by Congar at Vatican II which decidedly envisages the Church and its sacraments both in christic and pneumatic categories. Congar's contribution to this line of development is considered in the next sub-section.

3. The Conciliar Role of Congar: Reaffirmation of the Church as the Continuation of the Salvific Missions of the Son and of the Spirit

For a considerable length of time ecclesiology in the West was narrowly preoccupied with clarifying issues raised first by the Papalist – Conciliarist disputes, and later by the Protestant Reformation. The Church was understood as the organization founded by Jesus and directed by the members of the hierarchy, who guarantee the faithful execution of the functions he defined. The result was to reduce ecclesiology to hierarchology, so that theologians focused excessively on certain structural and institutional questions: «The Church as practically nothing more than a society in which some commanded and the rest obeyed; but above all it exalted authority. It considered the Church from the viewpoint of her rights and the powers that made her a social structure; in a word, as a juridical subject of authority and rights»[63]. In this hierarchical and juridical understanding of the Church there was little attempt to reflect on the Holy Spirit as its life-giving source. Although the Church in principle accepted the essential power and presence of the Holy Spirit, it seemed that the third divine Person simply legitimized the authority of the hierarchy, bound the consciences of the faithful in obedience to Church law, prevented the magisterium from pronouncing error in solemn declarations and established the perennial vigor of the social structure of the Church. Although for these functions the action of the Holy Spirit is important, they do not reveal the full scope of his very being, presence and activity. The Holy Spirit is not present in the Church merely to sanction certain visible forms; instead these external forms are there to minister to the internal working of the Holy Spirit in the Church, so that visible and invisible together form one incarnational reality, the Body of Christ[64].

---

63 Y. CONGAR, *Pour une Église servante et pauvre*, Paris 1963, 104 ; Eng. trans. J. Nicholson, *Power and Poverty in the Church*, Baltimore 1964, 109.

64 Cf. J. DUPUIS, *Jesus Christ and His Spirit*. Theological Approaches, Bangalore 1977, 24.

More than forty years of intensive theological research was already coming to fruition, when Pope John XXIII made the completely unexpected announcement of his plan to convoke the twentyfirst ecumenical Council of the Church on October 11, 1962[65]. As soon as the Council was convened, Congar was called upon to contribute his theological expertise. At the Council Congar helped to compose the message to the world at its opening[66], and worked on such major documents as *Dei Verbum* [Constitution on Divine Revelation], *Lumen Gentium* [Dogmatic Constitution on the Church], *Gaudium et Spes* [Pastoral Constitution on the Church in the Modern World], *Unitatis Redintegratio* [Decree on Ecumenism], *Presbyterorum Ordinis* [Decree on the Life and Ministry of Priests], *Dignitatis Humanae* [Declaration on Religious Freedom], and *Ad Gentes Divinitus* [Decree on the Church's Missionary Activity][67]. Almost all the major themes to be taken up by the Council were already anticipated in the earlier writings of Congar.

Looking back on how so much of his own study had prepared him to contribute to conciliar themes, he could only regard this as a sign of providence at work in his life: «I did not know [...] another knew it on my behalf [...] that this would pave the way for Vatican II. I was filled to overflowing. All the things to which I have given special attention issued in the Council: ecclesiology, ecumenism, reform of the Church, the lay state, mission, ministries, collegiality, return to the sources and Tradition»[68]. Congar's achievement at Vatican II consisted chiefly in underlining the pneumatological *leitmotiv* which ran through all these themes. Congar promoted reflections on pneumatology, since the Holy Spirit was the divine Person who enables the presence of Christ be felt

---

[65] Regarding the idea of the Council, Congar quoted the words of Pope John XXIII: «it is not the fruit of lengthy reflection. It is rather the spontaneous flower of an unexpected springtime. [...] With the grace of God, we are convening the Council. And we are intending to prepare it, bearing in mind all that is essential to bring strength and new vigour in the union of the Catholic family in conformity with the Lord's plan».Y. CONGAR, «A Last Look at the Council», in *Vatican II by Those Who Were There*, ed. A. STACOPOOLE, London 1986, 338.

[66] «October 21 was to see the very beautiful Message to the World drawn up, with the approval of John XXIII, by four French bishops [...] from a project proposed by a number of theologians, among whom were Fathers Congar and Chenu». J.P. JOSSUA, *Yves Congar*. Theology in the Service of God's People, 164.

[67] Cf. Y. CONGAR, *Entretiens d'automne*. Interview ed. by B. Lauret, Paris 1987, 12-13; Eng. trans. J. Bowden, *Fifty Years of Catholic Theology*. Conversation withY. Congar, London 1987, 6-7; see also J.P. JOSSUA, *Yves Congar*. Theology in the Service of God's People, 162; J.R. NELSON, «International Theological Congress on Pneumatology», *JES* 19 (1982) 675.

[68] Y. CONGAR, «Reflection on Being a Theologian», *NB* 62 (1981) 409.

within the community, and who induces new consciousness and initiatives[69]. Although at the beginning of the Council there was not much awareness of the need of the christic-pneumatic understanding of the Church, an essentially pneumatological measurement of ecclesial legitimacy was called for as the Council proceeded, since there was a remarkable consensus among the members that the Holy Spirit is indeed like the wind which blows where it wills (cf. Jn 3, 8). Although Congar was influential in formulating various themes in the documents of Vatican II, here his contribution towards a pneumatological understanding of the Church is emphasized. This understanding is most evident in *Ad Gentes Divinitus* [*Decree on the Church's Missionary Activity*.] .The chief reason for centering on this particular decree is that Congar drafted its first chapter, in which he puts forward his basic idea that the Church is the continuation of the missions of the Son and of the Spirit. After his text was wholeheartedly accepted by all the Council's Fathers, Congar considered working on *Ad Gentes* as the greatest grace in his life[70].

Congar attempted to link trinitarian theology and ecclesiology, since christology alone had become the central point of reference in the Catholic concept of the Church: «it is not our idea and our presentation of the Church which must be renewed in its source, it is our idea of God as a living God, and in this, our idea of faith»[71]. Thus, Congar asserted the need to rediscover the tradition of the undivided Church, and its insistence on the *ecclesia de Trinitate*. This tradition was marked by a theological vision in which the visible [christological or institutional] and the invisible [pneumatological or sacramental] aspects were harmoniously conjoined into the theology of the Church. Congar included this trinitarian economy of the Church in the following text: «According to the plan of the Father, it has its origin in the missions of the Son and the

---

69 Cf. Y. CONGAR, *Le Concile au jour le jour*. Deuxième session, Paris 1964, 111-112; Eng. trans. L. Sheppard, *Report from Rome*. On the Second Session of the Vatican Council, London 1964, 76.

70 After going through the first draft of *Ad Gentes*, many Fathers felt that the missionary propositions lacked an adequate theological foundation. Finally, because of pressure exerted by certain bishops, Card. Agagianian appointed Congar to formulate the first chapter of the Decree on Missionary Activity. Cf. J.B. ANDERSON, *A Vatican II Pneumatology of the Paschal Mystery*: The Historical – Doctrinal Genesis 1, 2-5, Roma 1988, 69-97; see also S. BRECHTER, «Decree on the Church's Missionary Activity; "Origin and History of the Decree; Doctrinal Principles"», in *Commentary on the Documents of Vatican II* vol. 4, ed. H. Vorgrimler, London 1989, 87-101.

71 Y. CONGAR, «The Council in the Age of Dialogue», *CC* 12 (1962) 148.

Holy Spirit»[72]. Here it is clear that the origin of the Church is found in the two self-communications of God the Father: in the Word made flesh in history and in the Spirit poured out in human minds and hearts. Therefore, first and foremost, Church is the creation of the Trinity, the extension of the divine life itself, a unity in plurality. In other words, the Church is an historical image of the trinitarian structure of the divine economy of human salvation: everything comes from the Father through the Son in the Spirit, and everything ascends to the Father in the Spirit through the Son[73].

Since the Church springs forth from the Trinity, it is a *communion* of persons sharing one and the same life[74]. Communion is a concept which, unfortunately, had not been developed for centuries in the West, although it had remained a central feature of ecclesiology in the East. Before the Council, Congar had anticipated that, among the notions describing the trinitarian nature of the Church, that of communion would hold central place in the ecclesiology of the future. This is quite explicit in many of his earlier writings. The Church, he stated, is not merely a society, but is «the divine Society itself, the life of God reaching out to humanity and taking humanity into itself»[75]. Similarly he maintained that the oneness of the triune God is the source of the unity of the Church:

---

[72] *Ad Gentes*, 2. The original draft of Congar reads: «the Church itself proceeds out of the sending of the Son and the Holy Spirit, which originate from the design of grace of God the Father». J.B. ANDERSON, *A Vatican II Pneumatology*, 234.

[73] Cf. Y. CONGAR, *Le concile de Vatican II*. Son Église peuple de Dieu et corps du Christ, Paris 1984, 82, 166; see also ID., *Je crois en l'Esprit Saint, I*: L'expérience de l'Esprit, Paris 1979, 229-230; Eng. trans. D. Smith, *I Believe in the Holy Spirit. The Experience of the Spirit*: vol. 1, London 1983, 168-169; ID., *Entretiens d'automne*, 77-78 (*Fifty Years of Catholic Theology*, 59). This idea was reflected very well in the first work of Congar: «The Church is in a sense an extension or manifestation of the blessed Trinity, the mystery of God in man: God, coming from God and returning to God, taking up humanity into himself. The final cause of the unity of the Church rests in God himself, and by appropriation, in the Holy Spirit». Y. CONGAR, *Chrétiens désunis*. Principles d'un oecuménisme catholique, Paris 1937, 68; Eng. trans. M.A. Bousfield, *Divided Christendom. A Catholic Study of the Problem of Reunion*, London 1939, 56.

[74] The concept *communion* is not a description of the Church's structure. It describes its nature or, as the Council puts it, its mystery. First of all *Lumen Gentium* 2, taking up the language of the Bible, says that the eternal Father has created us in accordance with his eternal design and has called us to share in his divine life [*Dei Verbum* 2, *Ad Gentes* 3, *Gaudium et Spes* 19]. Secondly, the Council says that the communion which is the purpose of salvation history is realized in a unique way in history in Jesus Christ [*LG*, 2, *GS*, 22]. Finally what took place in Jesus Christ once and for all is continued by the Holy Spirit [*LG*, 48; *AG*, 4]. Cf. W. KASPER, *Theology and Church*, London 1989, 152.

[75] Y. CONGAR, *Chrétiens désunis*, 59-60 (*Divided Christendom*, 49).

The Church is not a natural entity but a society of spiritualized beings, a community of human persons with the divine Persons. That a true plurality of persons should yet truly have one life as the mystery of the mystical body. *Unum corpus, multi sumus*. The unity of the holy and undivided Trinity which is the perfect unity in plurality is the model and principle of the unity of the Church, as St. Cyprian forcibly says[76].

Although the divine salvific economy in the world is one unique work, the two divine missions and all three divine Persons are involved in it. In one of his writings, Congar made use of different images to explain this truth: the Father as the arm or the power from which the movement arises, the Son as the hand, the Holy Spirit as the fingers forming humanity in the image of God. Yet another image: the Father is the root, the Son the stem and the Holy Spirit the fruit[77]. The missions of the Son and the Spirit begin from the Father, who is the principle without origin from whom all the activity of the blessed Trinity arises, and in particular the salvific self-communications in the Incarnation and in the Church[78]. In his writings, therefore, Congar claims that the point of departure for any discussion of the relationship between the mission of the Son and that of the Spirit should be the primary decision of the Father[79]. Although Congar attributes the primary role to the Father, he states that each of the three Persons imprints on salvation history its own characteristics traits, a truth which ought to be reflected in the theology of the Church.

The cause of the divine missions, which is the basis of the Church, is the love of the Father, which does not desire something for itself, but gives of itself gratuitously[80]. The two forms of the communication of this love are the missions of the Son and the Spirit. They reveal and establish the love of the Father among human beings[81]. When working in the draft

---

[76] Y. CONGAR, *Chrétiens désunis*, 71 (*Divided Christendom*, 58).

[77] Cf. Y. CONGAR, *La Pentecôte. Chartres 1956*, 37 (*The Mystery of the Church*, 157).

[78] Cf. *Ad Gentes*, 2; for the original draft of Congar, cf. J.B. ANDERSON, *A Vatican II Pneumatology*, 234.

[79] Cf. Y. CONGAR, *La Pentecôte. Chartres 1956*, 35-37 (*The Mystery of the Church*, 156-157); see also ID., *Théologie du laïcat*, 86-87 (*Lay People in the Church*, 59-60); ID., *Le Concile au jour le jour*. Quatrième session, Paris 1966, 142-176.

[80] Cf. *Ad Gentes*, 2; for the original draft of Congar, cf. J.B. ANDERSON, *A Vatican II Pneumatology*, 234.

[81] Cf. Y. CONGAR, «Theology of the Apostolate», *WM* 7 (1956) 285; see also ID., *Sacerdoce et laïcat*, 13-14 (*Priest and Layman*, 5). Whenever Congar writes about the origin of the divine missions and the origin of the Church, he considers the soul of the missions as the love of God. He uses several phrases from the New Testament to substantiate this: «In this love of God was made manifest among us, that God sent his

of *Ad Gentes*, Congar decided not to emphasize the usual Western thomistic notion of the divine *spiration*, whereby the Holy Spirit is breathed forth from the Father and the Son. Rather than stating that the Son is co-actor in the procession of the Holy Spirit, Congar proposed the phrase: from this fountain-like love, the Son is generated and from it the Holy Spirit proceeds through the Son[82]. Yet, Congar never expected that the Council Fathers would pass the draft. When he was informed of the Council's unconditional acceptance of the text of *AG*, 2, «Congar reacted with astonishment and joy, because he had introduced with the phrase, "the Holy Spirit proceeds through the Son" a little of Eastern theology»[83].

Congar underlined the fact that the Church, as a human organism enlivened by divine knowledge and love, is entirely dependent on the two missions originated by the Father[84]. In his later writing Congar also acknowledged that, regarding the decision to formulate an ecclesiology in relation to these missions, he was primarily influenced by the imagery of the two hands of God used by St. Irenaeus[85]. Furthermore, so as not to subordinate the mission of the Holy Spirit to that of Christ, Congar in his early writings often made use of the schema: *the structure and the life*[86].

---

only Son into the world, so that we might live through him. It is not that we loved God, but that he loved us, and sent his Son to be the expiation for our sins (1 Cor 1, 17; 2 Cor 10, 7-8; 1 Thess 1, 1-7; 2 Tim 1,14)». Y. CONGAR, «Theology of the Apostolate», 285-286; see also ID., *Sacerdoce et laïcat*, 14-15 (*Priest and Layman*, 6).

[82] Cf. J.B. ANDERSON, *A Vatican II Pneumatology*, 234.

[83] J.B. ANDERSON, *A Vatican II Pneumatology*, 198. Congar always had very high regard for the Orthodox reflection about the mystery of the Trinity. Wherever he had a chance, he tries to bring out it. His approach towards the Orthodox Church was very positive due to his enriching encounters with them. He considers that the difference between the two traditions is due to different approaches to the relationship between the natural and the supernatural. There is also the problem of different anthropological understandings of the image and likeness of God. To him, the Western and Eastern Churches share the same faith although they have approached the mystery from different angles. He even comes to say that the differences between the West and East, from the historical point of view is something providential. Cf. Y. CONGAR, *Chrétiens en dialogue*, 264-270 (*Dialogue between Christians*, 223-229); see also ID., *Je crois en l'Esprit Saint, III*: Le Fleuve de vie coule en Orient et en Occident, Paris 1980, 32-33; Eng. trans. D. Smith, *I Believe in the Holy Spirit*: The River of Life Flows in the East and in the West: vol. 3, London 1983, 8; ID., *La Parole et le Souffle*, 187 (*The Word and the Spirit*, 117).

[84] Cf. *Ad Gentes*, 2-4; for the original draft of Congar, cf. J.B. ANDERSON, *A Vatican II Pneumatology*, 236-238. The same idea is reflected in many of Congar's writings: *Chrétiens désunis*, 68-69 (*Divided Christendom*, 55-56); see also ID., *Laïcat, Église et monde*, 30-31 (*Laity, Church and World*, 17).

[85] Cf. Y. CONGAR, *Il est Seigneur et Il donne la vie*, 19 (*Lord and Giver of Life*, 9).

[86] To expatiate this schema Congar took the *Genesis* account of creation and Ezekiel's vision of the valley of dry bones. He applies the same pattern of God's action with regard

By applying this schema, he maintained that the form of the Church comes from Jesus Christ, the true mediator between God and humanity: from his incarnation, public ministry, selection of the Twelve, institution of certain sacraments [Baptism and Eucharist], granting the primacy to Peter and finally from his death and resurrection[87]. This structure of the Church comes alive, however, through the mission of the Holy Spirit, which began at Pentecost. The function of the Spirit who descended onto the early Church is to manifest and bring to fulfillment the mission of the Son[88]. The same idea that the Holy Spirit perfects the mission of Christ is reflected in the *Dogmatic Constitution on the Church* and the *Decree on the Missionary Activity of the Church*. Here, the Holy Spirit is perceived not simply as the energy by which the Son completes his own redemptive mission, but as the divine Person who extends the mission of Christ and builds up his Body in the world. For this reason, Congar considers that the theology of the Council is protected from the extreme of either christocentrism or pneumatocentricism[89].

Some Orthodox critics, notwithstanding the introductory paragraphs of *Lumen Gentium* and *Ad Gentes* on the function of the three divine Persons in salvation-history, have observed that the ecclesiology of the Council is still essentially christocentric[90]. It is true that, in the Conciliar documents, the Holy Spirit is not sufficiently presented as the divine Person without whom the Church could not exist, because the *Pneuma* gives it being, and not merely power. In spite of the Orthodox accusation of *christocentrism*, it is necessary to understand that Vatican II made an effort to integrate christology and pneumatology. It is evident that the Council Fathers, through the successive sessions, moved towards an ever fuller awareness of the christic-pneumatic foundation of the Church. In

---

to the foundation of the Church. Cf. Y. CONGAR, *La Pentecôte*. Chartres 1956, 42 (*The Mystery of the Church*, 160); see also ID., *Laïcat, Église et monde*, 29 (*Laity, Church and World*, 16); ID., *Mystère de l'Église*, 158-159 (*Mystery of the Church*, 128).

[87] Cf. *Ad Gentes*, 2-3; for the original draft of Congar, cf. J.B. ANDERSON, *A Vatican II Pneumatology*, 237-238.

[88] Cf. *Ad Gentes*, 4-5; see also Y. CONGAR, *La Pentecôte*. Chartres 1956, 116-118 (*The Mystery of the Church*, 188); ID., *Laïcat, Église et monde*, 30-31 (*Laity Church and the World*, 17).

[89] Cf. Y. CONGAR, *Le Concile de Vatican II. Son Église peuple de Dieu et corps du Christ*, 175-176; see also ID., *L'expérience de l'Esprit*, 227-228 (*The Experience of the Spirit*, 167).

[90] Cf. N. NISSIOTIS, «The Main Ecclesiological Problem of the Second Vatican Council», *JES* 2 (1965) 34; see also J. ZIZIOULAS, «The Pneumatological Dimension of the Church», 147; H. MAROT, «The Decrees of Vatican Council II: First Orthodox Reactions», *Con* 2 (1966) 70-78.

this regard, the efforts of the theological experts at the Council, such as those of Congar, were considerable. His understanding of the *ecclesia* as the continuation of the missions of the Son and the Spirit, especially as this is stated in the *Decree on the Church's Missionary Activity*, helped the Council Fathers to express the proper relation of the two divine missions in building up the Body of Christ.

From what has been stated in this chapter, it becomes clear that in the first half of this century there had taken place a steady shift in Catholic theology from a predominantly christocentric understanding of the Church and the sacraments to a christic-pneumatic one. This development had come about mainly due to the renewed study of biblical, patristic and liturgical sources[91]. By making use of these derivations, Congar tried to restate the original perception of the role of the Holy Spirit in the Church and the sacraments. What enabled him, apart from source studies, to formulate a christic-pneumatic approach to these theological tracts were his frequent ecumenical encounters with representatives of the Eastern Churches. Since their understanding of the Church and the sacraments is a synthesis of long-standing liturgical practices and of faithful adherence to biblical and patristic traditions, Congar found that it was truly complementary to his own thinking. Finally, he introduced the shift from a christic to christic-pneumatic understanding of Church and sacraments into the documents of Vatican II, in which the *ecclesia* and its signs of salvation are viewed as the continuations of the salvific missions of the Son and the Spirit. In view of what is to be exposed in the following major part of this study on the epicletic nature of the sacraments according to Congar, it can be said at this point that his consistent emphasis on both the christic and the pneumatic aspects of all dimensions of the Church form the solid basis of his particular effort to offer an integrated understanding of the christologico-commemorative and of the pneumatologico-invocative structure of the solemn acts of the liturgical assembly.

---

[91] Cf. Y. CONGAR, *Vraie et fausse réforme dans l'Église*, Paris 1950, 24-28; see also ID., *Mystère de l'Église*, 47 (*Mystery of the Church*, 44); ID., *Théologie du laïcat*, 8-9 (*Lay People in the Church*, xii).

PART TWO

AN ANALYSIS OF
CARDINAL YVES CONGAR'S
PRESENTATION OF THE INVOCATION
OF THE HOLY SPIRIT AS CONSTITUTIVE
OF THE SACRAMENTS

CHAPTER II

The Foundation of the Epicletic Dimension of the Sacraments: Pentecost as the Animating Event of the Body of Christ

Having developed the major influences which led Congar to formulate an epicletic understanding of the Church and the sacraments, this second part comprises a detailed analysis of his writings, so as to illuminate how he expressed this understanding. On examining the writings of Congar, one notices that there is a gradual development in his comprehension of the mission of the Holy Spirit from his earlier publications to those written after the Second Vatican Council[1]. When Congar began to emphasize the role of the Holy Spirit in his reflections on the Church and the sacraments, the *Pneuma* was considered chiefly as the *divine agent* of the risen Christ who gives life and movement to the ecclesial community and all its activities. Although the Spirit is sent in order to animate the community that Jesus founded through re-enacting the Paschal mystery in word, sacrament and love, Congar did not regard this work as that of the *Pneuma*: «the work of the Holy Spirit's mission is not his work, something independent and self-contained: it is the work of Christ»[2]. In

---

[1] Congar began to work on the second volume of *La Tradition et les traditions. Essai théologique*, while Vatican II was proceeding. After many of the Fathers had read Congar's text, the doctrinal commission established a new subcommission to rework the schema *De fontibus revelationis* in accordance with the directives of the Pope and the co-ordinating committee, in which along with K. Rahner, Y. Congar was asked to draw the final draft. Cf. A. DULLES, *The Reshaping of Catholicism*: Current Challenges in the Theology of Church, New York 1988, 75-76; see also A. NICHOLAS, *Yves Congar*, London 1989, 11.

[2] Y. CONGAR, *Laïcat, Église et monde*, 31 (*Laity, Church and World*, 17); see also *Mystère de l'Église*, 136 (*Mystery of the Church*, 110).

his later writings, however, Congar admitted that, by following the theology of Luke-Acts rather than that of Paul, he could not present the role of the glorified Christ and the role of the Holy Spirit after Pentecost as functionally the same. From then on, Congar intended to give proper weight to the distinct personality and work of the Spirit[3]. Because of his change of comprehension with regard to the Spirit, it is feasible to refer to the «*first*» and the «*second*» Congar. Hence, in order to facilitate the study of the theme of this thesis, this chapter is divided into two sub-sections which investigate the earlier writings of Congar, that is, those until 1962, concerning the constitutive role of the epiclesis of the Holy Spirit in enacting the sacraments.

The first sub-division places emphasis on the sending of the Holy Spirit as the historical extension of Christ's lordship in the Church and as the forceful efficacy of the symbolic signs he instituted. Although the signs enacted by Jesus were part of his public ministry, their full value was attained with his death and resurrection. For Congar, the Pasch is the center of the whole salvific event of Christ since, through his death and resurrection, he was made Lord, and thus able to send the *life-giving* power of the Holy Spirit to his followers. The novelty of the Holy Spirit poured out on the day of Pentecost is that he is no more to be perceived as the energizing force given to some judges, kings and prophets, but as the divine Person dwelling in all the Christian faithful who form his temple. In the salvation of the humanity, the co-ordination of the missions of Jesus Christ and of the Holy Spirit can be compared to a child who is brought into the world [the mystery of Pentecost] after several months of preparation within the womb of his mother [the mystery of Christmas]. Similarly, the sacraments which Jesus of Nazareth inaugurated during his public ministry received life and effectiveness at the coming of the Holy Spirit. At this time Congar views the work of Jesus Christ as primary, and that of the Holy Spirit as its continuation while he is physically absent.

In the second sub-section the roles of the Holy Spirit and of the apostles as the dual actors in bringing about the sacraments are analyzed. The saving signs that Jesus of Nazareth instituted during his public life and made fully efficacious through the paschal mystery, are extended after Pentecost by two agents: the Paraclete and the Twelve. The Holy Spirit is sent in a new way on the day of Pentecost as the principle of divine sanctification, since he is to assure that the salvation attained by the Son is

---

3 Cf. Y. CONGAR, *Il est Seigneur et Il donne la vie*, 23-24 (*Lord and Giver of Life*, 11-12); see also *La Parole et le Souffle*, 184 (*The Word and the Spirit*, 115).

established in the minds and hearts of human beings. The role of the Holy Spirit, therefore, is to render actual the salvific value of the sacraments instituted by Christ. And the Twelve whom Jesus chose during his public mission (cf. Mk 3, 13-15; Lk 4, 12-13) share in his unique mission to extend the merciful love of the Father towards all people. Thus, Congar links the mission of the Twelve to that of the Holy Spirit. These are considered by him as two «*concelebrating agents*» from the very day of Pentecost. As soon as the Twelve received the Spirit, they began to speak and to witness to what Christ achieved through the cross and the resurrection. Hence, the divine *Pneuma* not only co-operates in their ministry to word and sacrament, but also consecrates them and molds them according to his own holiness. Because of the active co-operation of the Spirit with the Apostles, Congar emphasizes that all the definite acts of their ministry have an unquestionably divine warrant. Therefore, when the ordained ministers of the Church act to communicate salvation through sacred signs, they do so only in the power of the Holy Spirit.

1. The Sending of the Holy Spirit as the Extension of Christ's Lordship and as the Efficacy of the Sacraments

In his early writings Congar often points out that the sending of the Holy Spirit after the glorification of Jesus does not mean that the divine *Pneuma* was not at work in Israel before Pentecost. Congar notes, however, that in the Old Testament the Holy Spirit is very often depicted as an impersonal power or force[4]. Even at the later period of the Hebrew Scriptures, when the covenant with God had attained more or less interior and moral nature, the presence of the Holy Spirit was regarded as something collective: «There was never any question of the Holy Spirit or of God taking up his dwelling in souls as persons who are his temple»[5]. Although the Holy Spirit was understood to have worked among the judges, kings and prophets of Israel as a source of empowerment, a new mode of his presence was foretold as one of the specific manifestations of the messianic age. The Spirit of God would rest upon the Messiah (cf. Is 11,2; 61,1) and be poured out on the witnesses of the new era he ushered in. For Congar, this prophecy was fulfilled both when the Spirit descended on Jesus at his baptism (Mk 1, 9-11), and when Jesus affirmed

---

4 Cf. Y. CONGAR, *Le mystère du temple ou l'économie de la présence de Dieu a sa créature de la Genèse à l'Apocalypse*, Paris 1958, 185; Eng. trans. R.F. Trevett, *The Mystery of the Temple*, Westminster 1962, 154-155.

5 Y. CONGAR, *Le mystère du temple*, 31 (*The Mystery of the Temple*, 16); see also *Chrétiens désunis*, 145-146 (*Divided Christendom*, 113).

that the divine *Pneuma* was upon him (Lk 4, 18-21)[6]. This is quite evident during Jesus' public mission, even if he consistently maintained that the gift of the Spirit was not to be given to his followers until his glorification[7]. The supreme gift of the risen Jesus was the outpouring of the very Holy Spirit by whom he had been raised from the dead[8]. The event of Pentecost, as this word indicates, refers to the fullness of the Passover of the Lord: «Pentecost is the fiftieth day of the feast of the Passover. It came about "when fifty days [the paschal period] was accomplished" (Acts 2,1). The fiftieth day, that is to say, the fullness, according to the laws of ancient symbolism [so important for an understanding of the real meaning of things], for $7 \times 7 + 1 = 50$ [super-fullness]»[9]. Because of the connection of Pentecost with the Passover of Christ, Congar considers that the former is an integral part of the liturgical year, just as are Christmas and Easter. It is also the commemoration of a specific aspect of the mystery of salvation in Jesus Christ[10]. Pentecost is truly meaningful only in connection with the christological cycle, since the work of the Holy Spirit invariably fulfills that of Jesus Christ[11]. In this way, Congar formulated the theology of the double divine missions: that of the Son and that of the Spirit, existing in interdependence and harmony[12]. According to Congar, Jesus during his public ministry established a certain *structure* which was to continue after his physical absence. Through the purification he received from John the Baptist, the selection of the Twelve, the appointment of Peter as their head, the breaking of the bread and giving of the wine at the Last Supper,

---

[6] Cf. Y. CONGAR, *Les voies du Dieu vivant*, 167 (*The Revelation of God*, 150); see also *Mystère de l'Église*, 24 (*Mystery of the Church*, 25-26).

[7] Cf. Y. CONGAR, *Le mystère du temple*, 322 (*The Mystery of the Temple*, 276).

[8] Cf. Y. CONGAR, *La Pentecôte*. Chartres 1956, 94 (*The Mystery of the Church*, 179); see also *Le mystère du temple*, 326 (*The Mystery of the Temple*, 155).

[9] Y. CONGAR, *La Pentecôte*. Chartres 1956, 31 (*The Mystery of the Church*, 155); see also *Les voies du Dieu vivant*, 124 (*The Revelation of God*, 111).

[10] Cf. Y. CONGAR, *La Pentecôte*. Chartres 1956, 14 (*The Mystery of the Church*, 148). For Congar, a mystery of salvation «means one of those decisive acts or moments selected by God's grace, an event which somehow re-shapes forever the existing relation between man and God. For that reason, the celebration of mysteries like Christmas, Easter or Pentecost is not a simple commemoration in the sense of recalling to mind. In celebrating one of these, Christians put themselves into the current of God's gift, a gift ever working to effect in time what he initiated on a particular day». Y. CONGAR, *La Pentecôte*. Chartres 1956, 14 (*The Mystery of the Church*, 148).

[11] Cf. Y. CONGAR, *Mystère de l'Église*, 141 (*Mystery of the Church*, 114-115); see also *Laïcat, Église et monde*, 31 (*Laity, Church and World*, 17).

[12] Cf. Y. CONGAR, *Théologie du laïcat*, 400 (*Lay People in the Church*, 289); see also *Laïcat, Église et monde*, 36-37 (*Laity, Church and World*, 21).

and finally the outpouring of water and blood from his pierced side on Calvary, Jesus inaugurated a sacramental body, so that his followers could enter into a common experience of renewed life[13]. If the mission of Jesus is necessary so as to provide his followers a communal structure, the mission of the Holy Spirit is essential so as to grant it *life* and *movement*.

In order to illustrate more clearly the relationship between *structure* and *life*, or the double divine missions, Congar made use of the image of the temple: «If we speak of the Temple of God, it was Christ who built it (Eph 2,22), and the Holy Spirit dwells in it (1 Cor 3, 16-17). What about our status as adopted sons of God? It was Christ who, by his incarnation, acquired the right for us, but the Holy Spirit brings it about and causes us to act accordingly»[14]. Thus, according to Congar, the Holy Spirit is sent essentially for the purpose of dwelling in the ecclesial structure built by Christ. Consequently, as the indwelling presence in the ecclesial body, the Holy Spirit is the soul of the Church. As such, the divine *Pneuma* acts not only as its *life-giving soul* animating all the activities to be carried by the faithful, but also as its *indwelling soul* perfecting them in holiness through sanctifying grace[15]. For Congar, these two related modes of the activity of the Holy Spirit in the temple of the Church are particularly evident in sacramental worship. Accordingly, the re-creative work, that Jesus Christ has definitively begun, is continued by his Spirit in an invisible manner, but through a visible means: the symbols of the Church. Congar thus considers the ecclesial sacraments not simply as signs of hope as were those of Israel, but as signs of a definitive act of salvation[16]. For him, they are the means of bringing each individual Christian, in all ages and times, into contact with the single historical Paschal mystery of Christ from which their efficacy flows[17]. Therefore, they are not independent realities, for the core of all the sacraments is the one redemptive mystery of Christ. Yet, whereas the sacrament of the Eucharist effects the real presence of Christ for his followers, Baptism and the other sacraments bring his sanctifying power into their lives[18]. Since the Holy Spirit renders all the acts of the Church *life-giving*, he enables the sacraments to bring forth fruit here and now in the Church.

---

13 Cf. Y. CONGAR, *Théologie du laïcat*, 49-50 (*Lay People in the Church*, 31); see also *Mystère de l'Église*, 157 (*Mystery of the Church*, 127).

14 Y. CONGAR, *La Pentecôte*. Chartres 1956, 43 (*The Mystery of the Church*, 160).

15 Cf. Y. CONGAR, *La Pentecôte*. Chartres 1956, 96 (*The Mystery of the Church*, 180).

16 Cf. Y. CONGAR, *Le mystère du temple*, 340 (*The Mystery of the Temple*, 297).

17 Cf. Y. CONGAR, *Mystère de l'Église*, 107 (*Mystery of the Church*, 87).

18 Cf. Y. CONGAR, *Mystère de l'Église*, 107 (*Mystery of the Church*, 87).

Hence, it becomes evident for Congar that the Holy Spirit is the divine Person who renders all the Christian sacraments efficacious: «Not only is the action of the Holy Spirit wholly related to Christ and is to do for the disciples, after Christ's departure, what he did while still with them, but the Spirit came to give life, motion and effectiveness to a body, to sacraments, to an apostolic ministry already constituted by Christ in the time of his earthly life»[19]. By studying the liturgical, patristic and theological tradition, Congar finds that both the eucharistic consecration and the specific grace of all the other sacraments are effected by the Holy Spirit who is their «true unseen artificer»[20]. Furthermore, the Holy Spirit acts as the result of the invocatory prayer of the whole liturgical assembly. Therefore, the sacrament of Eucharist is the sovereign actualization of Christian worship carried out in the unity of the Holy Spirit, since at its celebration the faithful become ever more authentic members of the mystical Body of Jesus Christ. According to Congar, although the faithful appear to receive Christ, he actually assimilates them to himself, and dwells among them, as in a temple. In fact, during the messianic age there is no temple other than the faithful themselves who receive the sacramental body of Christ and are filled with the Holy Spirit[21]. Thus, when the faithful approach the Eucharist, the Spirit not only enables them to become members of the mystical Body of Christ, but also dwells in him through the outpouring of divine grace. This teaching is surely the basis for what Congar will later state about the effect of the post-consecratory epiclesis.

If the Eucharist is for the faithful the perpetual sacramental commemoration of the self-giving of Jesus Christ, made possible by the sending of the Holy Spirit, Baptism is the unique sacramental act which transfers the faithful from the realm of sin and death to that of forgiveness and life, that is, to the benefits of the reconciliation with the Father which Jesus accomplished once for all time on the cross[22]. The sign of this reconciliation is the gift of the Holy Spirit which the faithful receive through the rite of Baptism. In line with the Fathers, Congar

---

[19] Y. CONGAR, *Mystère de l'Église*, 157-158 (*Mystery of the Church*, 127-128); see also «Conclusion», in *Le Concile et les conciles*, eds. B. Botte – H. Marot, Paris 1960, 326.

[20] Y. CONGAR, *Théologie du laïcat*, 285 (*Lay People in the Church*), 216); see also «Conclusion», 313-314.

[21] Cf. Y. CONGAR, *Le mystère du temple*, 184-185 (*The Mystery of the Temple*, 154).

[22] Cf. Y. CONGAR, *Mystère de l'Église*, 31, 33 (*Mystery of the Church*, 31, 33); see also *Chrétiens désunis*, 77 (*Divided Christendom*, 63).

comments that the desire of John the Baptist to be purified by Jesus, although he himself was baptizing with the water (cf. Jn 1,33), means that he longed to possess the gift of the Holy Spirit[23]. Congar notes that in the *Gospel of John* the water that flows from the side of Jesus exalted on the cross symbolizes the outpouring of the Holy Spirit at Christian Baptism so as to bestow new life on the catechumens[24]. This intrinsic relation of the Holy Spirit with the Baptism is well presented in the liturgical ritual of the Latin Church. There, as Congar points out, it is said that through Baptism candidates expect to receive faith and eternal life: «The ceremony of Baptism in which we are thus born anew of water and the Spirit begins in the Latin rite with the following dialogue, "What will faith give you? Eternal life". It is not for nothing that Baptism is called illumination»[25]. The faith and the eternal life that the candidates desire to receive at Baptism constitute the interior illumination which derives from the unending light of the Holy Spirit who enables Christians to perceive all things from the divine viewpoint. Thus, Congar states that, without the faith that derives from the gift of the Holy Spirit at Baptism, no one could know God: «it is only in eternity that we shall have the open vision. But even now, incompletely but nonetheless truly, we have eternal life by faith»[26]. Moreover, an integral component of the baptismal rite is the anointing with the oil of catechumens which Congar maintains, in line with liturgical and patristic thought, is a further symbol of the gift of the Holy Spirit[27].

If Baptism marks the beginning of the imparting of the Holy Spirit, this process is completed through Confirmation. Since both sacraments impart the Holy Spirit to the faithful, the theological problems involved in the question of their relationship are quite central: Does the Holy Spirit indwell in Christians from the moment of the Baptism or only from the moment of Confirmation? How can these two sacraments be seen within the mystery of being united to Christ? Congar notes that the relation between Baptism and Confirmation can be understood only through

---

23 Cf. Y. CONGAR, *Le mystère du temple*, 318 (*The Mystery of the Temple*, 272).

24 Cf. Y. CONGAR, *Mystère de l'Église*, 21 (*Mystery of the Church*, 24); see also *Les voies du Dieu vivant*, 124 (*The Revelation of God*, 111).

25 Y. CONGAR, *Chrétiens désunis*, 66 (*Divided Christendom*, 54). Here Congar notes that «faith and Baptism are two distinct realities, but they are so connected that one [Baptism] is, so to speak, the body of the other, or its consummation. Faith is not Baptism, [...] but it is as it were its clothing and its consummation». Y. CONGAR, *Sacerdoce et laïcat*, 149 (*Priest and Layman*, 120).

26 Y. CONGAR, *Chrétiens désunis*, 66 (*Divided Christendom*, 54).

27 Cf. Y. CONGAR, *Théologie du laïcat*, 370-371 (*Lay People in the Church*, 273).

reflection on the missions of the Word and of the Spirit, that is, on the work achieved in the Paschal mystery and on that achieved at Pentecost: «The intimate connection and the duality of the two sacraments have to be seen together in the light of the duality of the Persons and missions and the unity of work of Christ and the Holy Spirit. The Spirit comes to complete Christ's own work and the two phases of a single work are signified and effected in the liturgy»[28]. Thus, although there are two sacramental actions, that enacted at Confirmation is related to that enacted at Baptism. While the sacrament of Baptism places the faithful under the influence of the Holy Spirit (cf. 1 Pet 2,9), the sacrament of Confirmation strengthens this influence, granting a prophetical function to the faithful so that they can witness to Christian faith publicly[29]. Therefore, for Congar, the sacrament of Confirmation fosters the efficacy of the one work of Christ which the Holy Spirit actualizes by consecrating Christians for the task of witnessing to the faith in society:

> Baptism finds its completion in Confirmation. One of the essential effects of Confirmation is that it makes the baptized persons witnesses to Jesus Christ in the world. They cease to be children in Christ, living, as little children do, for themselves alone; they become adult in Christ, with their own place in the world with the mission and the grace to bear witness to the Lord in it, by the profession, or better, the confession of the faith[30].

Here Congar highlights Confirmation as the communication of the power of the Holy Spirit, so that the baptized can bear ever more prophetic witness to Christ[31].

A further consequence of these sacraments of initiation is the reception, on the part of the faithful, of *adoptive filiation* with Christ. By becoming the sons and daughters of the Father, the faithful not only bear in themselves the image of Christ, but also are incorporated into his social Body, and obtain the privilege of participating in all the other sacraments of the Church[32]. Hence, through Baptism and Confirmation the faithful enter an *ordo* of the Church, becoming sons and daughters of the Father with Christ through the power of the Holy Spirit: «First of all they are

---

[28] Y. CONGAR, *La Pentecôte*. Chartres 1956, 45 (*The Mystery of the Church*, 161).

[29] Cf. Y. CONGAR, *Théologie du laïcat*, 35-36 (*Lay People in the Church*, 16); see also *Sacerdoce et laïcat*, 293 (*Priest and Layman*, 261).

[30] Y. CONGAR, *Laïcat, Église et monde*, 99 (*Laity, Church and World*, 67-68).

[31] Cf. Y. CONGAR, *La Pentecôte*. Chartres 1956, 126 (*The Mystery of the Church*, 192).

[32] Cf, Y. CONGAR, *Chrétiens désunis*, 146 (*Divided Christendom*, 113); see also *Sainte Église, études et approches ecclésiologiques*, Paris 1963, 340; «Structure du sacerdoce chrétien», 72.

made sons and daughters in Christ and then there is breathed into them the Spirit which cries "Abba, Father" [...]. Secondly, the Spirit builds up their interior life. It pertains to him to abide in them and to make them live according to Christ, so that their life may be theirs and yet also his»[33]. By thus bestowing the gift of adoptive filiation on the faithful, the Holy Spirit brings into existence a third race, a *tertium genus*: Christians made up of different sexes, ages, cultures and social standings (cf. Gal 3,28); they are in the true sense *paroikoi*, or foreigners, in this world with a commonwealth in heaven[34]. Moreover, with the sacraments of initiation, a priestly quality is communicated to all the faithful, so that no one in the community is «secular», but all are «ordained»[35]. Yet, since Christ is the sole priest of the New Testament for evermore, the priesthood which the faithful acquire through Baptism and Confirmation is a sharing in his being:

> What is given to one alone on behalf of all is then extended and communicated to all; what has been done by one alone on behalf of all must still be, in a way, done by all. Christ is Son, and as such, heir: The faithful become *filii in Filio* and *cohaeredes Christi*. Christ alone is temple: the faithful are temples with him. Christ alone is priest: the faithful are priests with him[36].

As sharers in the filiation of Christ the eternal high priest through the Spirit, the faithful are also his *co-heirs*, and possess his priestly character (cf. 1 Pet 2,9).

Although Congar regards the ordained ministers as the official agents of Christ, he views the faithful, whose priesthood is based on the efficacious power of the Holy Spirit at work in sacraments of Baptism and Confir-mation, as true participants in the priestly identity and activity of Christ. In other words, with the outpouring of the gifts of the Holy Spirit «there is a mission of life and love, a mission *ex spiritu*, added to the juridical mission *ex officio*, which had previously constituted, in the Twelve, the Church as institution»[37]. Therefore, it is essential that there

---

33 Y. CONGAR, *Le mystère du temple*, 185 (*The Mystery of the Temple*, 154).

34 Cf. Y. CONGAR, *Sacerdoce et laïcat*, 322 (*Priest and Layman*, 293).

35 Cf. Y. CONGAR, *Sacerdoce et laïcat*, 318 (*Priest and Layman*, 289); see also *Les voies du Dieu vivant*, 204 (*The Revelation of God*, 186); *Jésus Christ. Notre médiateur et notre Seigneur*, Paris 1965, 210-211; Eng. trans. L. O'Neil, *Jesus Christ*, New York 1966, 191-192.

36 Y. CONGAR, *Théologie du laïcat*, 174 (*Lay People in the Church*, 133).

37 Y. CONGAR, *Théologie du laïcat*, 457 (*Lay People in the Church*, 326). Congar always considers the Twelve as those who first received the authorization to continue the mission of Christ, since their authority and action are normative. Therefore the faithful's

exist a co-ordinated action, or a «*con-celebration*», between the baptized and the ordained. In order to explain this close relation, Congar makes use of the pair of words «*priesthood-laity*» and compares it to the pair of words used to designate the marital partnership, «*husband - wife*»[38]. Just as husbands make all the decisions which pertain to the whole family, only after consultation with their wives, similarly the ordained ministers should take into consideration the opinions of the faithful with regard to the various activities of the Church: «It is the ordained who celebrates, but the whole body offers: it is he who teaches, but all bear witness and are active in the knowledge of faith; it is he who has the care of souls, but all have the mission to the apostolate, and all, moreover, have to share the charge of the cares and needs of people[39]. Congar states that, although the faithful participate in sacramental worship, they do not do so by presiding at it, as do the ordained ministers. He argues that the New Testament never indicates that the faithful conduct the public worship of the Church[40]. Consequently, for him, the priestly qualification of the faithful, although it is integral to the Church, does not pertain to its structure as such; it only expresses its nature and aids in accomplishing its mission[41]. The faithful exercise the cultic dimension of their priesthood mainly by leading a holy life, undertaking an apostolate of prayer, and being committed to works of charity and compassion[42]. Congar maintains that the worship of God which the faithful exercise through such an existence corresponds to the prophetic understanding of religion (cf. Heb 13,16; Hos 6,6; 14,3) which is *spiritual-real* in nature and content[43].

---

mission is only a sharing in, an association with and complement to that of the Twelve. Cf. Y. CONGAR, *Théologie du laïcat*, 496-497 (*Lay People in the Church*, 354-355).

[38] Cf. Y. CONGAR, *Sacerdoce et laïcat*, 119 (*Priest and Layman*, 99).

[39] Y. CONGAR, *Sacerdoce et laïcat*, 119 (*Priest and Layman*, 99).

[40] Cf. Y. CONGAR, *Théologie du laïcat*, 176 (*Lay People in the Church*, 135); see also *Sacerdoce et laïcat*, 148 (*Priest and Layman*, 119).

[41] Cf. Y. CONGAR, *Théologie du laïcat*, 296 (*Lay People in the Church*, 224-225).

[42] Cf. Y. CONGAR, *Théologie du laïcat*, 177 (*Lay People in the Church*, 136).

[43] Cf. Y. CONGAR, *Sacerdoce et laïcat*, 99 (*Priest and Layman*, 81); see also *Théologie du laïcat*, 177 (*Lay People in the Church*, 136). From studying the different terminologies, which are being used for the priesthood of the faithful – common priesthood, universal priesthood, inward priesthood – Congar concludes that not a single one fully expresses the reality for which it stands. He prefers to call it *spiritual priesthood*. Congar points out very clearly that the word «spiritual» is not used in a metaphorical sense, and does not mean that the ministerial priesthood is not spiritual. What he wants to suggest is simply the idea of a priesthood which does not involve any powers which distinguish one member of the body from another. Cf. Y. CONGAR, *Théologie du laïcat*, 241-242 (*Lay People in the Church*, 186).

Congar ascribes this *spiritual-real* worship on the part of the faithful to the work of the divine *Pneuma*, because «it comes not by flesh and blood but is put in motion by a working of the Holy Spirit, the gift proper to the new and final dispensation»[44]. Hence, the baptized and the confirmed can say «Abba Father» (Rom 8,15) and «Jesus is Lord» (1 Cor 12,3). For, the Father of the Lord Jesus Christ is contented neither with fruits nor with animals, but desires to have no sacrifice other than the human person[45]. Accordingly, the faithful who are filled by the Spirit are called to offer the Father and the Son nothing less than what they are:«What God wants to be offered is nothing but the human person; not irrational beasts but the spiritual, *rational*, worship and sacrifice of his reasoning creatures, who are made that they may as sons and daughters render up again to God the image that they bear»[46]. Thus, for Congar, the sacrifice of oneself is the spiritual worship which the Holy Spirit enables the members of the universal priesthood to offer. The faithful offer pneumatic worship to God, for their spiritual priesthood consists in a life of grace, one lived in Christ, the head of the ecclesial body. In short, the gift of the Holy Spirit that faithful receive through the sacraments of initiation enables them to conduct a life of sacrifice which is proper to the nature of the spiritual priesthood. The basis of the efficacious action of the Holy Spirit in the sacraments of Baptism and Confirmation is the faithfulness of the Lord Jesus Christ, the founder of the Church and the source of its salvific signs.

Furthermore, Congar identifies the *charismata* as the gifts proper to the spiritual priesthood, and roots this teaching both in the farewell discourse of Jesus as recorded in *John* chapters 14-16, and in the Pentecost account. The expressions in *John* «I will give you», «I will send to you», and «he will teach you» indicate to Congar that the Spirit was to be given both to individuals and to the community. In the Pentecostal experience, the same theme is found: «On that day, the Holy Spirit was given to each one, but he was, too, given to the disciples gathered together, and gathered in oneness of mind. That is what is expressed in *Acts* by the constant use of the formula *epi to auto*, "all together" (Acts 1,15; 2, 1.44.47)[47]. The use of the phrase *epi to auto* demonstrates that, from the beginning of Christianity, charisms were given to individuals

---

44 Y. CONGAR, *Théologie du laïcat*, 221 (*Lay People in the Church*, 158).

45 Cf. Y. CONGAR, *Sacerdoce et laïcat*, 110 (*Priest and Layman*, 91).

46 Y. CONGAR, *Théologie du laïcat*, 166 (*Lay people in the Church*, 126).

47 Y. CONGAR, *La Pentecôte*. Chartres 1956, 15-16 (*The Mystery of the Church*, 149).

for the well-being of the entire community. Although the *charismata* that the faithful receive do not form the Church as a sacral organism, there is no opposition between them and the hierarchical ministry, because even the ordained ministers were chosen from among those who had been given the gifts of the Spirit, who in turn had intervened in their appointment (cf. Acts 13, 2.4; 1 Tim 4,14)[48]. Congar expresses this idea quite clearly when he conjoins the functional and the fraternal forms of mediation which exist in the Church:

> The Body of Christ is built up by the regular mediation, functional and hierarchical, of the appointed ministers, the sacraments and the other rites of the Church, but also by the unpredictable, occasional and fraternal mediation of the various encounters and unexpected happenings brought about by the Spirit, which he offers to souls ready to accept them[49].

The sacraments of the Church are the regular or functional means by which the mission of Christ is continued in history. Yet, the sacraments and all other liturgical celebrations of the Church can be carried out only by the grace of the Holy Spirit in response to the invocatory prayer of the Church[50]. Therefore, for Congar, the Church must pray that the efficacious presence and power of the Holy Spirit accompany the enactment of the sacraments. In other words, an epiclesis, that is, an invocation of the Holy Spirit should be evident in each sacramental rite. Unfortunately, the epiclesis is made explicit only at the Eucharist, and even there it is restricted to the precise moment in which the bread and wine become the body and blood of Christ[51]. According to Congar, such an understanding of the epiclesis does not fully respect the theological insight that the Holy Spirit is the activating principle of the sacraments of Christ which are enacted by the Church. From what Congar affirms in the passage quoted above, the regular or functional mediation of the epiclesis, which is the task of the ordained praying in the name of the whole liturgical assembly, would not be fully efficacious without reference to the «unpredictable, occasional and fraternal» forms of invoking the Holy Spirit which arise among the baptized and the confirmed. The presupposition of the liturgical epiclesis, therefore, is an entire priestly people which enjoys various forms of the mediation of the Holy Spirit, and which carries out a co-ordinated life of love and service in the Church and in the world.

---

48 Cf. Y. CONGAR, *Mystère de l'Église*, 164-165 (*Mystery of the Church*, 133).

49 Y. CONGAR, *Mystère de l'Église*, 170-171 (*Mystery of the Church*, 137).

50 Cf. Y. CONGAR, *Théologie du laïcat*, 288 (*Lay People in the Church*, 218-219).

51 Cf. Y. CONGAR, *Mystère de l'Église*, 155 (*Mystery of the Church*, 125).

2. The Role of the Holy Spirit and the Apostles as the Concelebrating Agents of the Sacraments

With the passage of Christ to the Father, the social body which he founded was still to be activated in history through the very means which he determined. According to Congar, this is the reason why Christ sent the Holy Spirit to the Apostles he had appointed. With regard to the effective extension of the salvific signs of Jesus, the roles assumed by the Holy Spirit and the Apostles can be compared to those of agents[52]. In other words, with the completed public life and paschal mystery of Jesus Christ, the formative period of the sacraments was over. However, they would be brought to a new stage of efficacy only through the invisible agency of the Holy Spirit and the visible agency of the Twelve. In the *Gospel of John*, Congar finds explicit mention of these two agencies: the Paraclete to be sent by Christ (cf. Jn 14, 16.26; 15,26) and the Apostles already sent by him (cf. Jn 13,16)[53]. By granting the role of the Holy Spirit and that of the Apostles equal status in advancing the means of salvation which Christ instituted, Congar does not confuse their respective identities. Rather he claims that the activities of these two agents of the sacraments are exercised in a complementary way which can be designated as a «*con-celebration*»[54].

Certainly, Congar does not envisage the agency of the Holy Spirit in the same way as he does that of the Twelve in enacting the sacraments. The mission of the Holy Spirit was not definitively inaugurated during the public life of Jesus, but was only announced as a promise to be realized in the future. The mission of the Holy Spirit began with the transition of Christ to the Father, and particularly with his glorification[55]. Therefore, the Holy Spirit, the gift peculiar to the messianic age (cf. Jn 7,39; 16,7), was sent in an absolutely new way on the day of Pentecost as the result of the exaltation of the crucified Jesus. This sending of the Holy Spirit, in order to actuate the means of salvation which Christ instituted, was made

---

[52] Cf. Y. CONGAR, *Mystère de l'Église*, 130 (*Mystery of the Church*, 105); see also *Sainte Église, études et approches ecclésiologiques*, 158-161.

[53] Cf. Y. CONGAR, *Les voies du Dieu vivant*, 172 (*The Revelation of God*, 155); see also «Le Christ, l'Église et la grâce dans l'économie de l'espérance chrétienne», *Ist* 1 (1954) 146.

[54] Y. CONGAR, *La Pentecôte*. Chartres 1956, 106 (*The Mystery of the Church*, 185); see also *Le mystère du temple*, 340 (*The Mystery of the Temple*, 297); *Jésus Christ*, 208 (*Jesus Christ*, 196); «Le Christ, l'Église et la grâce dans l'économie de l'espérance chrétienne», 141.

[55] Cf. Y. CONGAR, *Mystère de l'Église*, 132 (*Mystery of the Church*, 107); see also *Jésus Christ*, 101-102 (*Jesus Christ*, 92-93).

possible due to his state as *kyrios*, the Lord of all things[56]. Since the Holy Spirit was to assure the fullness of the mission of Christ (cf. Lk 24,49; Jn 14,16), the sacraments received from the divine *Pneuma* their vitality and efficacy. Consequently, the Holy Spirit was poured out so that the sacraments could be the vital principles of the nascent organism of the Church[57].

Although the Holy Spirit was indeed sent in order to fulfill the redemptive work of Christ, Congar never regards the *Pneuma* as effecting a *continuation* of the mission of the *Logos*. The activity proper to the Holy Spirit comprises an *interiorization* of that of Christ, since he is depicted in the Scriptures as the divine being who has a distinct personality and mission: «The New Testament frequently implies that the Spirit possesses a real and fully personal character. Christ speaks of him as "another Paraclete", personal like himself (Jn 14, 16.17). Paul, like John, shows him as the object of a second mission (Gal 4, 4 - 6)[58]. Thus, just like the Word, the Holy Spirit is a Person, and not simply a vague energy by which the glorified Christ acts in and among the faithful. Congar describes this distinct and proper mission of the *Pneuma* in the following way: «the Holy Spirit is the sun of the soul and, at the same time, the wind "blowing where it wills" (Jn 3,8), sowing the seed of its choice where no human hand has planted»[59]. However, although the *Pneuma* as a divine Person other than the *Logos* has a particular mission other than that of the latter, Congar maintains that the goal of their activities is identical. Since all the actions of the Trinity *ad extra* are accomplished in unison by the three Persons to whom the divine essence, wisdom and power are strictly common, Congar affirms that the mission of the Spirit is perfectly equal in dignity and in efficacy that of the Son[60].

---

[56] Cf. Y. CONGAR, *Mystère de l'Église*, 132 (*Mystery of the Church*, 107).

[57] Cf. Y. CONGAR, *Mystère de l'Église*, 159 (*Mystery of the Church*, 128); see also «Le Christ, l'Église et la grâce dans l'économie de l'espérance chrétienne», 141, 147. Congar states that «the Holy Spirit, the Spirit of the Son, sent by him and proceeding from him, gives force and efficacy to these powers when used in proclaiming the faith and in celebrating the sacraments of faith, as is affirmed in countless passages of the Scripture». Y. CONGAR, *Mystère de l'Église*, 172 (*Mystery of the Church*, 139).

[58] Y. CONGAR, *La Pentecôte*. Chartres 1956, 39-40 (*The Mystery of the Church*, 159).

[59] Cf. Y. CONGAR, *Chrétiens en dialogue*, 102 (*Dialogue between Christians*, 73); see also *Laïcat, Église et monde*, 30-31 (*Laity, Church and World*, 17); *La Pentecôte*. Chartres 1956, 40 (*The Mystery of the Church*, 159); *La Tradition et les traditions*. Essai historique, Paris 1960, 30-31; Eng. trans. M. Naseby, *Tradition and Traditions*. An Historical and a Theological Essay: vol. 1, London 1966, 19.

[60] Cf. Y. CONGAR, *Mystère de l'Église*, 135 (*Mystery of the Church*, 110).

Accordingly, one of the activities most explicitly attributed to the Holy Spirit is to illumine others regarding the truth of Christ (1 Jn 4,1ff; Jn. 1,26; Apoc 19,10; Acts 1,8). Congar notes that Jesus described the Paraclete as the one who would bring to mind all that he had said: «I have said these things to you while still with you. But the *advocate*, the Holy Spirit, whom the Father will send in my name, will teach you everything and recall to your minds all that I have said to you» (Jn 14,26; cf. 16,12)[61]. In other words, the role of the Holy Spirit is «to actualize, to interiorize, to personalize what Christ said and did once for all people and all times»[62]. Although there is an identical goal which marks the missions of the Son and the Spirit, they each have a distinctive content[63]. While Christ established the objective form of the means of salvation, by instituting different sacraments, the Holy Spirit is to render these means actual, interior and personal in the lives of Christians:

> Christ proclaimed the word of God; the Spirit brings it to mind and inclines the heart to understand it. Christ built the house and the Spirit comes to dwell there (Eph 2,22). Christ gives us the status of adopted children; the Spirit puts in our hearts the consciousness of this status and enables us to carry out the corresponding acts and duties[64].

As this text indicates, Congar does not claim that the Holy Spirit accomplishes something new, independent and self-contained, but states that the *Pneuma* interiorizes in many the essential elements fixed by the incarnate *Logos*. However, the distinction is a real one between the mission of Christ and that of the Holy Spirit, in spite of the fact that they are co-ordinated[65]. Thus, between what the Son and the Spirit achieve within the faithful there is no *radical autonomy*[66]. Consequently, the

---

[61] Cf. Y. CONGAR, *Les voies du Dieu vivant*, 173 (*The Revelation of God*, 156); see also *La Pentecôte*. Chartres 1956, 36 (*The Mystery of the Church*, 157).

[62] Y. CONGAR, *La Tradition et les traditions*: vol. 1, 30-31 (*Tradition and Traditions*: vol. 1, 19).

[63] Cf. Y. CONGAR, *Mystère de l'Église*, 133 (*Mystery of the Church*, 108). Congar comments that, while in the *Acts of the Apostles* the Holy Spirit is the «other Paraclete» who simply acts as an agent of Christ in his Body, in the letters of Paul, with regard to the life of the Christians, Christ and the Holy Spirit are almost identified. Cf. Y. CONGAR, *Mystère de l'Église*, 24 (*Mystery of the Church*, 26).

[64] Y. CONGAR, *Mystère de l'Église*, 134 (*Mystery of the Church*, 109); see also *Laïcat, Église et monde*, 32 (*Laity, Church and World*, 18); *Le mystère du temple*, 328 (*The Mystery of the Temple*), 283; *La Pentecôte*. Chartres 1956, 67 (*The Mystery of the Church*, 169).

[65] Cf. Y. CONGAR, *Mystère de l'Église*, 135 (*Mystery of the Church*, 110); see also «Le Christ, l'Église et la grâce dans l'économie de l'espérance chrétienne», 147.

[66] Cf. Y. CONGAR, *Mystère de l'Église*, 166 (*Mystery of the Church*, 134).

Spirit relates his mission wholly to that of the Son, just as Christ entrusted his mission fully to the Spirit[67].

Therefore the sacraments, as the objective means of salvation Jesus instituted through his public life, death and resurrection, become interiorly effective in the faithful through the work of the Holy Spirit. In other words, the sacraments that are rooted in the mission of divine *Logos* become actual in each age by the mission of the divine *Pneuma*[68]. Moreover, the Holy Spirit communicates to the faithful in the «now-time» the redemptive mysteries of Christ, so as to orient the Church towards its absolute future:

> To the past but ever active and efficacious reality of Christ's passion, in which the reconciliation of us all and the whole world is already accomplished; to a present reality of grace, which gives us eternal life and builds up the mystical Body; finally, to the future reality of the consummation in glory, which the sacrament proclaims and of which it is the pledge[69].

Here, the mission of the Holy Spirit is not perceived as limited only to the attainment of salvation by the faithful while they are on earth, but is also viewed as guaranteeing that this salvation extend into eternity. Therefore, by comprehending the role of the Holy Spirit in terms of the vicar or agent of Christ, Congar stresses the one eternal goal which the two co-dependent yet distinct missions of the *Logos* and the *Pneuma* carry out within history[70].

As has been mentioned, Congar designates the Holy Spirit and the Twelve as the agents who carry on the salvific mission of Christ in his absence. Although the apostolic mission of the Twelve gradually came into existence during the public life of Jesus, its abounding efficiency was realized only with the descent of the Holy Spirit at Pentecost. From then on, according to Congar, the Apostles appointed by Christ to extend his mission began to act jointly with the Holy Spirit (cf. Acts 1,2; 13,4):

---

[67] Cf. Y. CONGAR, *Laïcat, Église et monde*, 47 (*Laity, Church and World*, 29). Taking inspiration from the *Gospel of John*, Congar states that «the Spirit is sent to us at the prayer of Christ (Jn 14,16), in his name (14,26), by him (15,26; cf. 19,30; 20,22; Apoc 21,6). We must go still further and say that the Holy Spirit proceeds from the Father (15,26), but also that he receives from the Son (16,15)». Y. CONGAR, *La Pentecôte*. Chartres 1956, 51-52 (*The Mystery of the Church*, 164).

[68] Cf. Y. CONGAR, *La Pentecôte*. Chartres 1956, 41 (*The Mystery of the Church*, 159).

[69] Y. CONGAR, *Mystère de l'Église*, 18 (*Mystery of the Church*, 20-21).

[70] Cf. Y. CONGAR, *Mystère de l'Église*, 142-143 (*Mystery of the Church*, 115-116).

The Holy Spirit and the Apostles are manifested jointly at Pentecost; not that the apostolate had not been founded beforehand or that the Spirit had not been given, but it was at Pentecost that the Church was definitely set up in the world and manifested as a new creation with its own specific energies, which consist precisely in the Holy Spirit and the apostolic ministry acting conjointly (cf. Jn 20, 22–23)[71].

The official joining together of the apostles and the Holy Spirit, for Congar, has enormous significance for the future of the Church. The Apostles and those they ordained to be the official representatives of Christ in the Church are united to the Holy Spirit by a covenant which grants a basic infallibility to the acts of Christian ministry. This covenantal tie is especially operative in the exercise of the cultic function of the ministry, the offering of the Eucharistic sacrifice and the celebration of the other sacraments: «The essential tie then is simultaneously divine and human, the invisible Spirit, soul of the Church and effective source of its life, and the visible framework of its organization, the priesthood and the sacraments, by which truth and grace are mediated to mankind»[72]. In this text Congar succinctly links together the transcendent mediation of the Holy Spirit and the immanent mediation of the ordained in effecting the sacraments. For him, the seven signs of the salvation are nothing less than the means by which the uniqueness of the divine-human mediation of Christ is made actual for the faithful through the co-operation of the Holy Spirit and the ordained[73]. Since the intervention of the Holy Spirit enables the ritual actions of the presider to be efficacious, the epiclesis, or invocation of the divine *Pneuma*, is an inherent aspect of the celebration of the sacraments. Therefore, the Holy Spirit not only renders effective the signs of salvation but also permeates the members of the apostolic body and those who are to participate in the celebration of the mysteries. In short, the *Pneuma* creates an organic unity among the baptized and the ordained. Consequently, even if, as Congar maintains, the New Testament does not explicitly mention the joint action of the Holy Spirit and the Apostles in the sacraments, it can be said that this truth is presupposed, not only because of the positive data concerning Pentecost and its effects, but also because of the theological implications of the rapid growth and extension of the early Church.

---

71 Y. CONGAR, *Mystère de l'Église*, 146 (*Mystery of the Church*, 119); see also *Sainte Église, études et approaches ecclésiologiques*, 158-161.

72 Y. CONGAR, *Le Christ, Marie et l'Église*, Paris 1952, 15; Eng. trans.S.J. Henry, *Christ, Our Lady and the Church*, Westminster 1957, 7; see also «Ordre et juridiction dans l'Église», *Iré* 10 (1933) 30.

73 Cf. Y. CONGAR, *Chrétiens désunis*, 75-76 (*Divided Christendom*, 62).

Congar finds that the faithful approach the sacraments in order to express and deepen their faith, which itself is the result of the interior prompting of the Holy Spirit. Since they seek to participate in the sacraments with faith, they can understand that the efficacious Spirit operates among them through the mediation of the ordained ministers: «The specific function of the Holy Spirit is, on the one hand, to give the institution life and movement "and in this sense of the word, efficacious" and, on the other hand, to bring home to individuals and to their innermost being the gifts of God»[74]. In order to illumine this vital role of the Holy Spirit in the sacrament of Baptism, Congar notes that in the New Testament membership in the mystical body is always accomplished by means of a symbolic washing which is an actual entrance into the paschal mystery of Jesus Christ. This is very evident in the case of Paul of Tarsus. Congar dwells on the uniqueness of Paul's baptism (cf. Acts 9,18), since the other disciples who enjoyed the privilege of being with Jesus during his public ministry (cf. Acts 1, 21-22) were not obliged to receive this sacrament. Accordingly, the baptism of Paul indicates that in and through the symbolic activity of the apostolic body, the Holy Spirit makes possible in a believer an interior and personal experience of the risen Christ. The sacrament of Baptism, therefore, is brought about by the joint action of the Holy Spirit and the ordained ministers. Through their *con-celebration*, the faithful attain saving grace, that is, a participation in the unique gift of salvation in Christ[75]. In causing this effect in many persons, the Holy Spirit acts as the divine agent who mystically transfers mortal human beings into spiritually reborn creatures, while the successors of the Apostles provide a visible, external sign of the divine mediation through their liturgical one.

This joint action of the ordained ministers and the Holy Spirit can be discovered in the other sacraments as well. If in the sacrament of Baptism the Holy Spirit bestows on the faithful the grace of salvation, which Jesus Christ obtained through his death and resurrection, in the sacrament of Confirmation the *Pneuma* anoints them so that with hope they might give testimony to it in their cultural context[76]. In these rites, the Holy Spirit enables the ordained ministers who perform them to preside visibly that

---

[74] Y. CONGAR, *Mystère de l'Église*, 155 (*Mystery of the Church*, 125).

[75] Cf. Y. CONGAR, *Chrétiens désunis*, 75-76 (*Divided Christendom*, 62).

[76] Cf. Y. CONGAR, *Sacerdoce et laïcat*, 293 (*Priest and Layman*, 261). Congar finds that in the Fathers and in the Liturgy, the Church is first of all a community formed by Baptism by which persons attain their state as Christians, and in Confirmation they are *ipso facto* incorporated into the state of those who give witness in the world. Cf. Y. CONGAR, *Sacerdoce et laïcat*, 293 (*Priest and Layman*, 261).

which the *Pneuma* communicates transcendentally. In fact, the ordained fulfill their own reception of Confirmation and Orders when they carry out their ministry: «Do we, priests and preachers, think of this when we carry out, even with authority, the ministry of the word, the sacraments, or spiritual government. Let us ask the Holy Spirit to add his witness to our own, as Scripture phrases it; to celebrate with us»[77]. Likewise, in the celebration of the sacrament of Penance, the grace of the Holy Spirit is conjoined to the words and actions of the ordained ministers so that the faithful be strengthened through the visible gesture of making the sign of the cross by which one is made to realize that he is a sinner in need of being forgiven: «At all events, one essential aspect of the testimony of the Holy Spirit is to manifest the sin of the world and to strengthen the faithful interiorly. We know that he does not leave the ministers of the Gospel to themselves, but acts as their guide»[78]. Thus, the bestowal of sacramental absolution on the part of the ordained cannot be explained apart from the gifts of forgiveness and peace which the Holy Spirit grants to the baptized and confirmed who have failed to live according to justice and hope.

In the case of the Eucharist, the authority to consecrate the elements of bread and wine pertains exclusively to the ordained ministers. While they exercise this ministry, they are carrying out a pneumatological act, that is, «a divinely-ordained application of the might of God, who is faithful to his covenant and to his ordinance»[79]. Similarly, the imposition of hands on the part of bishops, so as to consign spiritual gifts (cf. Acts 8, 14-18; 9,17; 19,6) for the effective practice of the ordained ministry (cf. Acts 13, 2-4; cf. 1 Tim 4,14 and 2 Tim 1,6), is possible only through the combined action of the Holy Spirit and the successors of the Twelve. According to Congar, the sacrament of the Anointing of the Sick is closely connected with the power of the Holy Spirit, since the presbyters perform this rite by praying over the faithful, that is to say, by formulating an epiclesis (cf. Jam 5,14)[80]. In short, Jesus Christ, although physically absent from his followers, continues to carry out his saving mission among them by means of two agents: his Spirit and his ministers. These two concelebrating vicars act in unison, the one inwardly and the

---

[77] Y. CONGAR, *Les voies du Dieu vivant*, 171 (*The Revelation of God*, 154).

[78] Y. CONGAR, *Mystère de l'Église*, 151 (*Mystery of the Church*, 123); see also Jn 16,8.

[79] Y. CONGAR, *Théologie du laïcat*, 288 (*Lay People in the Church*, 218); see also «Structure du sacerdoce chrétien», 70; «Le Christ, l'Église et la grâce dans l'économie de l'espérance chrétienne», 148.

[80] Cf. Y. CONGAR, *Mystère de l'Église*, 155 (*Mystery of the Church*, 125).

other outwardly so as to constitute the Church continually as the community made holy by grace. Consequently, for Congar, in the process by which Jesus Christ builds up his social Body in history through the very means which he instituted, the complementary mission of the Holy Spirit is absolutely necessary. The pneumatic mission is meant «to give life, motion and effectiveness to a body, to a sacrament, to an apostolic ministry already constituted by Christ in the time of his *acta et passa in carne*»[81].

From the content of the sub-divisions of this chapter, one can deduce that for Congar the indispensable role of the divine *Pneuma* in assuring the ceaseless efficacy of the sacraments is conjoined to the salvific mysteries of the incarnation, passion, death and resurrection of the divine *Logos*. In the public ministry of the incarnate Word, Congar isolates symbolic gestures by which a body of followers is prepared to continue the saving mission of their master between the time of his glorification and his second coming. Although the institution of the sacraments had taken place during the public ministry of Jesus of Nazareth, their vitality and efficacy was linked to his death and resurrection which made possible the outpouring of his Spirit. According to Congar, only the risen Christ was able to send forth the divine efficacy itself, the Holy Spirit. This does not mean that the divine *Pneuma* was not active in the world before the glorification of the incarnate *Logos*. Yet, the new presence of the Holy Spirit at Pentecost revealed that he is more than an energizing force emanating from the Father; he is a divine Person, who takes up his dwelling in the souls of the followers of Christ, rendering the preaching, the rituals and the pastoral love of the Church sources of salvation. Although there is a fundamental difference between the roles of the Holy Spirit and the ordained as agents of the risen Christ, Congar admits that in the execution of their activities, especially in the enactment of the sacraments, there exists a true *con-celebration*. For Congar when the ordained act visibly and publicly through the sacraments, they are accompanied invisibly and spiritually by the Holy Spirit. This truth is the basis of a valid theology of the *epiclesis* of the Holy Spirit as a constitutive element of the enactment of every sacrament.

---

81 Y. CONGAR, *Mystère de l'Église*, 158 (*Mystery of the Church*, 128); see also *Théologie du laïcat*, 493-494 (*Lay People in the Church*, 352).

CHAPTER III

Ordination by the Laying on of Hands
as the Solemn Imploration of the Empowerment
of the Holy Spirit

The previous chapter, which was mainly based on the writings of Congar before Vatican II, dealt with the efficacious role of the Holy Spirit in interiorizing in the faithful the salvation which Jesus associated with the sacraments he instituted. There it was explained how Congar understood that the different symbolic acts performed by Jesus during his public mission attained their salvific value through his death and glorification. Congar considered the sending of the Holy Spirit at Pentecost as a definitive sign of the eternal validity of the paschal mystery. The Spirit was to perfect and complement the mission of Christ by enabling the re-enactment of his salvific signs to sanctify his followers of each age. However, Congar did not isolate this mission of the Holy Spirit from that entrusted by Jesus Christ to the Twelve. While the Holy Spirit acts invisibly, the Apostles and their successors do so visibly. Although Congar did not place the missions of the Holy Spirit and the Apostles on an equal footing, he strongly held that both concelebrated, so as to extend and personalize the salvation wrought by Christ.

This chapter protracts this theme by investigating how Congar further understood the invocation of the Holy Spirit as constitutive of the sacrament of Ordination. Here emphasis is given to his conciliar and post-conciliar writings [from 1962 to 1986]. The two sub-sections deal respectively with Ordination as a Pentecostal bestowal of the Spirit on those who have the charism of leadership, and as the laying on of hands which renders them representatives both of Christ and of the Church.

The first sub-section elucidates Congar's vision of Ordination as a share in the mission of the Holy Spirit and in that of the Apostles. Although Jesus Christ selected the Twelve during his public life, they initiated their mandate to announce salvation in word and sign only when the Holy Spirit came upon them at Pentecost. Congar further noted that at Pentecost the Twelve really understood not only the message of Jesus Christ but also the task he had entrusted to them. The Spirit who first activated the mission of the Apostles remained with them on all the important occasions in which they were to communicate the salvific event of Christ to others through speech and symbols. Similarly, Ordination is a bestowal of the Holy Spirit that renders its recipients members of that chain of authoritative witnesses to salvation of which the Twelve are the first links. Congar affirmed that, with the gift of the Holy Spirit, the ordained are empowered to execute their mission of effecting signs of salvation for many others in the community. As the divine Person who guarantees the efficacy of Ordination, the Holy Spirit guides all the efforts of ecclesial ministers to impart grace to humankind.

In the second sub-section, the conferral of the Holy Spirit at Ordination through the laying on of hands by the bishop is viewed as enabling the ordinandi to act both *in persona Christi* and *in persona ecclesiae*. Congar maintained that, although Jesus Christ granted special authority only to the Twelve of his many disciples, they received the Holy Spirit, and could thus exercise their function in the community, solely at the moment when they were sitting together with the other disciples and with Mary. Similarly, the laying on of hands by the bishop during the celebration of the sacrament of Ordination takes place within the believing community gathered in prayer. However, Congar does not limit the bestowal of the Spirit on the ordinandi to the moment in the rite when the bishop lays his hands on them, for the reception of the grace of ministry entails a continuous process. Thus, the members of the community have a part not only in the formation of the candidates but also in the invocation of the Spirit upon them as the bishop prays in silence for this gift. With the imparting of the Spirit at Ordination, ecclesial ministers are enabled to join with the divine *Pneuma* in extending the benefits of salvation, through word, symbol and service, to all those who believe in Christ. This means that, within the entire community of priestly people, the ordained ministers serve as representatives both of Christ, the Head, and of the Church, that is, of all the baptized and confirmed members of the social Body. In this sense, the Spirit renders the ordained living symbols of the unity of Christ and his followers.

1. Ordination as a Pentecostal Bestowal of the Holy Spirit and as a Prolongation of the Mission of the Twelve

By their anointing with the Holy Spirit in the sacraments of Baptism and Confirmation, believers attain the status of sons and daughters of the Father in Christ Jesus, and of members of the common priesthood. Through these sacraments, the Holy Spirit continually forms the mystical body of Christ by means of the grace and charisma granted to all its members[1]. Hence, according to Congar, although there exists a variety of ministries arising from the anointing of the Holy Spirit given at Baptism and Confirmation, the sacrament of Order comprises a decisive ministry[2]. For Congar, the significance of the ordained lies primarily in their mandate to «extend to all those who believe the benefit of the incarnation and the promise of the resurrection, and to make them members of the Body of the Son of God»[3]. In other words, the sacrament of Order is one of the principal sacraments[4], since it joins humankind to the work of the incarnate Word by fostering the unity of the Church and the perpetuation of the mission of the Twelve:

> The role of the ministries brought into being by this sacrament is to signify and to ensure the continuous relationship to the work of the Word incarnate, on the one hand by assuring unity within each and every community and between communities, and on the other hand by

---

[1] Cf. Y. CONGAR, «Actualité d'une Pneumatologie», *POC* 23 (1973) 127; Eng. vers.«Pneumatology Today», *AER* 167 (1973) 443; see also *Ministères et Communion ecclésiale*, Paris 1971, 17; *Un Peuple messianique*. L'Église, sacrement du salut. Salut et libération, Paris 1975, 78; *Essais oecuméniques*: Le mouvement, les hommes, les problèmes, Paris 1984, 305-306.

[2] Cf. Y. CONGAR, «Réflections et recherches actuelles sur l'assemblée liturgique», *LMD* 115 (1973) 14-15; Eng. vers. «Reflections on the Liturgical Assembly», *TD* 22 (1974) 151; see also «Actualité d' une Pneumatologie», 129 («Pneumatology Today», 445); «Le monothéisme politique et le Dieu Trinité», *NRT* 113 (1981) 16. According to Congar, the ministries should be found in the concept of the people of God to which Christians belong by Baptism and in which they are ordained by Confirmation and Order. He differentiated these ministries into sacramental structures and recognized ones. While the sacramental structures come from above although at the same time they belong very much within the community, the recognized ministries are undoubtedly needed to ensure the unified character of the community. Cf. Y. CONGAR, *Cette Église que j'aime*, 13 (*The Church That I Love*, 13); see also «My Path-Findings in the Theology of Laity and Ministries», 178; *Appelés à la vie*, 123 (*Called to Life*, 116).

[3] Y. CONGAR, *Cette Église que j'aime*, 49 (*The Church That I Love*, 47).

[4] Cf. Y. CONGAR, «L'idée de sacrements majeurs ou principaux», *Con* 4 (1968) 31; Eng. vers. «The Idea of "Major" or Principal Sacraments», *Con* 4 (1968) 15; see also *L'Ecclésiologie du haut moyen age*: de saint Gregoire le Grand à la désunion entre Byzance et Rome, Paris 1968, 92-98.

witnessing to the unbroken link with the apostolic institution and guaranteeing its continuance[5].

Since the existence of Order assures the link of each local Church with the apostolic body that was founded by Christ, Congar dedicates much attention to the institution and the mission of the Twelve in order to probe the ecclesial significance of this sacrament[6].

Congar states that the constitution of the Twelve took place when Jesus selected them and designated them to be with him during his public ministry. This election stood in the place of a consecration, since they did not receive water baptism from the hands of Jesus. This consecration empowered them to take up the mission on which Jesus sent them. Yet the full exercise of their mission began only with the outpouring of the Holy Spirit on the day of Pentecost[7]. This reception of the Holy Spirit by the Twelve was necessary, so that they could actualize the mission that Christ had entrusted to them: «Christ uttered the words of his gospel once; he accomplished our salvation and gave his life, once and for all time; he instituted the sacraments and consecrated the Apostles once only. Thus did he establish the pattern of life for his people. The role of the Holy Spirit is to actualize all in his absence»[8]. If the mission of the Twelve is that of perpetuating the work of Christ, Congar finds that the mission of the Holy Spirit is precisely the same. After the departure of Christ from the world, the Holy Spirit and the Twelve create a vital recollection in others concerning what had happened to Jesus of Nazareth in the past, and at the same time a dynamic looking forward to what would happen in the future to him and to all who are in him[9].

However, Congar made it extremely clear that the collaboration between the Holy Spirit and the Apostles is meant to form a union of alliance with many others. For when the Holy Spirit is bestowed on

---

[5] Y. CONGAR, *Appelés à la vie*, 78 (*Called to Life*, 70); see also *La Parole et le Souffle*, 133-134 (*The Word and the Spirit*, 82).

[6] Cf. Y. CONGAR, «L'*ecclesia* ou communauté chrétienne, sujet intégral de l'action liturgique», 259; see also «Ministères et structuration de l'Église», *LMD* 102 (1970) 11.

[7] Cf. Y. CONGAR, *L'expérience de l' Esprit*, 150-151 (*The Experience of the Spirit*, 106); see also *Ministères et Communion ecclésiale*, 92.

[8] Y. CONGAR, *La Tradition et les traditions*. Essai théologique, Paris 1963, 104-105; Eng trans. M. Naseby – T. Rainvorough, *Tradition and Traditions. A Theological Essay*: vol. 2, New York 1966, 342; see also *L'Église, une sainte, catholique et apostolique* in *Mysterium Salutis*: vol. 15, eds. J. Feiner – M. Löhrer. Paris 1970, 165; «Le Personne l'Église», *RT* 71 (1971) 637.

[9] Cf. Y. CONGAR, *Il est Seigneur et Il donne la vie*, 59-60 (*Lord and Giver of Life*, 42); see also *L' Église de Saint Augustin à l'époque moderne*, Paris 1970, 182; «L'*ecclesia* ou communauté chrétienne, sujet intégral de l'action liturgique», 251.

members of the community, they act as his free and dynamic partners: «The union of the Holy Spirit with the apostolic institution and with the Church is a union of alliance: he is given as the one Promised proper to the new and eternal alliance, he is united to a created being in such a way as to make of it his associated organ, animated and free»[10]. Congar notes that at Pentecost the Holy Spirit was poured out on the Twelve and on all the other disciples, so that the life of the Church would be marked by diversity and by communion at the same time. Hence, since the Holy Spirit descended on the Twelve and on all the disciples, they could each attain a personalized form of sanctification that would enable them to speak convincingly about what they had experienced by being with Jesus. For Congar, the significant terms that are employed in the account of Pentecost are *epi to auto* [gathered together or in the same place] and *humothumadon* [of one mind]. These terms reveal that the working of the Holy Spirit requires a certain initial unity, which he marvelously brings about, so that he can bestow himself on a community[11]. This community «is not only the enclosure or *sheepfold* [*aulë*], but also the flock of individual sheep [*poimnë*], each of which the shepherd calls by its own name (Jn 10, 1-3.16)»[12]. Hence, each Christian is to have a share in building up the unity of the mystical Body of Christ. Consequently, the difference between the gift given by the Spirit to the Twelve and that given to the other disciples is not as important as is the truth that they are two modes of existence and activity which complete and condition each other. In short, they should function together, if the union of alliance desired by the Spirit is to be realized.

It follows for Congar that the gift of the Holy Spirit to all the baptized and that to the ordained are two sides of the same coin, even if they form

---

10 Y. CONGAR, «Pneumatologie ou christomonisme dans la tradition latine?», 412; see also *La Foi et la Théologie*, Tournai 1962, 164.

11 Cf. Y. CONGAR, *Il est Seigneur et Il donne la vie*, 25-26 (*Lord and Giver of Life*, 15); see also *Le Concile au jour le jour*. Deuxième session, 30 (*Report from Rome II*. On the Second Session of the Vatican Council, 194-195); «The Conciliar Structure or Regime of the Church», *Con* 19 (1983) 5. In this text Congar is very much inspired by Möhler's comment on *epi to auto* and *homothumadon*. This he considers as something original in Möhler's work: «When they received the strength and the light from on high, the leaders and members of the new-born Church were not scattered in different places, but gathered together in the same place and in one heart. They formed a single community of brothers. [...] Each disciple therefore was filled with the gifts from on high only because he formed a moral unity with all the other disciples». Y. CONGAR, *Il est Seigneur et Il donne la vie*, 25 (*Lord and Giver of Life*, 15); see also «The Conciliar Structure or Regime of the Church», 6; *Le Concile au jour le jour*. Deuxième session, 23-24 (*Report from Rome II*. On the Second Session of the Vatican Council, 188).

12 Y. CONGAR, *Il est Seigneur et Il donne la vie*, 28 (*Lord and Giver of Life*, 17).

two realities that determine a proper and necessary order in the community. Although the Holy Spirit is given to the whole community, Congar finds that it is justified to attribute a certain priority to the ordained: «The ministry of the Spirit is first and foremost something that has to be carried out by the Apostle, who lays the foundation (1 Cor 3,10; Rom 15,20)»[13]. Thus, Congar maintains that the animating power of the Holy Spirit is not given to a deacon, presbyter or bishop only at the moment of their ordination. Through the mediation of the entire ecclesial community, the Holy Spirit commences to animate them long before the act of ordination itself. Although one cannot be considered as a «candidate» in the modern understanding of the word, from the moment of being elected or called, the prompting of the Holy Spirit actually starts from then onwards[14]. The New Testament and Church history show that the Holy Spirit inspires not only the call to ministry but also its exercise:

> In the actual naming and institution or ordination of ministers, it is clear that the Spirit intervenes. The New Testament bears witness to this in a way that suggests rather than states it clearly (Acts 13, 1-3; 20,28; 1 Tim 1,18; 4,14; 2 Tim 1,6ff). The testimony borne by history, on the other hand, is clear: the Spirit inspires the choice of ministers and enables them to exercise their function by encouraging the qualities required[15].

If Congar clearly states here that the activity of the Holy Spirit begins from the call to prepare for Ordination, he notes that «not everyone possessing the gifts of the Spirit is instituted as a minister, but those who are instituted do in fact possess such gifts»[16]. In other words, the graces bestowed on candidates at their calling by the Holy Spirit are fully actualized in the sacrament of Ordination. Thus for Congar, the structure does not come first with regard to this sacrament, but the Holy Spirit, the Lord who encourages Christians to serve and constitute the Church[17]. For this reason, Ordination is not something unexpected, but a culmination of the whole process during which candidates have answered the call of the Holy Spirit. For Congar, the sacrament is the full expression of the

---

[13] Y. CONGAR, L'expérience de l'Esprit, 56 (The Experience of the Spirit, 33); see also Il est Seigneur et Il donne la vie, 55-56 (Lord and Giver of Life, 39); Ministères et Communion ecclésiale, 19; «Le diaconat dans la théologie des ministères», 124-125.

[14] Cf. Y. CONGAR, Le Fleuve de vie, 344-345 (The River of Life, 268).

[15] Y. CONGAR, Il est Seigneur et Il donne la vie, 20-21 (Lord and Giver of Life, 10).

[16] Y. CONGAR, Il est Seigneur et Il donne la vie, 21 (Lord and Giver of Life, 10).

[17] Cf. Y. CONGAR, Ministères et Communion ecclésiale, 67; see also Le Concile au jour le jour. Deuxième session, 31 (Report from Rome II. On the Second Session of the Vatican Council, 196).

continuity between the initial calling of the candidates and the juridical mission which they assume once they are ordained.

If the empowerment with the Holy Spirit that the ordained receive through Ordination is meant to bring people into contact with Jesus Christ, then it follows that they act according to it by carrying out the two main functions of preaching the Word and celebrating the sacraments. Congar designates these functions as the two tables at which the Holy Spirit enables Christ the Head to nourish his members through the mediation of the ordained:

> Both tables are Christ given to us so that we shall live, and this requires the activity of the Holy Spirit. Each of these realities has an external aspect, which it is possible to consider alone – it is possible to see nothing in scripture but a literary text, nothing in Tradition but a human history, nothing in the Eucharist but a ceremony and nothing in the Church but a sociological phenomenon. Each, however, also has a deep spiritual aspect to which God is committed through his Spirit[18].

Relying on the Pauline understanding of ecclesial ministry, Congar states that the primary responsibility of the ordained is to preach the Word effectively since it is a service rendered to fortify those who exist in Christ Jesus (cf. 2 Cor 1,24)[19]. Considering the intrinsic relationship between the Word and the Spirit, Congar argues that all preaching should be preceded by an invocation of the Spirit, in other words, by an epiclesis[20]. Just as during his public life Jesus of Nazareth manifested the Father, so during his physical absence it is the Holy Spirit who manifests him. Therefore, it is a pre-requisite that, before the Word enshrined in a fixed text be announced, the Holy Spirit be invoked, since the divine *Pneuma* enables those who hear the divine *Logos* to engage in a pneumatic or spiritual listening[21]. For Congar, if the living Word is to touch the inner core of Christians, the ordained must sincerely implore the Spirit to assist with his divine power not only those who announce but

---

[18] Y. CONGAR, *Il est Seigneur et Il donne la vie*, 42-43 (*Lord and Giver of Life*, 28-29).

[19] Cf. Y. CONGAR, *L'expérience de l'Esprit*, 56 (*The Experience of the Spirit*, 33); see also «Institutionalized Religion», in *The Word in History*: The St. Xavier Symposium, ed. P. Burke, New York 1966, 146; «Magisterium, Theologians, the Faithful and the Faith», *DL* 31 (1981) 549; *Il est Seigneur et Il donne la vie*, 50 (*Lord and Giver of Life*, 33-34).

[20] Cf. Y. CONGAR, *Le Fleuve de vie*, 347-348 (*The River of Life*, 270).

[21] Cf. Y. CONGAR, *Appelés à la vie*, 47 (*Called to Life*, 40); see also *Le Fleuve de vie*, 348-349 (*The River of Life*, 270).

also those who hear the Gospel (Acts 16,14)[22]. The implication is that, if the presence of the Holy Spirit in the ordained makes their preaching truly spiritual, those who hear them can experience the living presence of Christ in their midst[23].

The ordained also depend on the power received from the Holy Spirit so as to render the Word most intensely active in the sacraments. Congar thus states that the effective enactment of the sacraments results from the imploration of the Holy Spirit on the part of the ordained[24]. Consequently, the ordained invoke the Holy Spirit at the liturgical celebrations because of the salvific grace granted to them at their Ordination[25]. Moreover, Congar asserts that, through the preaching of the Gospel [*munus docendi*] and through the administration of sacraments [*munus sanctificandi*], the ordained fulfill their mandate to foster the spiritual growth and fraternal unity of the faithful [*munus pascendi*]. Therefore, for Congar, the ministry of the ordained is not only a hierarchic transmission of power based on the presence of the Holy Spirit in them, but also a charismatic service ordered in view of forming the members of the community evermore into a single body[26]. In this body, the ordained represent Christ as the transcendent Head of the baptized and confirmed members, just as the latter represent his immanent closeness in those who are gathered in his name: «Since the Church is constituted as the active sign of God's design for salvation, the sacrament of Order plays a decisive part along with the Baptism and the Eucharist: it structures the people of God by representing visibly Christ as head and as sanctifier»[27]. Although lay people can represent the immanence of Christ in the Church, they cannot give full expression to his identity as the head

---

22 Cf. Y. CONGAR, *Le Fleuve de vie*, 348 (*The River of Life*, 270); see also *Il est Seigneur et Il donne la vie*, 41 (*Lord and Giver of Life*, 27-28); *La Parole et le Souffle*, 49 (*The Word and the Spirit*, 23).

23 Cf. Y. CONGAR, *La Tradition et les traditions*: vol. 2, 45 (*Tradition and Traditions*: vol. 2, 272).

24 Cf. Y. CONGAR, «La pneumatologie dans la théologie catholique», *RSPT* 51 (1967) 257; see also *Il est Seigneur et Il donne la vie*, 21 (*Lord and Giver of Life*, 10).

25 Cf. Y. CONGAR, *Le Fleuve de vie*, 344-345 (*The River of Life*, 269-270); see also *Le Concile de Vatican II*. Son Église peuple de Dieu et corps du Christ, 167.

26 Cf. Y. CONGAR, «La hiérarchie comme service, selon le nouveau testament et les documents de la tradition», in *L'épiscopat et l'Église universelle*, eds. B.D. Dupuy – Y. Congar, Paris 1962, 94; see also *The Church Peaceful*, Dublin 1977, 11; *Appelés à la vie*, 113 (*Called to Life*, 106).

27 Y. CONGAR, «L'idée de sacrements majeurs ou principaux», 31 («The Idea of "Major" or "Principal" Sacraments», 14); see also «L'Église, comme peuple de Dieu», 17-18 («The Church, People of God», 8-9).

of his social body. For this reason, Congar states that an ordained person «is not only, as a Christian, the offerer of his own spiritual sacrifice: he is also, as a minister, the servant of other Christians»[28]. Hence, the ordained function as a living anamnesis of Christ's self-giving, so that they might help all the faithful arrive at the *res* of the Eucharist, that is, the unity of the members in their head. In other words, the ordained sanctify the community, because in the synaxis they invoke the Holy Spirit to consecrate not only the gifts of bread and wine but also the faithful who receive them[29].

Congar comments that in the liturgical formula: «The Lord be with you» – «And with your spirit» intends to call to mind the special presence of the Holy Spirit in the member of the ministerial priesthood who is to preside. Although the formula could be said simply to denote a greeting in keeping with the proper religious atmosphere of the celebration, Congar insists that it signifies a pneumatological truth: «The formula "the Lord is (be) with [...]" is frequently used in the Old Testament and it is often concerned with an action that has to be done according to God's plan and is connected with the presence of the Spirit in the one who has to perform this action»[30]. In the Hebrew scriptures, this greeting meant that the presence of the Holy Spirit in the official ministers is a reality essential to the salvific character of the event about to take place. Through the divine power which leaders receive at the moment of their Ordination, they possess a permanent charism of the Spirit. In other words, the phrases «The Lord be with you» – «And with your spirit» bear public witness to the fact that the Holy Spirit is to act in and through the mediation of those who perform a saving action for the good of the People of God[31].

Consequently, Congar argues that the ordained do not simply act spontaneously as they fulfill their spiritual functions, for these call for a constant epiclesis. This epicletic dimension of the official ministry does not deny the permanent presence of the Holy Spirit in them through Ordination, but makes them conscious of «the relationship between the Christian community and the minister who is the president and the pastor

---

[28] Y. CONGAR, «Institutionalized Religion», 146; see also *The Church Peaceful*, 22.

[29] Cf. Y. CONGAR, «Le Saint-Esprit dans la consécration et la communion selon la tradition occidentale», *Nic* 9 (1981) 384.

[30] Y. CONGAR, *L'expérience de l'Esprit*, 62 (*The Experience of the Spirit*, 36-37).

[31] Cf. Y. CONGAR, *L'expérience de l'Esprit*, 62-63 (*The Experience of the Spirit*, 37); see also *Le Fleuve de vie*, 306-307 (*The River of Life*, 236).

of that community»[32]. Therefore, under the following sub-section attention is given to how the epicletic dimension of Ordination renders the ordinandi capable of acting both *in persona Christi* and *in persona ecclesiae* by means of the laying on of hands and the epiclesis of the Holy Spirit.

2. The Laying on of Hands as the Recognition of a Special Charism which Represents both Christ and the Church

From what has been stated thus far, the rite of Ordination is viewed by Congar as essentially linked to the gift of the Holy Spirit received by the Twelve at Pentecost, and for this reason unites the mission of the ordained to theirs. In other words, the Church in the West has identified the ordained as the sacramental representatives of the Apostles whom Christ consecrated once for all time. For this reason, Congar states that «presbyterial priesthood binds the believers to the historical incarnation through means positively and historically instituted for it»[33]. Furthermore, Congar asked himself how the apostolic ministry, inaugurated by Jesus and animated by the Holy Spirit (cf. Acts 1,2), could be continued in the life of the Church after the original Twelve had died. The succession of their apostleship could be realized only through the power of the Holy Spirit transmitted in some tangible way[34]. It is, in fact, quite evident in the early Christian Church that, whenever the Apostles formally appointed the leaders of a particular community, they laid hands on them so as to signify their intention that the Holy Spirit be given them. In the case of Saul and Barnabas, it is said in Acts 13,3 that, before they were sent to build up the Church in Antioch, hands were laid on them. The verse that follows indicates that they were sent on their mission by the very Holy Spirit imparted to them through this laying on of hands (Acts 13,4). The same idea is operative in Paul's address to the elders of the Church at Ephesus: «Take heed to yourselves and to all the flock, in which the Holy Spirit has made you overseers, [...]»(Acts 20,28)[35]. Because of the presence of the Holy Spirit in Church leaders by means of

---

[32] Y. CONGAR, *L'expérience de l'Esprit*, 152 (*The Experience of the Spirit*, 107); see also «L'*ecclesia* ou communauté chrétienne, sujet intégral de l'action liturgique», 243.

[33] Y. CONGAR, *The Church Peaceful*, 27; see also «Actualité d'une pneumatologie», 129 («Pneumatology Today», 445).

[34] Cf. Y. CONGAR, *Il est Seigneur et Il donne la vie*, 21 (*Lord and Giver of Life*, 10).

[35] Cf. Y. CONGAR, *Il est Seigneur et Il donne la vie*, 60 (*Lord and Giver of Life*, 42-43).

the imposition of hands, Congar found that their words were so effective in convincing those who heard the message, and that their gestures were so inspired that ever new disciples of Christ were strengthened by them (cf. Acts 8, 14 -17).

This co-ordination between the activity of the Holy Spirit and that of the Apostles was continued in the members of the presbyterate or the episcopate who were ordained through the symbolic act of the laying on of hands. Therefore, this ritual, while it creates a direct relationship with Christ, is at the same time mediated through the Spirit-filled apostolic institution. In other words, the sacrament of Order is a prolongation in the identity and the mission of the Twelve, so as to guarantee the fact that the priestly people founded by Jesus is served by the very institution which he established: «Let us briefly say that Jesus instituted a structured community, a community entirely holy, priestly, prophetical, missionary, apostolic at the heart of its life. Some are promoted liberally by the Holy Spirit, others join to this with an imposition of hands which is connected to the institution and to the mission of the Twelve»[36]. Thus, in the ecclesial sacrament of Order through the invocation of the Holy Spirit and the imposition of hands on the part of the bishop, the ordained are linked to the apostolic mission initiated by the *Logos* and set in motion by the divine *Pneuma*. Just as at Pentecost the Holy Spirit permeated the Apostles with his power, so at Ordination the same empowerment is historically prolonged for the good of the priestly people who form the Church. It is therefore clear that Congar does not develop a theology of Order apart from consideration of the service to be rendered to the ecclesial community. His aim in presenting the sacrament of Order as an epicletic event is to conjoin it to the life of the community.

From the studies of ancient liturgical texts, Congar concluded that almost all the prayers of Ordination formally implore the Father that the Spirit be communicated to the new ministers, who receive the laying on

---

[36] Y. CONGAR, *Ministères et Communion ecclésiale*, 19; see also «My Path-Findings in the Theology of Laity and Ministries», 178; *La Parole et le Souffle*, 185 (*The Word and the Spirit*, 116). «[Ordination] provides a link with the apostolic institution that comes from Christ, the founder of the new people of God. The Ordination that one has received from his bishop in the communion of the *ecclesia* makes the priest a member of that chain of mission and ministry in which the Twelve were the first links. He is the presence in a certain sense of the bishop, who is himself the presence of the apostolic Body. He is therefore qualified to link the community, which is living from its foundation, to the institution in its apostolicity and its catholicity. The ordained minister therefore possesses in his own right the sacramental actions – the forgiveness of sins and the Eucharist – that were handed over to the Apostles». Y. CONGAR, *La Parole et le Souffle*, 134-135 (*The Word and the Spirit*, 82-83).

of hands from the bishop. This ritual act is the outward sign that the Holy Spirit has been bestowed on those who are to teach, sanctify and unite the community of Jesus Christ. Congar explicitly states that this ritual act comprises an epiclesis:

> This is in itself a gesture pointing to the communication of the Spirit, but it has always been accompanied or followed by prayer. It is also a gesture that was practiced by the Apostles and the first disciples (Acts 6,6; 13,3; cf. 1 Tim 4,16; 2 Tim 1,6). The "form" of Ordination is the preface which is a deprecative expression and for this reason it is clearly an epiclesis[37].

With regard to the administration of Ordination, Congar observes that in the theological tradition the phrase has always been used «give the Holy Spirit for sanctifying». Thus, one cannot separate the gift of the Holy Spirit from his divine Person. In receiving the Spirit through the laying on of hands, the candidates enter into a permanent relationship with the divine *Pneuma* who is uncreated grace itself. Therefore, the Holy Spirit unites the candidates to Jesus Christ the Head and to all his members so that, once sent on mission, they can perform the holy mysteries which sanctify the mystical Body[38]. Thus, the epiclesis enacted at the sacrament of Order renders the candidates holy in an objective manner, so that they are conjoined to the Head and the members of the Church and can make visible the holiness being communicated from the One to the many. However, although the laying on of hands is viewed by Congar as the form of the sacrament of Order, he is reluctant to isolate the precise moment when the formal epiclesis first was effective in the candidates. For Congar, the sanctifying action is possibly initiated at the election of the candidates, and is completed in the solemn act of Ordination and in the ministry which follows it.

---

[37] Y. CONGAR, *Le Fleuve de vie*, 345 (*The River of Life*, 268). Congar found this is well developed in the epiclesis for the Ordination of the priests in the *Eucology of Serapion*. It reads: «We raise our hand, sovereign God of heaven, Father of your only Son, over this man and we pray that the Spirit of truth may fill him. Grant him the understanding and the knowledge of a right heart. May the Holy Spirit be with him so that he may govern your people with you, un-created God. Through the Spirit of Moses, you have poured out your Holy Spirit over those whom you have chosen. Grant also to this man the Holy Spirit, through the Spirit of your only Son, in the grace of wisdom, growth and right faith, so that he may serve you with a pure conscience through your only Son Jesus Christ. Through him may glory and honour be given to you for ever and ever. Amen». Y. CONGAR, *Le Fleuve de vie*, 345 (*The River of Life*, 273).

[38] Cf. Y. CONGAR, *A mes frères*, Paris 1968, 20; see also «Réflections et recherches actuelles sur l'assemblée liturgique», 14-15 («Reflection on the Liturgical Assembly», 151); *Ministères et Communion ecclésiale*, 46; «My Path-Findings in the Theology of Laity and Ministries», 180, 188.

Therefore, for Congar, the ministerial function of the ordained springs neither from their capacity nor from their initiative; rather they arise from acting «*in persona Christi or in nomine Christi*»[39]. According to Congar, the theology underlying this Western understanding of ministerial actions is based on the biblical notion *Salïah*, which implies that those sent represent the one who sends them. Consequently, the bishops and the priests are to be viewed as the images of the Father or of the Son acting in the midst of the ecclesial community through the Holy Spirit, and thus representing the transcendent character of the mystical Body:

> This idea has antecedents of a very firm kind in the biblical notion of the *Salïah* the messenger commissioned by an authority that he makes present by representing, and also in the idea so well known in the early centuries of Christianity that the bishop [the priest] was the image of the Father or the image of Christ in the midst of the Christian community and over and against the people[40].

This is very much evident especially in the case of the Eucharistic liturgy, for the early Christians believed that the role of the presiders had an *iconic* value; they officiate in the name of Christ, the eternal High Priest, and re-actualize what he did once and for all time. This Western understanding of the bishops or priests as acting *in persona Christi* does not deny that «the one who acts *in nomine Christi* acts through the power of the Spirit bestowed at the time of ordination. He acts effectively *in persona Christi* for the fulfillment of the *oikonomia* of the mystery»[41]. Hence, for Congar, the gift of the Holy Spirit enables functions to be performed *in persona Christi*, for the authority of the ordained is not their own; it is received from Christ and the Spirit. However, Congar acknowledges that due to certain theological trends, evident in the West from the twelfth century onwards, the term *in persona Christi* was

---

39 Y. CONGAR, *Le Fleuve de vie*, 305 (*The River of Life*, 234); see also «L'*ecclesia* ou communauté chrétienne, sujet intégral de l'action liturgique», 263-264.

40 Y. CONGAR, *Le Fleuve de vie*, 305 (*The River of Life*, 234-235); see also «Actualité renouvelée du Saint-Esprit», *LV* 27 (1972) 558-559; Eng. vers. «Renewed Actuality of the Holy Spirit», *LV* 28 (1973) 29.

41 Y. CONGAR, *Le Fleuve de vie*, 309 (*The River of Life*, 237); see also «Le diaconat dans la théologie des Ministères», 131. Clear evidence can be found in the renewed ritual of the Ordination of priests and the acceptance of Hippolytus' prayer for the consecration of the bishop. The new prayer for the Ordination reads: "Make your servants here present priests of Jesus Christ through renewing them by your Holy Spirit". With regard to the ordination of the bishop, the consecratory prayer from Hippolytus' *Apostolic Tradition* has been adopted. Cf. Y. CONGAR, *L'expérience de l'Esprit*, 230 (*The Experience of the Spirit*, 169).

severed from its original ecclesial context. For example, he states that «such a term as *sacerdos alter Christus* has to be understood in its true sense»[42].

In order to maintain the proper meaning of the notion *in persona Christi*, Congar insists that it is to be linked to the co-related concept *in persona ecclesiae*, according to which the ordained represents the entire worshiping community: «He represents not only Christ, the sovereign high priest, in whose person he acts, but also the *ecclesia*, the community of Christians, in whose person he acts also. He therefore acts *in persona Christi* and *in persona ecclesiae*. One of these aspects cannot be isolated from the other – the one is contained within the other»[43]. In this text, and especially in its last phrase, Congar is indirectly criticizing the normal Western mode of understanding the notion *in persona ecclesiae* as subordinated to the notion *in persona Christi*, thereby granting more significance to christology than to pneumatology with regard to Order[44]. Congar in fact proposes that the notion *in persona Christi* be included within the concept *in persona ecclesiae*. So as to support this position, he appeals to the Eastern theological tradition which, due to its emphasis on the pneumatic origin of the community, stresses that the spiritual power that the ordained receive through the laying on of hands at the rite of Ordination exists solely for building up the community of the faithful. Following this view, Congar firmly states that the sanctifying power of the ordained is not something inherent in them, over which they could exercise dominion; «this power is rather the grace of the Holy Spirit which is operative, and even ensured, through them *"in the Church"*»[45]. Thus, Congar argues that the sacrament of Order should never be isolated from particular pastoral needs, since every Ordination actually serves to meet these. By reflecting on the use of such words as, *ordinare* and *ordinatio*, Congar demonstrates that, from the early centuries onwards, the ministry of the ordained was understood in relation to a specific

---

[42] Y. CONGAR, *Le Fleuve de vie*, 308 (*The River of Life*, 236).

[43] Y. CONGAR, *Le Fleuve de vie*, 306 (*The River of Life*, 235); see also «L'*ecclesia* ou communauté chrétienne, sujet intégral de l'action liturgique», 282.

[44] «An insistence on the Christological aspect – this has occurred in the West – means that the *in persona ecclesiae* is situated within the *in persona Christi*, which is consequently seen as the basis and the reason for the first. *Mediator Dei* presents the teaching in this way». Y. CONGAR, *Le Fleuve de vie*, 306 (*The River of Life*, 235); see also «Ministères et structuration de l'Église», 10.

[45] Y. CONGAR, *Le Fleuve de vie*, 306 (*The River of Life*, 236); see also *Le Concile au jour le jour*. Deuxième session, 30 (*Report from Rome II. On the Second Session of the Vatican Council*, 196).

service in the community of the faithful which is the place in which the Holy Spirit constantly dwells[46].

Because of this essentially communitarian dimension of ordained ministry, which is based on the epicletic nature of the act of Ordination itself, Congar situates the priest within the body of the baptized: «The priest is truly a member of the community. In a sense he emerges from it. But he does not derive from it his role as president. That he owes to his Ordination, which is derived by succession down the ages from the mission of Christ to the Apostles»[47]. Here, Congar distances himself from the sequences which he used in the early stages of his writings, marked by an overemphasis on christology: *from Christ – to the priest – to the laity*. Instead he proposes the sequence: *from Christ – to the community – with its ordained ministries*[48]. This thought pattern does not deny, however, that through the laying on of hands at the rite of Ordination the candidates acquire a permanent character which is not the same as those imprinted at Baptism and Confirmation: «These two sacraments establish the being of the Christian. The sacrament of Ordination establishes a ministerial representation; it is charism of function»[49]. Therefore, although the ordained represent the community, they are not its delegates as such. In this context it is worthwhile to cite the saying of St. Cyprian to which Congar often refers: «The bishop is in the Church and the Church is in the bishop»[50]. Although, through the laying on of hands, the candidates are linked to the apostolic body and thus to Christ, the eternal High Priest, their election arose from within the community in which the Holy Spirit resides permanently. For this reason, the community has an indispensable role in the formation and in the imparting of the Spirit to the candidates.

Through studies concerning the understanding of the early Church regarding the rite of Ordination, Congar found that the involvement of

---

[46] Cf. Y. CONGAR, *Ministères et Communion ecclésiale*, 21, 93-94; see also «My-Path Findings in the Theology of Laity and Ministries», 180; «Ministères et structuration de l'Église», 11.

[47] Y. CONGAR, *Appelés à la vie*, 128 (*Called to Life*, 121-122).

[48] Cf. Y. CONGAR, *Appelés à la vie*, 122 (*Called to Life*, 115); see also «My Path-findings in the Theology of Laity and Ministries», 176; «Réflexions et recherches actuelles sur l'assemblée liturgique», 14 («Reflections on the Liturgical Assembly», 151); *La Parole et le Souffle*, 184-185 (*The Word and the Spirit*, 115); «Ministères et structuration de l'Église», 13.

[49] Y. CONGAR, *The Church Peaceful*, 21; see also «Le diaconat dans la théologie des Ministères», 125.

[50] Y. CONGAR, «The Conciliar Structure or Regime of the Church», 5 as cited from G.V. Hartel, *S. Thasci Caecili Cypriani*: vol. 2, Vindobonae 1871, 732.

the faithful in it is quite pronounced. The community, even without a previous consultation, presented to the bishop one of its members to be ordained as a deacon or presbyter[51]. Even today, Congar notes, the share of the community in the whole process of Ordination is not explicitly taken into consideration. The consequence is that those who are ordained in and for the community often forget its role: «Is vocation a controlled, personal *attraction*, verified by superiors and then consecrated, or is it not rather the recognition, by the community and its head, of gifts which mark someone out for the receipt of a *mission* by being consecrated at the hands of the bishop? And is not that the case for the bishops themselves?»[52] The share of the community in the imparting of the Holy Spirit to the candidates, Congar argues, concerns not only their selection and formation but even the liturgical act of Ordination itself[53]. Thus, at the rite, the Holy Spirit is communicated to the candidates through the laying on of hands by the bishop and through the prayer of invocation, in which the community takes part: «The Spirit is not a gift communicated merely by the laying on of hands. He is invoked in the epiclesis in which the whole community shares. The community has already taken part in the awakening and maturing of a vocation and in the choice of an individual or the approval of his selection»[54]. This truth is well illustrated in the revised liturgies of Ordination since, while the bishop officially calls upon the Holy Spirit to consecrate the candidates, the entire assembly remains in silence, and prays along with him[55].

Although in the early Christian communities the episcopate, the presbyterate and the diaconate seem to have been understood primarily as charisms by which to build up the Church, Congar does not deny that

---

[51] Cf. Y. CONGAR, *Ministères et Communion ecclésiale*, 20; see also «My Path-findings in the Theology of Laity and Ministries», 179; «Vocation sacerdotale et vocation chrétienne», *Sem* 19 (1967) 8-9.

[52] Y. CONGAR, *Ministères et Communion ecclésiale*, 20; see also «My Path-findings in the Theology of Laity and Ministries», 179.

[53] Concerning its execution Congar suggests the following: «In the course of his formation the candidate should go through a probationary stage before the diaconate or as a deacon. In this way he inserts himself in a community of Christians who will intervene in a very effective way to form him. The community will effect the maturation of a minister who, in a certain way, will emanate from it: before the Ordination, in a visit to the bishop, and on the day of Ordination publicly, some faithful will come to bear witness in regard to the one whom they have known and assisted in becoming a minister of the Gospel». Y. CONGAR, *The Church Peaceful*, 82.

[54] Y. CONGAR, *La Parole et le Souffle*, 70-71 (*The Word and the Spirit*, 35).

[55] Cf. Y. CONGAR, *La Parole et le Souffle*, 184-185 (*The Word and the Spirit*, 116); see also *L'expérience de l'Esprit*, 152-153 (*The Experience of the Spirit*, 107); *Il est Seigneur et Il donne la vie*, 64-66 (*Lord and Giver of Life*, 44-45).

these rites confer a juridical and liturgical form of power as well. This empowerment, which the candidates receive through the symbolic act of the laying on of hands and not from a later conferral of jurisdiction, indicates that Ordination is effected not only by the institution of Christ but also by the gift of the Spirit. In and through the anamnesis and epiclesis enacted at the liturgical celebration of Ordination, the divine missions of the Son and of the Holy Spirit complement one another[56]. The complementarity of the two missions is expressed in theological texts, in iconography and in the liturgy itself, which in this respect is particularly noteworthy. In the rite for the consecration of bishops, Congar finds theological significance in the act of placing the Gospel on the head and the shoulders of the elect before proceeding with the laying on of hands. The first action depicts graphically that the bishop is to carry out the mission of Christ, and the laying on of hands which follows signifies that the bishop can do so only because he shares in the Pentecostal gift conferred on the Twelve:

> Before the laying on of hands by the consecrating bishop, the Gospel is placed on the head and shoulders of the bishop elect. This gesture has several meanings. The Gospel is Christ and the laying on of hands that follows makes the gesture of blessing which Christ, when he ascended into heaven, made over the Apostles as a sign of the imminent bestowal of the Spirit a present reality[57].

Congar states that this impressive ritual effectively indicates the intrinsic relationship between Christ and the Spirit, which is operative not only at the rite of Ordination but also in every act of fulfilling the mission of the episcopacy. Consequently, Congar affirms that «the fine rite of placing the book of the Gospel on the head of the one elected symbolizes the tongues of fire, which at the first Pentecost inaugurated Christian preaching»[58]. Moreover, Congar notes that, in the part of the *Apostolic*

---

[56] Cf. Y. CONGAR, *Il est Seigneur et Il donne la vie*, 65-66 (*Lord and Giver of Life*, 45-46); see also *Ministères et communion ecclésiale*, 40.

[57] Y. CONGAR, *La Parole et Souffle*, 50-51 (*The Word and the Spirit*, 24). «For the consecration of a bishop, the rite of the imposition of the Gospel, attested in the East from the end of the fourth century, at Rome in the sixth, and in Gaul in the seventh; or there is the ceremonial accompanying the solemn liturgical proclamation of the Gospel, especially the "*Gloria tibi, Domine*", of Eastern origin which entered the West through the Gallican liturgy». Y. CONGAR, *La Tradition et les traditions*: vol. 2, 45 (*Tradition and Traditions*: vol. 2, 272).

[58] Y. CONGAR, *L'expérience de l'Esprit*, 153 (*The Experience of the Spirit*, 107). In Severian of Gabala's (A. D. 400) comments on this ritual, Congar discovered that the imposition of the Gospels on the elect is similar to the tongues of fire that the Apostles received on the day of Pentecost: «The presence of tongues on their [that is, the Apostles]

Constitution which concerns the ritual of Ordination, it is stipulated that, while the ordaining bishop pronounces a prayer during the imposition of the Gospel, the other bishops, the priests and all the faithful pray in silence for the descent of the Holy Spirit[59].

In order to conclude this chapter, it can be said that Congar develops an explicitly epicletic understanding of Order by means of the following logical process: During Jesus' public ministry he selected the Twelve from the other disciples in order to continue his ministry after he would be physically absent from the nascent community he had established. As soon as he was glorified, he could send his own Spirit upon the community gathered around the Twelve, so that it could activate the mission entrusted to it. For Congar, the ecclesial rites of Ordination to the diaconate, the presbyterate or the episcopate center on a solemn imploration of the Holy Spirit, so that each grade of ministry might participate in the chain of empowerment of which the Twelve are the first links. However, Congar considers this empowerment more as a process than as a rite. Ordination with the Holy Spirit actually begins at the moment when the vocation or election of the candidates takes place, a choice in which the active participation of the entire community is an invaluable factor. As an approval of their selection, the sacrament of Order is conferred by the bishop of the community who lays his hands on the head of the candidates and invokes on them the presence of the Holy Spirit who was bestowed on the Apostles on the day of Pentecost. Just as the community takes part in the selection and maturing of ecclesial vocations, at the rite of Ordination itself it also participates in the most important moment, that is, in the act of invoking the divine *Pneuma* on the ordinandi. This fact does not mean to negate that through the sacrament of Ordination the whole being of the ordained is consecrated to Christ, the sole and sovereign Priest of the New Testament and that they possess the empowerment to preach the Word, to administer the sacraments and to guide the people in unity. Yet, it should not be forgotten that the ordained act in all these ways *in persona Christi* and *in persona ecclesiae*. Although Congar dedicated much time to research on the sacrament of Ordination, he never lost sight of its sure foundation in

---

heads is therefore the sign of the Ordination. Indeed, as custom demands, down to the present time, since the descent of the Spirit is invisible, the book of the Gospels is placed on the head of the person who is to be ordained archpriest and, when this imposition is made, all that should be seen is a tongue of fire on the head – a tongue because of the preaching of the Gospel and a tongue of fire because of the words: "I have come to bring fire on earth"». Y. CONGAR, *La Parole et Souffle*, 51 (*The Word and the Spirit*, 24).

[59] Cf. Y. CONGAR, *La Parole et Souffle*, 51 (*The Word and the Spirit*, 24).

the sacraments of Baptism and Confirmation. Hence in the following chapter, the epicletic dimensions of both these sacraments are considered.

CHAPTER IV

Baptism and Confirmation:
Dual Anointing with the Holy Spirit
and Progressive Incorporation into the Body of Christ

This chapter on the first two sacraments of Christian initiation further illustrates the way in which Congar viewed the invocation of the Holy Spirit as a constitutive factor of all the sacraments of the Church. Like the previous one, this chapter examines his writings from 1962 to 1986, by means of two sub-sections dealing respectively with the epicletic dimensions of Baptism and Confirmation. Since these sacraments are explained by Congar in terms of a pneumatological christology, this theme is briefly exposed at the beginning of the chapter. The mutual relation between the Word and the Breath who originate from the Father is operative from the outset of salvation history, and yet becomes fully explicit in the redemptive event. As the divine *Logos* is conceived in the womb of the virgin Mary, is anointed in the Jordan, undertakes a public mission of words, signs and service and offers himself in death on the cross, the divine *Pneuma* renders these actions universal and definitive sources of spiritual rebirth for humankind. According to Congar, since the entire life of Jesus of Nazareth was pervaded with the eschatological power of the Spirit, he could communicate the same power to his followers, once he achieved glorification. With the coming of the Spirit at Pentecost, the signs which Jesus instituted during his public life could constitute his Church as the universal sacrament of salvation in the world. Thus, although the sacramentality of the Church is dependent on its founder, it can perpetually serve as the means of salvation for all peoples only because the Holy Spirit of Jesus Christ permeates all its sacred actions.

Thereafter, it is shown in the first sub-section that, since the sacraments of Baptism and Confirmation are to extend the benefits of Easter and Pentecost in a personal manner to all those who come to Christian faith, they are effected through the collaboration of the Word and the Spirit. Accordingly Congar finds the roots of the sacrament of Baptism in Jesus' intention to fulfill all justice at the Jordan, for which he received the anointing with the Holy Spirit who accompanied him throughout his mission, and into death and glory. The ecclesial rite of Baptism thus plunges believers into the water so as to share in Jesus' death and, on emerging from the water, to share in his glory. Then they are anointed with his Spirit, so as to enjoy the new status of being children of God the Father along with him. This new status of being anointed and guided by the Holy Spirit should continue throughout their entire existence, in order to be fully realized only in the future Kingdom of God. The constitutive role of the invocation of the Holy Spirit in the sacrament of Baptism thus guarantees that the justification of believers in Christ perdures not only in history but also in the world to come.

In the second sub-section on Confirmation, it is explained how Congar perceives that the new life of the baptized is made ever more explicit and effective. He bases the relation between Baptism and Confirmation on the two divine missions: that of the Son and that of the Spirit. For him, Confirmation is sharing in the messianic anointing of Jesus Christ, by which the Spirit enabled him to commit himself to the mandate he had received from the Father. Similarly, although the baptized continually live by the promptings of the Spirit, the sacrament of Confirmation strengthens them with charisms so that they might exercise more fully the threefold aspects of the priesthood of Jesus Christ: prophetic, cultic and pastoral. Through Confirmation, the baptized are inserted into the communitarian and missionary tasks of the social Body of Christ. In order to render the seriousness of this sacrament more clear, Congar highly recommends that it should be prepared for in a thorough manner, with the hope that the awareness of the gift of the Holy Spirit in the consciousness of adult Christians will greatly enhance their participation in all aspects of ecclesial life and mission.

1. Baptism as an Anointing with the Spirit of the Son for Regaining the Sonship of God within the Church

Although Congar's conception of the involvement of the Holy Spirit in the sacramental life of the Church gradually evolved, it became more explicit in the conciliar period. From then on, he began to consider pneumatology as more than the abstract dogmatic treatise about the third Person of the Trinity. According to his new understanding, pneumatology is meant to «describe the impact, in the context of a vision of the Church, of the fact that the Spirit distributes his gifts as he wills and in this way builds up the Church»[1]. Although the economy of salvation originates in the will of the Father and culminates in the self-giving of the Son, it is communicated in the power of the Holy Spirit. In the sacramental rites of the Church, which comprise the symbolic making-present of divine salvation, the same movement is to be discerned: grace comes from the Father, through the Son, and in the Spirit. Then the Spirit, through the Son, leads the faithful to union with the Father. Thus, the invocation of the Holy Spirit at the sacraments «does not first pertain to sacramental theology, but to theology as such, that is to say, to the doctrine of the Trinity, and then to the economy of salvation which reflects this theology»[2]. Therefore, in order to understand the role of the Holy Spirit in the sacraments of Baptism and Confirmation, a brief consideration should be given to Congar's trinitarian approach to the event of salvation.

God is the absolute Principle without origin from whom the missions of the Son [Word] and of the Spirit [Breath] eternally emerge[3]. If these divine missions first became manifest in history, this does not mean that they did not exist before, or that their existence was not relevant in the world: «The Word, then, was already in the world from the beginning (Jn 1,10), but he also came into the world (Jn 1, 11,14). The Spirit was also already there (Gen 1,2) and also he came»[4]. Consequently, for Congar, their respective salvific and sanctifying missions are gratuitous acts by which the eternal and divine processions freely grant salvation to humankind within the history of the world. The mutual relation between the mission of the Word and that of the Spirit becomes most explicit in the event of the incarnation. Congar notes that the divine *Pneuma* has an indispensable role in two aspects in this event. The first is the Holy Spirit's active intervention in bringing about the conception of Jesus in

---

[1] Y. CONGAR, *L'expérience de l'Esprit*, 216 (*The Experience of the Spirit*, 156); see also «Actualité renouvelée du Saint-Esprit», 557-558 («Renewed Actuality of the Holy Spirit», 20-21); «Initiatives locales et normes universelles», *LMD* 112 (1972) 67-68; Eng. vers. «The Need for Pluralism in the Church», *DL* 24 (1974) 353; «Actualité d'une pneumatologie», 125 («Pneumatology Today», 440).

[2] Y. CONGAR, «Pneumatologie ou christomonisme dans la tradition latine?», 397; see also *L'expérience de l'Esprit*, 147-148 (*The Experience of the Spirit*, 104); *Le Fleuve de vie*, 309 (*The River of Life*, 237-238).

[3] Cf. Y. CONGAR, *La Parole et le Souffle*, 35 (*The Word and the Spirit*, 15); see also *Il est Seigneur et Il donne la vie*, 116-117 (*Lord and Giver of Life*, 85).

[4] Y. CONGAR, *Il est Seigneur et Il donne la vie*, 17 (*Lord and Giver of Life*, 8).

Mary's womb, and the second is his consecration of Jesus at the baptism in the Jordan: «It is the Holy Spirit who, already, as the third Person, has anointed and consecrated or sanctified Christ in view of his mission of salvation: a first time in constituting Christ through the incarnation (Lk 1,35), a second time in anointing him for his ministry at the time of his baptism»[5]. This implies that Jesus of Nazareth not only possessed the Holy Spirit and was hallowed by him, but also carried out all his activities, even his self-giving on the cross at the prompting of the divine *Pneuma*.

According to Congar, at the event of his baptism Jesus began to understand that he was to give himself over to the salvific plan of the heavenly Father: «His baptism, his encounter with John the Baptist, the Spirit's coming to him and the word that accompanied that coming were certainly all events of decisive importance in making explicit his human consciousness of his identity as the one who was chosen and sent and as the Son of God and the Servant and Lamb of God»[6]. This consciousness of Jesus primarily entailed a sense of the type of servant he was to be, that is, one who would ultimately submit his total being to the Father for the sake of others (cf. Heb 10, 5 -10). Therefore, for Congar, the baptism of Jesus was the primordial moment of his death, and the latter the consequence of the radical service demanded by the former (cf. Mk 10,38; Lk 12,50). It follows that what occurred in the Jordan was not a mere rite, but the anointing with the Holy Spirit and the beginning of the messianic era: «Within this regime, "baptizing" should not be identified with the rite. It points to the whole of Jesus' activity and to his mission, which was declared when he received John the Baptist's water-baptism, followed by anointing by the Spirit, and which inaugurates the messianic era, which is characterized by the gift of the Holy Spirit»[7]. Congar points out that, according to Scripture, once the just Jesus had entered into the water, identifying himself with those who were unjust, the Spirit came down on him to initiate the end-time. In the same way, Christians are immersed into the water of Baptism as those passing from injustice to justice (1 Cor 5,21), and the Spirit is given to them as the pledge of eternal life. Therefore, it is a primary mystery of faith that those who have been baptized into Jesus Christ and anointed by the Holy Spirit have a new and messianic identity. They enjoy a common existence with their

---

[5] Y. CONGAR, «Pneumatologie ou christomonisme dans la tradition latine?», 398; see also *Il est Seigneur et Il donne la vie*, 272 (*Lord and Giver of Life*, 213-214).

[6] Y. CONGAR, *L'expérience de l'Esprit*, 38 (*The Experience of the Spirit*, 17).

[7] Y. CONGAR, *Il est Seigneur et Il donne la vie*, 244 (*Lord and Giver of Life*, 191); see also *La Foi et la Théologie*, 20.

Saviour since, in and through Baptism, «it is the same Spirit who is in Christ and in Christians»[8].

Congar compares this relationship between water and the Holy Spirit with the connection between these two realities in the creation account of *Genesis*. Just as at the beginning the Spirit hovered over the water (Gen 1,2), so Baptism as an initiation sacrament, entails water, over which the Spirit moves, so as to create a new reality in the universe. Commenting on this parallel, Congar says that «this water is like the womb of our mother, the Church, in which the Spirit gives birth to the Body of Christ»[9]. This reflection is based on the close affiliation made between the Holy Spirit and water in the Scriptures and in the writings of the Fathers. In fact, almost all the water images that are found in the Old Testament actually refer to the life-giving identity of the Holy Spirit[10]. Congar finds much evidence of this truth in the Fourth Gospel, especially in Jn 3,5:

> It is clear that the evangelist was thinking, in 3,5, of Christian baptism, which is a baptism both of water and of Spirit. This does not mean that the rite and the water are the instrumental cause of the gift of the Spirit. This may be a theological interpretation, for which there are good arguments in the Church's tradition. The text does not say this: the *kai* "and" points, as it does in Tit 3,5, for example, to two associated and combined causes, that is all. But baptism of Spirit and baptism of water are not two distinctly separate realities[11].

Furthermore, in the *Gospel of John*, Jesus mentions in his discourse with the Samaritan woman that the Holy Spirit is to be understood as the living water «welling up to eternal life» (Jn 4,14).

---

8 Y. CONGAR, «Pneumatologie ou christomonisme dans la tradition latine?», 412-413; see also *Il est Seigneur et Il donne la vie*, 278-279 (*Lord and Giver of Life*, 218).

9 Y. CONGAR, *Le Fleuve de vie*, 344 (*The River of Life*, 267).

10 «During the feast of Tabernacles, the priests went every morning to draw water from the spring of Siloam. They brought it back to the temple singing the Hallel (Ps 113–118) and the verse from the book of Isaiah (12,3): "With joy will draw water from the wells of salvation", and poured it out as a libation on the altar of sacrifice. This was a purification rite and at the same time a prayer for the autumn rains. In the Bible and for the Israelites, however, the symbolism of the water was very rich in several ways, in that it pointed to purification and life or fertility. It also pointed to the Law, the word of God and the wisdom that these brought (Is 55, 1ff.10-11) and, in connection with the memory of the water from the rock in the desert during the exodus, an eschatological announcement of new miracle (Isaiah) or fertility flowing from the Temple in the form of living water from a spring. The people of God had experienced or were to experience this water». Y. CONGAR, *L'expérience de l'Esprit*, 76-77 (*The Experience of the Spirit*, 50).

11 Y. CONGAR, *Il est Seigneur et Il donne la vie*, 246 (*Lord and Giver of Life*, 192); see also «Introduzione», to *La vita secondo lo Spirito, condizione del cristiano*, S. Lyonnet, Roma 1967, 7.

Congar thus views Baptism as the anointing with the Spirit of the Son and as an ecclesial event in which the missions of these two divine Persons are equally involved. Since the interrelation between the mission of the Son and that of the Spirit is based on their common origin in the Father, it is not possible to separate the christological and the pneumatological dimensions of Baptism. The Holy Spirit, who is Lord and giver of life, grants animation to those who are baptized into the Son, the Lord and achiever of salvation. Thus, Baptism illustrates, for Congar, that the missions of the glorified Lord and the Holy Spirit may be different in God, but functionally they are united. The Holy Spirit who anointed Jesus in the Jordan enabled him to complete his saving mission, just as after Pentecost he would help to complete the sanctifying mission of the *Pneuma* in the Church: «The Spirit is the Spirit of the Word, of the Lord, of the Son, of Christ. [...] But Jesus Christ is also of the Spirit, not only in his conception, but also in his messianic activity and in his being raised to the quality of Lord»[12]. Congar considers that the Holy Spirit acts in the rites of the Church as the Lord who renders present the former deeds of the Word incarnate, and anticipates his future coming in the here and now, that is, in what can be called the sacramental era[13]. Hence the Holy Spirit, who began to perfect the humanity of the Son of God at the Jordan, continued to do so throughout his public ministry, at his death on the cross, and at his glorification (cf. Rom 1,4; Eph 1, 20 - 22; Heb 5,5). Through Baptism the Spirit does the same in the faithful whom he recreates as children of the Father in the Son, and as heirs with him of the Kingdom (Rom 8, 14 -17)[14].

In the messianic era, which is marked by the presence and action of the Holy Spirit, the sacrament of Baptism has generally been closely connected with the confession of faith, as is evident in the history of the baptismal liturgy:

> Professions of faith, more or less stereotyped and answering to different needs, existed from the earliest times and is apparent from the New Testament itself. Baptism was always accompanied by a confession of faith; very soon, doubtless already in apostolic practice, this necessary

---

[12] Y. CONGAR, *La Parole et le Souffle*, 108 (*The Word and the Spirit*, 62); see also «Renewal of the Spirit and Reform of the Institution», *Con* 8 (1972) 40; *La Foi et la Théologie*, 105-106; *Il est Seigneur et Il donne la vie*, 24 (*Lord and Giver of Life*, 12).

[13] Cf. Y. CONGAR, *Le Fleuve de vie*, 193-195 (*The River of Life*, 144); see also *La Tradition et les traditions*: vol. 2, 34-35 (*Tradition and Traditions*: vol. 2, 261).

[14] Cf. Y. CONGAR, *L'expérience de l'Esprit*, 54-55 (*The Experience of the Spirit*, 32).

profession was made by replying to some questions on the fundamentals of saving faith[15].

Moreover, Congar notes that from the second century onwards the attention of the faithful was above all directed towards the celebration of water-baptism as a public act of faith. To be sure, Irenaeus specifically underlined the union that should exist between the reception of water-baptism and of the gift of the Spirit. However, in later centuries the water was considered simply to be sanctified by the Spirit in order that it be effective in the Baptism of the catechumens. This did not mean that the insight was lost that by the Spirit the catechumens attain the status of Christians[16]. Thus, becoming members of the body of Christ through Baptism entails two decisive events: firstly, the confession of faith, and secondly, being plunged into water. Since the catechumens are simultaneously baptized through faith and water, the gift of the Holy Spirit is operative in both of these decisive elements[17].

Yet, Congar states that in order to receive the Holy Spirit, the confession of faith must precede[18]. This does not suggest that faith and the Holy Spirit do not jointly bring about the birth and growth of Christ in the believers. Congar argues that this was the case at the very beginning of the salvific event: the conception of Jesus in the womb of Mary through the overshadowing of the Holy Spirit which could come about because of her active faith[19]. Similarly the catechumens enter into the new life of grace at Baptism through faith which is itself the gift of the Holy Spirit:

Faith and the Holy Spirit are constantly presented as jointly bringing about the birth and growth of Christ in us. That was so in the case of Mary [...] and it is so in our case too. There is an abundance of Scripture

---

[15] Y. CONGAR, La Tradition et les traditions: vol. 2, 22 (Tradition and Traditions: vol. 2, 245).

[16] Congar notes that at the end of the third century onwards, a trinitarian formula and a confession of faith were used in the celebration of Baptism. Cf. Y. CONGAR, La Tradition et la Vie de l'Église, Paris 1963, 29; Eng. trans. A.N. Woodrow, The Meaning of Tradition, New York 1964, 33; see also L'expérience de l'Esprit, 107-108 (The Experience of the Spirit 73-74).

[17] Cf. Y. CONGAR, Il est Seigneur et Il donne la vie, 243 (Lord and Giver of Life, 190).

[18] Congar finds that this is beautifully expressed in the Antiochian baptismal liturgy. There the anointing with the oil before the baptism by water is an illustration that faith is to precede the anointing by the Spirit. Cf. Y. CONGAR, Le Fleuve de vie, 76 (The River of Life, 42).

[19] Cf. Y. CONGAR Appelés à la vie, 84 (Called to Life, 76); see also Il est Seigneur et Il donne la vie, 132-133 (Lord and Giver of Life, 100).

texts bearing this fact out: "That we might receive the promise of the Spirit through faith", we read for instance in Galatians 3,14 (cf. also Gal 3, 2.5 and 5,5). And where there is mention of unction it is that of both faith and the Holy Spirit[20].

On the basis of this truth, Congar highlights the ecclesiological foundation of every act of Baptism. For him, this sacrament always involves an initiative on the part of catechumens so as to become members of the body of Christ in which the presence and power of the Holy Spirit are guaranteed[21]. Through the grace of Baptism, the faithful exist as living elements of the Body of Christ and of the temple of the Holy Spirit (cf. 1 Cor 12,13; Eph 4,4). Therefore, Congar affirms that the gift of the Spirit is bestowed through the anointing carried out in the sacrament of Baptism. This rite is not individualistic, but *ecclesial*, for it entails becoming a member of the Body of Christ, the Church.

According to Congar, the new life that is begun in and through Baptism with water and the Spirit is nothing less than a share in the very sonship of Christ. Just as the anointing of the Holy Spirit received at his baptism brought Jesus to know himself as the beloved Son of the Father, so in the sacrament of Baptism the faithful who receive the Spirit of the Son (cf. Gal 4,6; Rom 8,14) know that they have become sons and daughters of the Father. Thus, Congar affirms that the filiation of the baptized along with Christ is realized through the efficacious activity of the Holy Spirit in this sacrament: «the Spirit is not only the third in the intra-divine life, although he is equal in con-substantiality; he is also, in the economy of salvation, the agent of sonship as the effect of the grace and reality of holy living»[22]. Through the gift of filiation, the Holy Spirit grants the baptized a truly new state of existence in Jesus Christ, their first-born brother:

> The Spirit, who made the humanity of Jesus [who "was descended from David and from Mary according to the flesh", Rom 1,3; Gal 4,4] a completed humanity of the Son of God [through his resurrection and glorification, Rom 1, 4; Eph 1, 20-22; Heb 5,5], does the same with us, who are of the flesh from the moment of our birth, and makes us sons of God,

---

[20] Y. CONGAR, *Appelés à la vie*, 84 (*Called to Life*, 76); see also *Il est Seigneur et Il donne la vie*, 134-135 (*Lord and Giver of Life*, 101).

[21] Cf. Y. CONGAR, *Il est Seigneur et Il donne la vie*, 247-248 (*Lord and Giver of Life*, 194); see also *La Parole et le Souffle*, 135 (*The Word and the Spirit*, 83); «Unis dans le baptême, désunis dans l'eucharistie?», *Nic* 9 (1981) 249-251.

[22] Y. CONGAR, *Le Fleuve de vie*, 228 (*The River of Life*, 171); see also *Il est Seigneur et Il donne la vie*, 277-278 (*Lord and Giver of Life*, 217); *Appelés à la vie*, 82 (*Called to Life*, 72).

sons in the Son and called to inherit with him and to say after him: "Abba, Father" (Rom 8, 14-17)[23].

Consequently, the baptized begin a filial existence which consists in being freed from sin and death and having the gift of the Spirit (cf. Rom 7,6; 8,2). Congar acknowledges that, although the chosen people of Israel were sometimes called sons, and Yahweh was often depicted as their Father, they did not, however, possess the full identity of sons and heirs, since the Holy Spirit had not yet come to dwell personally in each of their souls[24]. The incarnation, death and glorification of the Word and the coming of the Spirit have changed the situation. Since then the Spirit is given to one and all, so that they may have faith in the salvific words and acts of Christ and receive the benefits of the paschal mystery. This explains why the sacrament of Baptism is an entrance into water and an anointing with the Holy Spirit. In and through the rite, the Spirit comes and dwells in the baptized, to incorporate them into the Son and to make them sons and daughters of the Father.

Since for Congar Baptism is an anointing with the Spirit so as to build up the mystical Body of the Son, there is no opposition between the *Pneuma* and the *Ecclesia*: «The Spirit plays a decisive part in building up the Church. By one Spirit we were all baptized into one body (1 Cor 12,13). The Spirit and the body are not opposed to each other – they have recourse to each other[25]. Here Congar makes it clear that the body of Christ formed by believers on earth is at the same time the dwelling place of the Spirit (Eph 2,22), a spiritual house (cf. 1 Pet 2,5; Phil 3,3), a temple in which authentic worship is offered to God. In this context, Congar departs from an excessively hierarchical notion of the community, and acknowledges that «the Church is the holy temple – and indeed every soul is also the Church»[26]. Moreover, this prominent theme of the indwelling of the Holy Spirit in the entire Christian community underscores the immanence of the third Person of the Trinity, while at the same time it affirms his absolute transcendence with regard to the Church. Thus, the Spirit whom all the baptized receive, is always the divine medium of communication not only between them and the Son and

---

23 Y. CONGAR, *L'expérience de l'Esprit*, 53-54 (*The Experience of the Spirit*, 31); see also «La tri-unité de Dieu et l'Église», *LVS* 128 (1974) 694.

24 Cf. Y. CONGAR, *Il est Seigneur et Il donne la vie*, 101-102 (*Lord and Giver of Life*, 74-75).

25 Y. CONGAR, *L'expérience de l'Esprit*, 55 (*The Experience of the Spirit*, 32); see also *Un Peuple messianique*. *L'Église, sacrement du salut. Salut et libération*, 79-81; *Le Fleuve de vie*, 193-194 (*The River of Life*, 144).

26 Y. CONGAR, *Il est Seigneur Il et donne la vie*, 148 (*Lord and Giver of Life*, 113).

the Father, but also among them, the members forming one body[27]. In this way, Congar reminds each ordained person in the community that neither the preaching nor the sacraments of the Church have the least autonomy with regard to Christ and the Holy Spirit, since «the two great activities of his ministry, the word and the sacraments, come from the Word and are life only through the action of the Spirit of truth»[28].

Furthermore, Congar regards the Spirit-filled life of the baptized in the present time to be a sure guarantee of their eternal inheritance until they acquire full possession of it (Eph 1,14; cf. 4,30). Although the baptized already enjoy the condition of being adopted sons and daughters, their filiation is still not complete. According to Congar, in the present era, the baptized have only the first-fruits of the Spirit, for the full harvest is to be gleaned in the end-time: «In the eschatological era, there will be a new communication of the Spirit which will provide the grace, the gifts and the indwelling, already part of the believers condition in the present messianic era, with their ultimate and definitive fruit»[29]. Therefore the Spirit that is given in Baptism is the guarantor not only of the present filiation of believers, but also of its full realization in the eschatological time. Just as the glorification of Jesus Christ was the fulfillment of the words «Thou art my son, today I have begotten thee» (Ps 2,7) which rested on the presence of the Holy Spirit in him, so the *eschaton* will be the fulfillment of the filiation which the baptized receive through the gift of the divine *Pneuma*. Therefore, for Congar, the state of being adopted sons and daughters both in the present and in the age to come is wholly dependent on the gift of the Holy Spirit: «The connection

---

[27] Cf. Y. CONGAR, *L'expérience de l'Esprit*, 55-56 (*The Experience of the Spirit*, 32-33).

[28] Y. CONGAR, *La Parole et le Souffle*, 201 (*The Word and the Spirit*, 130); see also «Actualité renouvelée du Saint-Esprit», 556-557 («Renewed Actuality of the Holy Spirit», 27); *Un Peuple messianique*. L'Église, sacrement du salut. Salut et libération, 35; *L'expérience de l'Esprit*, 48-49 (*The Experience of the Spirit*, 24-25); «Renewal of the Spirit and Reform of the Institution», 40-41; *L'Église, une, sainte, catholique et apostolique*, 165. The Church is the sacrament of salvation in virtue of its union with Christ. Here Congar draws on the biblical notions of the Church as spouse and as body to articulate this dependence. He states that the first implies otherness, the aspect of *vis-a-vis*, and the second implies identity and immanence. According to him, the Pauline notion points to a movement from one to the other. In order to become mother of the members of Christ, the spouse must be united to the Lord to receive from him the fruitful power of the Holy Spirit. The Church becomes sacrament of salvation in and through this same union while realizing the plenitude of Christ (cf. Eph 1, 9.22-23; Col 2,9). Cf. Y. CONGAR, *Un Peuple messianique*. L'Église, sacrement du salut. Salut et libération, 38-40.

[29] Y. CONGAR, *Il est Seigneur et Il donne la vie*, 104 (*Lord and Giver of Life*, 76).

between our present sonship and our eschatological sonship is in the first place obviously that of the reality itself: gift of the Spirit. [...] The Spirit is "sent" and given in the gift of grace [...] it is through his divine dynamism that we are able to return through the Son to the Father»[30]. Although Congar encourages the baptized to enrich their filiation through moral acts, in order to anticipate its full realization on the final day, he insists that the initiative of such good intentions is always given by the Holy Spirit with whom they can only co-operate.

Although believers receive the Spirit of sonship in Baptism, while they are in this world, they cannot avoid the spirit of evil, that is, of isolation, sin and death. Congar finds this truth illustrated in the life of Jesus who, after his baptism, passed forty days of temptation in the wilderness. Although he was filled with the Holy Spirit, he could not escape from the encounter with the evil spirit (cf. Lk 4, 1–13)[31]. Therefore, for Congar, the inauguration of the new life of believers at the moment of their Baptism should prepare them to resist evil and perform good actions: «Our actions, which may "merit" eternal life, are elements in a chain of grace in which the Holy Spirit as uncreated grace takes the initiative and provides the dynamism until the ultimate victory is reached in which God merely crowns his own gifts when he awards us a crown for our "merits"»[32]. In this text, Congar speaks of the ultimate victory over evil which is to be attained by the baptized in the Kingdom, once their good actions have ceased and the suffering they entailed is fully recompensed by the Father. Yet, lest it seem that the evil spirit and the Holy Spirit are two equally powerful forces, Congar makes it clear that, while evil is a created reality characterized by the absence of community, righteousness and immortality, the Holy Spirit is uncreated grace itself, the eternal source of love, justice and life. In fact, when human beings resist evil, the Holy Spirit should be acknowledged as the initiative and the dynamism which permeates the choice of the good[33]. If this is universally the case, it is particularly experienced by the baptized who have been anointed by the Spirit of the Father and the Son. Whatever merit the baptized attain is ultimately to be attributed to the uncreated grace who is the Holy Spirit

---

[30] Y. CONGAR, *Il est Seigneur et Il donne la vie*, 145 (*Lord and Giver of Life*, 107-108).

[31] Cf. Y. CONGAR, *Il est Seigneur et Il donne la vie*, 161 (*Lord and Giver of Life*, 122); see also *L'expérience de l'Esprit*, 37-41 (*The Experience of the Spirit*, 17-19).

[32] Y. CONGAR, *Il est Seigneur et Il donne la vie*, 146 (*Lord and Giver of Life*, 108).

[33] Cf. Y. CONGAR, *L'expérience de l'Esprit*, 53 (*The Experience of the Spirit*, 31); see also *Il est Seigneur et Il donne la vie*, 158, 160-161 (*Lord and Giver of Life*, 120, 121-122).

propelling them to choose love over hate, equity over iniquity, and mercy over violence. Thus, the merit won by the moral actions of the baptized is in fact a response to the gifts of the Holy Spirit, divine love, who leads them to the Son, divine justice, and to the Father, divine life.

Most important with regard to the theme of this study is the fact that Congar finds the epicletic dimension of Baptism to be well indicated in the liturgical texts of the Roman rite as early as the formulation of the *Gelasian Sacramentary*. For, the blessing of the baptismal water by invoking on it the Spirit of Christ constitutes a solemn epiclesis: «So I bless you [water] through Jesus Christ the only Son, our Lord, who [...] was baptized in you by John in the Jordan and who made you flow from his side with the blood. [...] May the virtue of your Spirit descend into the depth of this font»[34]. After this consecratory prayer follows the triple immersion of the catechumens and the formal confession of their faith. The present liturgical practice reflects these very same motifs. The dipping of the Paschal candle, which symbolizes Christ, into the water three times and the invocation of the Holy Spirit re-actualize the saving event which occurred in the Jordan[35]. Thus, with the words «may the virtue of your Spirit descend into the depths of this font», an explicit baptismal epiclesis is pronounced directly over the creature water. Thus it becomes the purifying element, permeated by the Spirit and employed by the Church, which washes away the evil of isolation, sin and death from the spiritual depths of the catechumens. Without the epiclesis, the creature water is not the saving symbol of the original creation, of the Exodus, of the drink from the rock in the desert, of the Jordan, of the pierced side of the crucified Jesus, and of the baptism performed on Pentecost. More precisely it can be said that water of itself does not immediately symbolize the life-giving Spirit, but that water prayed over by the Church assumes all the biblical associations mentioned above and becomes the privileged means by which the Spirit enables the events of salvation to be operative in the personal experience of the catechumens[36]. The mysteries of Israel and of the Messiah thus become, through the power of the Spirit,

---

[34] Y. CONGAR, *L'expérience de l'Esprit*, 149 (*The Experience of the Spirit*, 105).

[35] Cf. Y. CONGAR, *Le Fleuve de vie*, 343-344 (*The River of Life*, 267). Congar finds that the *consolamentum* of the Cathari is different from the other baptismal rituals, since the baptism of the Holy Spirit is done with an imposition of both hands and of the books (of the Gospels). Although this is the way the Ordination is conferred, here, it is for the forgiveness of sins and for individual salvation. Cf. Y. CONGAR, *La Parole et le Souffle*, 51-52 (*The Word and the Spirit*, 24).

[36] Cf. Y. CONGAR, *Il est Seigneur et Il donne la vie*, 245-246, 145-146 (*Lord and Giver of Life*, 191-192, 108); see also *L'expérience de l'Esprit*, 147-148 (*The Experience of the Spirit*, 104).

interior realities in the salvation history of the baptized. Thus, the epicletic aspect of Baptism is understood by Congar as rooted in its anamnetic aspect – Jesus in the Jordan and on Calvary – and yet is indispensable, if what the *Logos* once did in the past is to become actual in those living in successive moments of history.

In summary, it can be said that Congar considers the sacrament of Baptism as a washing with water and an anointing with the Holy Spirit, so that catechumens can have new life through the death and resurrection of Christ. Similar to the anointing received by Jesus at his baptism which made him aware of his own status as Son of God, in the ecclesial sacrament of Baptism, believers regain their lost filiation with the Father. The active agent here is none other than the Holy Spirit who through Baptism builds up the body of Christ, the Church. Therefore, the Church is the temple of the Spirit because it is composed of the people anointed by him. However, the filiation granted through the anointing with the Spirit at Baptism can fully be realized only in the glory of the *eschaton*. In this world, the baptized practice justice by following the initiatives of the Holy Spirit. Although the sacrament of Baptism renders the body of Christ an anointed community, the fruits of this status can be harvested only through Confirmation which strengthens the faithful so that their anointing and their justice take on a public form, and give courage and hope to many people living in despair. Therefore, in the next sub-section the epicletic aspect of Confirmation is considered.

2. Confirmation as Participation in the Messianic Anointing of Christ for Taking an Active Share in the Building up of theTemple of the Holy Spirit

If Baptism is an anointing with the Spirit (cf. Mk 1,8; Jn 1,33; 1 Cor 6,11; 12,13; Tit 3,5), which grants catechumens entrance into the totally new life of Christ, that is, into his ecclesial body (Rom 6,4f; 1 Cor 12,13; Gal 3,27), then this status must be organically developed, in relation to the good pleasure of the Lord. This is the basis of the sacrament of Confirmation, according to Congar. Confirmation is a participation in the messianic anointing of Christ which enables the baptized to bear public witness to saving grace[37]. In the Scriptures, the activity of the Holy Spirit is very much connected with the Christian task of bearing witness to the salvific words and actions of Jesus Christ: «In bearing witness, the Holy Spirit is not acting personally, in the sense that his work is new or different from Christ's; he realizes and gives an inner depth to what was

---

[37] Cf. Y. CONGAR, *Le Fleuve de vie*, 283 (*The River of Life*, 218).

said and done once and for all by Christ, which is the Gospel (cf. Jn
14,26; 16, 12-13)»[38]. Therefore, when the Holy Spirit bears witness, he
invariably remains faithful to what Christ said and did in the period of his
earthly life. It follows that, when the Holy Spirit inspires the baptized to
give witness to the truth of Christ, he assures that faithfulness to him
marks their activity. Although there is a certain element of tension, as
well as a bond of continuity, between what the pre-resurrection Jesus said
and did, and the later witness to it by believers after the outpouring of the
Holy Spirit at Pentecost, this fact is not primary. Essential is the
mysterious way in which «Christ's work is actualized by the Holy Spirit
in the course of human events»[39]. For Congar, through the sacrament of
Confirmation, the baptized share more intensely in the witness which the
Holy Spirit gives to Christ. Thus, he regards Confirmation as a special
empowerment to carry out the prophetic dimension of the common
priesthood, which involves confessing faith in Jesus Christ through word
and deed in any circumstances, even at the cost of death[40]. For this
reason, Confirmation can be designated as the sacrament which propels
the missionary task of the Church by means of a special anointing with
the Holy Spirit.

Although Confirmation may seem to be individualistic ritual, its
communitarian aspect nevertheless belongs to its specificity. Congar
illustrates this truth though reflection on two episodes in the *Acts of the
Apostles*: the Samaritans who were evangelized and baptized by Philip
and on whom Peter and John laid their hands (Acts 8, 14-17), and the
disciples of John from Ephesus whom Paul had baptized in the name of
the Lord and on whom he also laid hands (Acts 19, 1-6). Even if these
texts so not directly pertain to the sacrament of Confirmation, Congar
claims that they point to the ecclesiological significance of this rite:
«What takes place in the sacrament is that the baptized persons who are
confirmed are fully fitted into the apostolic community of the Church.
They are able to become full members of the Church when those who are
called to bear the Church's apostolicity have publicly accepted them»[41].
The stress which Congar places on apostolicity in this text indicates that,
for him as for Thomas Aquinas, the rite of Confirmation is connected
with the Pentecost-event. With the outpouring of the Holy Spirit on all
those who were sitting and praying together, the apostolicity of the

---

[38] Y. CONGAR, *La Tradition et la Vie de l'Église*, 45 (*The Meaning of Tradition*, 53).

[39] Y. CONGAR, *Appelés á la vie*, 78 (*Called to Life*, 69).

[40] Cf. Y. CONGAR, *Le Fleuve de vie*, 290-291 (*The River of Life*, 222).

[41] Y. CONGAR, *Le Fleuve de vie*, 286 (*The River of Life*, 220).

Church was activated, so that it could bear witness to the truths and values which Jesus stood for during his life on earth[42]. Similar to the gift of the Holy Spirit received at Pentecost, the grace of Confirmation is not meant for the benefit of individuals, but for the good of the entire Church which has a common apostolic goal. For this reason, Congar states that Confirmation renders the baptized «an integral part of the community which they help to form but which transcends them, taking them into itself»[43].

However, in pointing out the apostolicity of the confirmed, Congar does not depreciate the importance of the hierarchy who receive the gift of the Holy Spirit so as to carry out the apostolate with full authority. In other words, since Confirmation is the gift of the Holy Spirit by which the baptized are strengthened to be apostolic, Congar considers that its liturgical celebration must be presided over by the local head of the Church: the bishop who represents the apostolicity of the *ecclesia*. In addition, the general understanding among Christians that, whenever persons are baptized in an emergency, they should later to be taken to the head of the community also demonstrates the ecclesial aspect of Confirmation. At least in Western theology, and especially in the writings of Hippolytus and Cyprian, Congar finds clear evidence that Confirmation is normally to be administered by the bishop[44].

In the renewed Latin rite of Confirmation, promulgated after Vatican II through the Apostolic Constitution *Divinae Consortes Naturae* of August 15, 1971, Congar notes that the sacrament is conferred by anointing the forehead of the candidates with sacred chrism and by the imposition of the hand of the bishop along with the words: *Accipe signaculum doni Spiritus Sancti*. In paragraph twenty of this constitution Congar identifies many references to the ancient Eastern formula which explicitly mentions «the seal of the gift of the Spirit»[45]. This phrase no doubt calls to mind the outpouring of the Holy Spirit at Pentecost, as the constitution of Paul VI makes clear:

As far as the words that are pronounced at the time of anointing with chrism are concerned, we have certainly assessed the dignity of the

---

[42] Cf. Y. CONGAR, *Le Fleuve de vie*, 288-289 (*The River of Life*, 221); see also «Towards a Catholic Synthesis», *Con* 17 (1981) 70.

[43] Y. CONGAR, *Appelés à la vie*, 101 (*Called to Life*, 94-95); see also «Actualité renouvelée du Saint-Esprit», 546-547 («Renewed Actuality of the Holy Spirit», 17-18); *L'expérience de l'Esprit*, 58 (*The Experience of the Spirit*, 34).

[44] Cf. Y. CONGAR, *Le Fleuve de vie*, 282-283, 286-287 (*The River of Life*, 218, 220).

[45] Y. CONGAR, *Le Fleuve de vie*, 281 (*The River of Life*, 217).

venerable formula used in the Latin Church at its true value. We have, however, concluded that it was necessary to give preference to the early formula of the Byzantine rite, in which the gift of the Spirit himself is expressed and the pouring out of the Spirit on the day of Pentecost is recalled[46].

Consequently, the use of the formula «Receive the seal of the gift of the Holy Spirit» in the new ritual of Confirmation reflects the fourth and fifth-century Eastern understanding which associates two biblical terms: seal and gift. Both are inextricably linked in the New Testament with the self-communication of the Holy Spirit[47]. With regard to the practice of this sacrament, Congar points out that, in the early Church, the rite of Baptism consisted of two anointings. But in the Roman rite, from the fifth century onwards, these anointings were administered in stages, and that from then on Confirmation consisted of an anointing joined to an imposition of the hand by the bishop, which action directly referred to an apostolic gesture[48]. For this reason, the rite of Confirmation constitutes distinct a sacrament in itself, but one that essentially complements Baptism[49].

Congar was well aware of the many insufficiencies in the Catholic understanding of the relationship between the sacraments of Baptism and Confirmation:

> The Spirit, then, is given in Baptism. Why is it therefore necessary to add another sacrament in order to give the Spirit? It is not possible to be confirmed without having been baptized, but it is possible to be baptized, that is, it is possible to receive the gift of the Spirit and of Christian life without Confirmation? What does Confirmation bring?[50]

In answering this question, Congar first states that the difference between the two sacraments is a specifically theological issue, since it pertains to the economy of salvation, that is, to the activity of the economic Trinity. Accordingly he shows that both Baptism and Confirmation represent, at

---

[46] Y. CONGAR, *Le Fleuve de vie*, 282 (*The River of Life*, 217), as cited from Paul VI, «Constitutio Apostolica de Sacramento Confirmationis», *AAS* 63 (1971) 663.

[47] Cf. Y. CONGAR, *L'expérience de l'Esprit*, 230 (*The Experience of the Spirit*, 169).

[48] Cf. Y. CONGAR, «Actualité renouvelée du Saint-Esprit», 554-555 («Renewed Actuality of the Spirit», 25). By quoting L. Ligier, Congar puts forward that the present emphasis on anointing is not the right development. He argues that Confirmation is always based on the laying on of hands which really explicates the meaning of the sacrament. Cf. Y. CONGAR, *L'expérience de l'Esprit*, 150 (*The Experience of the Spirit*, 112).

[49] Cf. Y. CONGAR, *L'expérience de l'Esprit*, 150 (*The Experience of the Spirit*, 106).

[50] Y. CONGAR, *Le Fleuve de vie*, 283 (*The River of Life*, 218); see also *Il est Seigneur et Il donne la vie*, 202 (*Lord and Giver of Life*, 155).

the level of liturgical symbolism, the divine missions of the Son and the Spirit at work in the Church. In fact, the first two sacraments of Christian initiation reveal the unity and difference in the relation between the saving mission of the *Logos* and the sanctifying mission of the *Pneuma:*

> The work in question is the realization of the Body of Christ, his body as communion or Church and his sacramental body, after his physical or natural body. This was the work both of the Word, who assumed an individual human nature, and of the Holy Spirit, who sanctified the fruit that he had been brought about in the womb of the virgin Mary. Since then, we have had two closely combined aspects[51].

Here Congar points out that the basic christological and pneumatological design which is evident at the foundation of the Church also has a direct bearing on the two sacraments which initiate human beings into it[52]. Just as Easter was completed on Pentecost, so Baptism, which assimilates catechumens into the death and resurrection of Jesus (Rom 6, 3-11), is perfected in Confirmation, which grants them the benefits of the sending of the Spirit. To substantiate this claim, Congar finds that several Fathers of the Church have related Confirmation to Pentecost, and that the ancient liturgical celebrations of these sacraments indicate their affiliation with the two divine missions.

In order to make this affirmation more clear, Congar himself offered a diagrammatical illustration of the parallel between Easter and Baptism, and Pentecost and Confirmation:[53]

$$\frac{\text{Christ in his Pasch}}{\text{Pentecost}} = \frac{\text{Baptism}}{\text{Confirmation}}$$

As a further attempt to explain the difference between these two sacraments of Christian initiation, Congar states that Baptism bestows the gift of the Holy Spirit, and Confirmation is the seal of this gift: «In the one single process of initiation, which is consummated in the sacrament of the body and blood of the Lord, a symbolic aspect, which completes the

---

51 Y. CONGAR, *Le Fleuve de vie*, 291 (*The River of Life*, 222); see also «Actualité renouvelée du Saint-Esprit», 556-557 («Renewed Actuality of the Holy Spirit», 27); *L'expérience de l'Esprit*, 150-151 (*The Experience of the Spirit*, 106).

52 Congar acknowledges that in this approach he was very much influenced by authors such as L. S. Thornton and J. Lécuyer.

53 Cf. Y. CONGAR, *Le Fleuve de vie*, 284 (*The River of Life*, 219).

act of Baptism and seals the gift received in it, the sacrament of the "seal of the gift of the Spirit", has been distinguished from Baptism strictly so called»[54]. In short, Baptism, as the gift of the Spirit, and Confirmation, as its seal, are two stages in the one initiation process. Congar compares these stages to the activity of the divine *Pneuma* in the incarnation of the divine *Logos* and in his anointing for the messianic ministry. In the first case, the Spirit had an incomparable role in the conception of the Word in Mary's womb, which can be considered his anointing as the Christ. In the second case, the Spirit anointed Jesus of Nazareth at the Jordan for his unique mission[55]. A parallel occurs in the first two sacraments of initiation, since Baptism enables the catechumens to be re-born as sons and daughters of the Father along with Christ, and Confirmation grants them a part in his messianic anointing so as to carry out the will of the Father. This understanding of the relationship between Baptism and Confirmation is presented by Congar in the following diagram:[56]

$$\frac{\text{Incarnation}}{\text{Baptism of Jesus}} = \frac{\text{Baptism}}{\text{Seal of the Spirit}}$$

Hence the catechumens who are anointed by the Spirit at their Baptism subsequently receive Confirmation as its seal for the sake of their mission. Congar notes that in the ancient liturgies of Confirmation and in the writings of the Fathers, it is very evident that Christian initiation is fulfilled only when the spiritual anointing following Baptism is expressed visibly and tangibly in the rite of chrismation[57].

In considering the relationship and the difference between Baptism and Confirmation as anointings with the Holy Spirit, Congar refers to the biblical phrases «act *in*» [in Greek, «*en*»] and the «act *on*» [in Greek, «*epi*»]. These phrases which describe the work of the *Pneuma*, are used

---

[54] Y. CONGAR, *Le Fleuve de vie*, 291 (*The River of Life*, 222-223); see also «Actualité renouvelée du Saint-Esprit», 559-560 («Renewed Actuality of the Holy Spirit», 30).

[55] Cf. Y. CONGAR, *L'expérience de l'Esprit*, 34-41 (*The Experience of the Spirit*, 16-19); see also *Le Fleuve de vie*, 285 (*The River of Life*, 219); «Actualité renouvelée du Saint-Esprit», 556 («Renewed Actuality of the Holy Spirit», 27).

[56] Y. CONGAR, *L'expérience de l'Esprit*, 150 (*The Experience of the Spirit*, 106, 112).

[57] Cf. Y. CONGAR, *Le Fleuve de vie*, 285 (*The River of Life*, 219).

precisely by the prophet Ezekiel. According to him, the Spirit «acts *in*» people to purify them (Ez 36, 25-27), and thus grants them new life (Ez 37, 5-10). Yet, the Spirit «acts *on*» people in order to empower them for a mission, and his empowerment is usually followed by their external efforts to fulfill their mandate. Similarly, through the first anointing of Christians at Baptism, the Spirit «acts *in*» them, cleansing them from sin and giving them a share in the new life of Christ. Then, through Confirmation, which is the second anointing, the Spirit «acts *on*» them and grants them a share in the prophetic mission which Jesus took on from the moment of his baptism[58]. Therefore, for Congar, Baptism entails the fundamental consecration of the catechumens through the bestowal of the Spirit of the Son. Yet, the single process of initiation reaches a new stage at Confirmation, which seals the first gift of the Holy Spirit by sending the baptized on a prophetic, cultic and pastoral mission. This means that at the liturgical celebration of Confirmation, the common priesthood of the baptized is fully established, so that they can cooperate with the Spirit in accomplishing the sanctifying work of the Church which points back to what the Father has done in his Son, and forward to what the Son will hand over to the Father at the *eschaton*.

Regarding explicit mention of the epicletic dimension of Confirmation on the part of Congar, it must be said that this occurs rarely. In one text, in which he refers to the atmosphere of prayer and solidarity which should mark the commitment of young Christians to the mission they are capable of fulfilling because of the seal of the Holy Spirit. Congar suggests that the liturgical celebration should best take place within the framework of the parish Eucharist, «which would express in a pneumatological, epicletic and communitarian climate, the personal commitment of the young Christian»[59]. The use of the adjective «epicletic» between two others, namely «pneumatological» and «communitarian», is most indicative of Congar's conviction that the Holy Spirit communicates his very self to the *confirmandi*, and that he does this so that they be filled with his grace not only in the depth of their existence but also in their efforts to carry out the ecclesial mission entrusted to them, depending on their particular talents and charisms. Thus, this one explicit reference to the epiclesis enacted at Confirmation is most significant in revealing the essence of this second anointing with

---

[58] Cf. Y. CONGAR, *Il est Seigneur et Il donne la vie*, 253-254 (*Lord and Giver of Life*, 197).

[59] Y. CONGAR, «Actualité renouvelée du Saint-Esprit», 558 («Renewed Actuality of the Holy Spirit», 28).

the Holy Spirit: the incorporation into the prophetic mission of the Church.

Moreover, Congar insists that the recipients of Confirmation be well informed about the meaning of the rite, and that it be celebrated in an atmosphere of warmth and joy. Thus, there should be a proper preparation for the rite, and those who are involved in it should ideally be committed Christians, such as the members of the Charismatic Renewal, since they are most able to convince the candidates of the vitality and joy arising from dedicating themselves to the prophetic service of others: «I would very much like to see the members of the Renewal take part in such days of preparation and in the ceremony of Confirmation. They would bring to it their vital conviction that Jesus lives together with a warmth and a feeling of joy. It would be a feast of the Holy Spirit»[60]. In this text, Congar associates the epiclesis of the Holy Spirit on the candidates for Confirmation with the forceful sentiments of vitality, warmth, joy and festivity. For, in the end, if the sacrament of Confirmation is prepared for, celebrated and lived out well, it reinforces constantly the charismatic dimension of the Church.

From what has been considered in this chapter, it is clear that in and through the sacrament of Baptism the catechumens are anointed by the Holy Spirit so as to attain the gift of filiation along with the Son of the Father, Jesus Christ. Although the baptized receive this gift in the Church existing in history, its full realization is to occur only in the eschatological time. Throughout their journey towards the Kingdom, the Spirit fills the sons and daughters of the Father with the virtues of faith, hope and love. However, Congar did not consider the initial anointing with the Holy Spirit as an individualistic benefit, but as an empowerment for the task of building up the social Body of Christ. Thus Congar invariably links Baptism with Confirmation, the second anointing with the Holy Spirit for the sake of Christian prophetic witness to Christ. His entire theological argumentation with regard to these two sacraments is founded on the dual divine missions of the Son and of the Spirit, the Pasch being related to Baptism, and the Pentecost event to Confirmation.

---

[60] Y. CONGAR, *Le Fleuve de vie*, 293 (*The River of Life*, 224); see also *L'expérience de l'Esprit*, 151 (*The Experience of the Spirit*, 106). Congar's other observation in this regard is: «It would, of course, not be enough simply to take one bath of the Holy Spirit in a warm and cordial environment in order to be sure of living according to the Spirit. Life in the Spirit calls for perseverance, a daily recommitment to a generous effort and constant and repeated prayer. But if the practice of renewal in the Spirit formed part of parish life, it might well make a valuable contribution to the reanimation of the pastoral aspect of the sacraments of initiation». Y. CONGAR, *Il est Seigneur et Il donne la vie*, 203 (*Lord and Giver of Life*, 156).

The major advantage of underlining the epicletic dimension of both Baptism and Confirmation is that it indicates clearly that the entire Church is enriched by the gifts of the Spirit. This truth is fully realized when the baptized and the confirmed are gathered at the Eucharist through the action of the Holy Spirit who preserves ecclesial communion. Hence, in the following chapter the epicletic aspect of the sacrament of Eucharist is considered in detail.

CHAPTER V

Eucharistic Consecration
as Realized by the Account of the Institutional Words of Jesus
and by the Epiclesis of the Spirit

In the previous chapter it was explicated that, because of the epicletic role of the Holy Spirit in the sacraments of Baptism and Confirmation, the faithful take part in the messianic anointing and work of Jesus Christ. Yet, such a status and such a mission, which are to be fully realized only in the eschatological era, must be constantly renewed for Christian pilgrims who are journeying in history. Thus, the baptized and confirmed are repeatedly united and nourished on their way by participation in the eucharistic celebration. It follows for Congar that the Eucharist, as well as the other two sacraments of initiation, is actualized through a remembrance of Jesus Christ and an invocation of the Holy Spirit. Hence, this chapter treats, in two respective sub-sections: (1) the nexus between the invocation of the Holy Spirit and the pronouncement of the institutional words of Christ as the consecratory elements which are at the center of the eucharistic anaphora, and (2) the constitutive role of the post-consecratory invocation of the Holy Spirit in the Eucharist as the foundation of ecclesial communion.

In the first sub-division, it is shown how Congar's understanding of the consecratory role of the epiclesis of the Holy Spirit in the Eucharist is based on a decidedly pneumatological christology. Since the Eucharist makes actual the paschal mystery which is an event involving the missions of the Son and of the Spirit, it is a christic-pneumatic reality. There is in the Eucharist not only a christological moment [institutional narrative] in which the Last Supper and Calvary are commemorated, but also a pneumatological moment [formal invocation] in which this commemoration of an «*extra nos*» event becomes an «*in nobis*» reality for the faithful. However, Congar does not hold that solely the recital of the institutional words or of the epiclesis is determinative of the real presence of Christ and of the actual presence of his Pasch. He maintains instead that the conversion of bread and wine into the body and blood of Christ, as well as the re-enactment of the paschal mystery, take place in and through the entire eucharistic prayer. He finds abundant evidence by which to ground his theological position in various eucharistic prayers and patristic texts. Therefore, in this sub-section Congar's adherence to the dictum *lex orandi, lex credendi* is shown to be most fortuitous with regard to understanding the epicletic dimension of the eucharistic prayers of both the East and the West.

The second sub-section highlights the pertinence of the post-consecratory epiclesis of the Holy Spirit in the eucharistic celebration. For, the divine *Pneuma* acts to bring about not only the conversion of the bread and wine into the body and blood of the glorified Christ and the reactualization of the paschal mystery but also the reality of ecclesial communion. In other words, Congar maintains that the post-consecratory invocation of the Holy Spirit enables the faithful consciously to make their own the fruits of Christ's Pasch through efforts to strengthen ecclesial unity and to practice social charity. Although ecclesial communion is an ever-present gift of the Holy Spirit to the faithful who are aware of the divisions among them, perfect unity is a reality of the world to come, which is anticipated in the Eucharist. It can thus be said that, through the post-consecratory epiclesis, the Holy Spirit unites all three senses of the term «Body of Christ»: the glorified Body, the eucharistic Body and the mystical Body.

1. The Epicletic Dimension of the Eucharistic Celebration as an Expression of the Spirit's Involvement in the Salvific Event

In relation to the other sacraments, the Eucharist occupies an unparalleled position in the life of the Church. Congar states that the Eucharist is the synthesis, communicated sacramentally and spiritually, of what Jesus Christ has done for humanity in and through his Pasch: «Each and every one of the sacraments refers back to the Pasch of the Lord, his passion and resurrection, and it is these that the sacraments bring into the major decisive moments of human life. For the Eucharist links them all together since it is the celebration of that Pasch of Christ and the new alliance sealed in his blood»[1]. ccording to Congar, the Eucharist celebrates the very summit of the salvific event from which Christianity springs. Therefore, the eucharistic celebration synthesizes the co-ordination of the missions of the Son and of the Spirit in accomplishing the salvation of the world. Congar finds that the Eucharist is such a blending mainly for two reasons. First of all, Jesus Christ instituted this sacrament at the end of his public mission, and determined the way it should be celebrated in future as a commemoration of his self-giving love (cf. Mt 26, 26-29; Mk 14, 22-24; Lk 22, 19-20; 1 Cor 11, 23-25)[2]. Secondly, while the efficacy of all the sacraments depends on the salvific benefits of the death and resurrection of Christ, the Eucharist is the symbolic re-enactment of the Pasch in the midst of the believing community. Furthermore, since the mission of the Spirit is the result of the Pasch, the eucharistic celebration reflects the dual divine missions in its anamnetic and epicletic moments. However, Congar does not try to pinpoint the moment of consecration as do many other Western theologians. According to him, the whole eucharistic prayer is both anamnetic and epicletic, because of the concerted action of Christ and of the Spirit.

Congar states that the purpose of the epiclesis in the eucharistic celebration is to guarantee that all the benefits of the passion and resurrection of Christ may be made available to the celebrating community[3]. Although the active role of the Holy Spirit in converting the

---

[1] Y. CONGAR, *Appelés à la vie*, 108 (*Called to Life*, 101-102); see also «La relation entre culte ou sacrement et prédication de la Parole», *Con* 4 (1968) 55; Eng. vers. «Sacramental Worship and Preaching», *Con* 1 (1968) 28; «L'idée de sacrements majeurs ou principaux», 28 («The Idea of Major or Principal Sacraments», 13); *Un Peuple messianique. L'Église, sacrement du salut. Salut et libération*, 81. Having referred to the position of the Fathers of the Church, Congar was of the opinion that those sacraments which by their meaning and content are directly and fully link with Christ's passover and re-present the reality of this passover in a certain real way, have a special and an outstanding place in the overall sacramental structure. Accordingly for him, Baptism and Eucharist share the first place. Moreover, the incomparable insights of the other sacraments, such as the Anointing of the sick, holy Order, Reconciliation or Marriage do not clearly refer to the pasch of Christ immediately. Cf. Y. CONGAR, «La relation entre culte ou sacrement et prédication de la Parole», 55-57 («Sacramental Worship and Preaching», 28-30); see also «L'idée de sacrements majeurs ou principaux», 29-30 («The Idea of Major or Principal Sacraments», 13-14).

[2] Cf. Y. CONGAR, *La Parole et le Souffle*, 133-134 (*The Word and the Spirit*, 79); see also *Appelés à la vie*, 90 (*Called to Life*, 82).

[3] Cf. Y. CONGAR, *L'expérience de l'Esprit*, 114 (*The Experience of the Spirit*, 77); see also «Actualité renouvelée du Saint-Esprit», 558-559 («Renewed Actuality of the Holy Spirit», 29).

bread and wine was generally admitted, there is no attempt, until the Middle Ages, to stipulate when the epiclesis took place:

> There is ample testimony that the consecration of the bread and wine into the body and blood of Christ is brought about by the Holy Spirit. [...] The texts that in fact allude to an invocation [of the Spirit] may refer to the whole of the canon or even to the whole eucharistic celebration, which includes prayers which have the value of an epiclesis[4].

To substantiate this point, Congar refers to the Churches of the East, which had developed the pneumatic aspect of eucharistic theology, and especially to the liturgy of the Hispano-Visigothic Church which was celebrated by St. Isidore. Congar states that in the Orthodox liturgy the anaphora invariably constitutes a whole, so that neither the anamnesis nor the epiclesis can be isolated and treated separately. With regard to the Hispano-Visigothic liturgy, in which the Holy Spirit is clearly invoked over the elements during the eucharistic prayer, they are said to be consecrated by the *oratio sexta*, which includes all the prayers between the *Sanctus* and *Pater noster*[5]. Furthermore, in order to expatiate on the epicletic dimension of the entire eucharistic prayer, Congar culls much evidence from the various liturgical traditions. Although the anaphorae differ in their formulations of the role of the Holy Spirit, their common objective is to remind the faithful that the divine *Pneuma* prolongs the efficacy of the salvation attained for the humankind by the incarnation, death and resurrection of Jesus Christ[6]. Congar categorizes these eucharistic prayers under five headings.

---

4 Y. CONGAR, *Le Fleuve de vie*, 320 (*The River of Life*, 250). «There is no explicit epiclesis invoking the Holy Spirit in the *Roman rite* from the time of Gregory the Great until our own century, although the *Quam oblationem* before the consecration and the *Supplices te rogamus* after the consecration certainly have the value of an epiclesis. In the practical use of this liturgy, however, this relative gap has been filled by a great number of prayers, which were sufficiently widespread to show that they must have been commonly used. From a number of texts Congar has cited the following text: "Lord, may your Holy Spirit descend on this altar, we beseech you; may he bless and sanctify these gifts offered to your Majesty and may he deign to purify all those who receive them". Until the present century, the Missal of Pius V contained a prayer, the fourteenth-century version of which was, according to a manuscript of the period: "*Veni, sancte Spiritus invisibilis sanctificator, veni et sanctifica sacrificium istud tibi hodie praeparatum ad laudem et gloriam nominis tui. In nomine Patris et Filii et Spiritus Sancti*"». Y. CONGAR, *Le Fleuve de vie*, 322 (*The River of Life*, 251).

5 Cf. Y. CONGAR, *L'expérience de l'Esprit*, 154 (*The Experience of the Spirit*, 107-108); see also *Le Fleuve de vie*, 323 (*The River of Life*, 252); *L'Église de saint Augustin à l'époque moderne*, 37-38.

6 Cf. Y. CONGAR, *Le Fleuve de vie*, 296 (*The River of Life*, 229).

The first category of eucharistic prayers are categorized by a correlation between the Eucharist and the incarnation. Congar finds that they accentuate the divinity of the incarnate Word, and the deifying power of his flesh and blood. This means neither that the power of sanctifying the elements is attributed solely to the mystery of the incarnation to the exclusion of the passion and resurrection, nor that a purely christological view of the Eucharist is affirmed, without any pneumatological emphasis. Although this type of anaphora is found in the descriptions of the Eucharist provided by Justin Martyr and Irenaeus[7], Congar deems it to have been best articulated by Germanus I of Constantinople:

> From the womb, before the dawn, I have begotten you (Ps 110,3). Once again he [the priest] pleads [*parakalei*] that the mystery of the Son may be accomplished [*teleiōsai*] and that the bread and the wine may be begotten [*gennēthēnai*] and transformed into the body and blood of Christ and God and that the "today I have begotten you" will be accomplished (Ps 2,7). In this way, the Holy Spirit, invisibly present by the pleasure of the Father and the will of the Son, demonstrates the divine energy and, by the hand of the priest, consecrates and converts the holy gifts that are presented into the body and blood of our Lord Jesus Christ[8].

In this text, the eucharistic celebration is regarded as a sacramental begetting of the very body and blood of Christ, and the role of the Holy Spirit in the consecration and sanctification of the gifts is described in terms of divine energy. In another text, the Spirit is said to change the individualistic tendencies of the faithful, and to unite all in the ecclesial body of Christ[9].

Regarding the second category of anaphorae, Congar follows Louis Bouyer in stating that the epiclesis is closely associated with the

---

[7] Cf. Y. CONGAR, *Le Fleuve de vie*, 296 (*The River of Life*, 229). Congar cites the following text in the Justin Martyr's description of the Eucharist: «We do not receive these gifts as ordinary food or ordinary drink. But as Jesus Christ our Saviour was made flesh through the word of God, and took flesh and blood for our salvation, in the same way the food over which thanksgiving has been offered [= the "eucharistized bread") through the word of prayer [or "the prayer of the Word" or "word") which we have from him – the food by which our blood and flesh are nourished through its transformation – is, we are taught, the flesh and blood of Jesus who was made flesh». Y. CONGAR, *Le Fleuve de vie*, 296 (*The River of Life*, 244-245), as cited from H. Bettenson, *The Early Christian Fathers*, Oxford 1969, 61-62.

[8] Y. CONGAR, *Le Fleuve de vie*, 297 (*The River of Life*, 229, 245), as cited from Germanus, *Historia ecclesiastica et mystagogica* [PG 98, 436-437].

[9] Cf. Y. CONGAR, *Le Fleuve de vie*, 297 (*The River of Life*, 230).

anamnesis[10]. In these eucharistic prayers, the invocation of the Spirit is pronounced soon after thanking God for the good things of creation and for the wonders of the history of salvation. This pattern is quite evident especially in the *Eucharistic Prayer of John Chrysostom*, in the *Apostolic Tradition* of Hippolytus, and in the *Roman Canon*, whose essential aspects were determined in the fourth century. In all three anaphorae, Congar finds that the presider, serving as the icon of Christ and as the representative of the community, offers the bread and wine and implores God the Father to send the Holy Spirit upon them:

> In the eucharistic prayer of *John Chrysostom*, the account of the institution is introduced as follows: "When he had come and had accomplished the whole economy of salvation which was for us, the night when he handed himself over [...]". This is followed by the account of the institution, which is in turn followed by the anamnesis: "Mindful [...] of everything that has been accomplished for us – of the crucifixion, of his burial, of his resurrection on the third day – we offer these things that come from you. [...]" Then the [...] epiclesis begins with the words: "We offer you this spiritual sacrifice". The same applies to the *Apostolic Tradition*: "Mindful of his death and resurrection, we offer you the bread and wine [...] and we ask you to send your Holy Spirit upon the offering of your holy Church". In the *Roman Canon*, [...] we also find, after the account of the institution, "*Unde et memores* [the anamnesis] *offerimus* [...]", a little later, "*Supplices te rogamus*", which has frequently been regarded as the equivalent of an epiclesis[11].

According to Congar, it is most fascinating that these eucharistic prayers are considered to form an undifferentiated whole. The faithful who participate in the Eucharist are enabled by the Holy Spirit to derive grace not only from the commemoration of past salvific actions, but also from their actual experience of the Saviour, Jesus Christ[12].

The third category of eucharistic prayers contains an epiclesis which invokes the Spirit not only to bring about the conversion of the gifts into the body and blood of Christ, but also to sanctify those who receive the sacrament. In other words, the Holy Spirit is the divine agent of both the conversion of the gifts and the communion. Congar further notes that, while in the *Apostolic texts* the invocations over the bread and wine and over the assembly are joined together[13], in the *Greek patristic texts* the

---

10 Cf. Y. CONGAR, *Le Fleuve de vie*, 297 (*The River of Life*, 230).

11 Y. CONGAR, *Le Fleuve de vie*, 298 (*The River of Life*, 230); see also «Le Saint-Esprit dans la consécration et la communion selon la tradition occidentale», 384.

12 Cf. Y. CONGAR, *Le Fleuve de vie*, 298 (*The River of Life*, 230).

13 Cf. Y. CONGAR, *Le Fleuve de vie*, 298 (*The River of Life*, 230), as cited from F.E. Brightman, *Liturgies Eastern and Western*: vol. 1. Eastern Liturgies, Oxford 1896,

epiclesis of the Holy Spirit is chiefly meant to sanctify the faithful. Thus, these eucharistic prayers imply that the benefits of salvation are bestowed on the faithful in and through the reception of the Spirit-filled flesh and blood of Christ. In fact, it is for this purpose that Jesus filled the bread and wine with his Spirit at the final meal he had with his disciples during his earthly life[14].

The fourth category of anaphorae emphasizes that, since the epiclesis is closely connected with the anamnesis, it is wrong to isolate one from the other. According to Congar, the Egyptian rite contains an invocation of the Holy Spirit which is pronounced before the institutional words of Christ[15]. Moreover, Congar notes that in the Byzantine liturgy, and in the liturgies of John Chrysostom and the Basil the Great, the dialogue between the priest and the deacon at the end of the "great entrance" explicitly states that the epiclesis is the means by which the divine *Pneuma* concelebrates with the ordained ministers: «Priest: The Holy Spirit will come upon you and the power of the most High will cover you with his shadow. Deacon: The Holy Spirit himself will concelebrate with us all the days of our life»[16].

The fifth and final type of anaphorae is characterized by an epiclesis which asks the Spirit to consecrate the bread and wine soon after the words of the institution narrative have been spoken. According to Congar, many scholars doubt whether, at the early stages of Christian worship, there existed a consecratory epiclesis to be said after the words of institution[17]. Most probably, such an invocation was introduced, once the divinity of the Holy Spirit had to be affirmed so as to counter those who negated it. Congar observes that the same tendency arose with regard to the baptismal epiclesis: «Before the First Council of Constantinople in 381, the descent of Christ into the water of Baptism was invoked, whereas, after the council, it was the coming of the Spirit that was

---

20ff and also from L. Bouyer, *Eucharisty*. Theology and Spirituality of the Eucharistic Prayer, Notre Dame 1968, 264-266.

[14] Cf. Y. CONGAR, *Le Fleuve de vie*, 299 (*The River of Life*, 231).

[15] Cf. Y. CONGAR, *Le Fleuve de vie*, 299 (*The River of Life*, 231), as cited from S. Salaville, «Epiclèse eucharistique», in *Dictionnaire de théologie catholique*: vol. V, eds. A. Vacant – E. Mangenot , Paris 1939, 205-206.

[16] Y. CONGAR, *Le Fleuve de vie*, 299 (*The River of Life*, 231), as cited from *La Prière des Églises de rite byzantin*: vol. I, eds. E. Mercenier – F. Paris, Amay-sur-Meuse 1937, 235.

[17] Cf. Y. CONGAR, *Le Fleuve de vie*, 300 (*The River of Life*, 231), as cited from L. Bouyze, *Eucharist*. Theology and Spirituality of the Eucharistic Prayers, 146ff.

invoked»[18]. Congar claims that, in order to quell the doubts raised by Macedonius and the Pneumatomachi, liturgical texts attempted to stress the equal divinity of the Spirit in relation to the Father and the Son.

Having made such a categorization of the various anaphorae, Congar considers the content of major patristic texts. In the *Mystagogic Catecheses* of Cyril of Jerusalem, he finds that the change of the bread and wine into the body and blood of Christ is clearly said to take place in and through an invocation of the Holy Spirit, since he is the divine Person who brings about all transformation and sanctification: «After having been sanctified ourselves by these spiritual hymns (the Trisagion), we implore the God who loves men to send the Holy Spirit on to the gifts placed here, so as to make the bread the body of Christ and the wine the blood of Christ, since everything that the Holy Spirit touches is sanctified and transformed»[19]. Therefore, in his writings Cyril does not limit the epiclesis to a particular moment of the eucharistic anaphora, but views it as enveloping the entire celebration. Congar points out, moreover, that the text of Cyril does not make any reference to an account of the institution or to the anamnesis[20]. The same can be said of the liturgy of Basil the Great, in which can be found a most pronounced emphasis on the epiclesis as causing the gifts to be changed into the precious body and blood of Jesus Christ:

> We sinners also [...] dare to approach your holy altar and, bringing forward the symbols [*prosthentes*] [...] of the holy body and blood of your Christ, we implore you and invoke you, Holy of Holies, through the benevolence of your goodness, to make your Holy Spirit come down on us and on these gifts that we present to you: may he bless and sanctify them and present to us [*anadeixai*] [in] this bread the precious body itself of our Lord, God and Saviour Jesus Christ and [in] this cup the precious blood itself of our Lord, God and Saviour Jesus Christ, poured out for the life of the world, *changing them by your Holy Spirit*[21].

From the analysis of this and other texts, Congar becomes aware that the epicletic prayer is regarded as capable of consecrating the eucharistic gifts. Then he poses the question: does this understanding of the epiclesis

---

[18] Y. CONGAR, *Le Fleuve de vie*, 300 (*The River of Life*, 231), as cited from J. Quasten, «The Blesssing of the Font in the Syrian Rite of the Fourth Century», *TS* 7 (1946) 309-313.

[19] Y. CONGAR, *Le Fleuve de vie*, 301 (*The River of Life*, 232).

[20] Cf. Y. CONGAR, *Le Fleuve de vie*, 301 (*The River of Life*, 245-246).

[21] Y. CONGAR, *Le Fleuve de vie*, 301 (*The River of Life*, 232), as cited from L. Bouyer, *Eucharist*. Theology and Spirituality of the Eucharistic Prayer, 295-296.

as consecratory necessarily exclude that the same function be attributed to the words of institution in the eucharistic celebration?[22]

According to Congar, the epiclesis that extends throughout the canon of the Mass does not eliminate the necessity of the words of institution. In other words, he affirms that the conjoining of the epiclesis and the institutional narrative bring about the consecration of the bread and wine. There is no doubt that the eucharistic prayers which contain an epiclesis almost always include either the words of institution or else a clear allusion to them. In order to illumine the reason why the words of institution, along with the epiclesis are an essential element in realizing the Eucharist, Congar appeals to the logic employed by John Chrysostom, since he is the Eastern theologian who best explains their role in the consecration. According to Chrysostom, a word spoken once by God within history has a lasting effect, since it is meant to create life and to nourish it with grace:

> The words *increase* and *multiply*, although they were only said once, continue to have an influence and to give you the power to procreate children. The same applies to the words: *This is my body*. Although they were only spoken once, they give, and will continue to give until the end of the world, their existence and their virtue to all sacrifices[23].

If the eucharistic consecration is realized by means of the enduring efficacy of the words of institution pronounced by Jesus at the Last Supper, by what means or mediation are they pronounced over the bread and wine brought to the altar in a particular ecclesial community? Relying on the theological tradition of both East and West, Congar holds that this occurs through the cultic action of the ordained ministers[24]. Therefore, to admit the perennial causality of the words of institution entails facing the question concerning how the sanctifying function of the ordained is related to the christic and pneumatic dimensions of the eucharistic consecration.

Congar explains this relationship by considering the representative roles which the ordained exercise at the eucharistic celebration. First of all, in consecrating the eucharistic gifts, they represent Christ, the

---

22 Cf. Y. CONGAR, *Le Fleuve de vie*, 302 (*The River of Life*, 232-233).

23 Y. CONGAR, *Le Fleuve de vie*, 303 (*The River of Life*, 233), as cited from J. Chrysostom , *De proditione Iudae*, *Hom*. 1, no: 6 [PG 49, 380]; see also «Pneumatologie ou christomonisme dans la tradition latine?», 403.

24 Cf. Y. CONGAR, *Le Fleuve de vie*, 303-304 (*The River of Life*, 233-234); see also «Actualité renouvelée du Saint-Esprit», 558-559 («Renewed Actuality of the Holy Spirit», 29).

sovereign high priest, who chooses to act through them for the benefit of all the members of his social Body. Thus, the ordained serve as the icons of Christ, by acting in his name and nourishing his followers: «It is being recognized that the priest who is the sacramental representative of Christ, brings about the application of the consecration that Christ accomplished once, and which he has to accomplish every time in the Church's celebrations, to the offerings»[25]. Yet, even though they are the living images of Christ acting in the Cenacle, the ordained cannot be said, according to Congar, to act «directly and vertically in terms of Christ-priest», without taking into account that they do so for the community they serve, which is composed of living members of his mystical Body. Secondly, therefore, in consecrating the elements the ordained represent the Church of which they are members, since Order presumes Baptism and is oriented to the baptized[26]. Yet, even if the ordained belong to the community, since their calling emerges from it and is meant to edify it, they do not receive from it their cultic function of presiding at its liturgical celebrations[27]. Thus, they can act as presiding ministers at the Eucharist and pronounce the words of institution because they represent both the transcendent Head of the community, Jesus Christ in glory, and its members existing in this moment of history and in this concrete place.

However, Congar admits that in the Churches of the East and the West differing theological conceptions exist regarding the role of the ordained at the eucharistic celebration. Since in the West the words of institution are viewed fundamentally as an objective recital of the Gospel account of the Last Supper, it is necessary that the ordained ministers have the explicit intention of speaking in the name of Christ, and of doing what he did. Yet, in the East what is necessary is not the intention of the presiders but the power granted them through the invocation of the Holy Spirit[28]. This is very well illustrated in the *Liturgy of John Chrysostom*:

---

[25] Y. CONGAR, «Pneumatologie ou christomonisme dans la tradition latine?», 403; see also *Le Fleuve de vie*, 312-313 (*The River of Life*, 239); *Il est Seigneur et Il donne la vie*, 65-66 (*Lord and Giver of Life*, 45). It is something very positive now that the ordained priest is considered in relation to the priestly laity. Here, the ordained priesthood is seen in the perspective of the community rather than directly and vertically in terms of Christ-priest. Cf. Y. CONGAR, *Appelés à la vie*, 122 (*Called to Life*, 115).

[26] Cf. Y. CONGAR, «L'*ecclesia* ou communauté chrétienne, sujet intégral de l'action liturgique», 243; see also *Le Concile de Vatican II*. Son Église peuple de Dieu et corps du Christ, 156.

[27] Cf. Y. CONGAR, *Le Fleuve de vie*, 305-306 (*The River of Life*, 235); see also *Appelés à la vie*, 128-129 (*Called to Life*, 122).

[28] Cf. Y. CONGAR, *Le Fleuve de vie*, 302-303 (*The River of Life*, 233), as cited from N. Cabasilas, *Commentary on the Divine Liturgy*, London 1960, 29. To

We offer you this spiritual and bloodless worship and we invoke you, imploring you to send your Holy Spirit upon us and upon these gifts presented, and to make this bread the precious body of your Christ, changing it by your Holy Spirit [Amen], and of what is in this cup the precious blood of your Christ, changing it by your Holy Spirit [Amen], so that they may be for those who partake of them, for the soberness [...] of the soul, the remission of sins, the communication of your Holy Spirit, the fullness of the Kingdom, free access to you [...], and not judgement or condemnation[29].

As this text makes clear, whereas the West views the efficacy of the consecration as dependent on the spiritual intention of the ordained in pronouncing the words of institution, the East regards the epiclesis itself as the source of their spiritual power. Yet, Congar argues that this position of the East does not mean to suggest that the conversion of the bread and wine into the body and blood of Christ occurs only because the Holy Spirit is invoked at this moment in the history of the Church. In other words, «the epiclesis does not make the historical account unnecessary. How would it be possible for the Spirit to be present if there were not the historical reality of the economy?»[30]

Congar welcomes the fact that the pneumatological dimension of the Eucharist is being recognized in the West as a complement to its emphasis on the christological one. But it has to be asked in what measure this theoretical recognition is evident in the liturgical texts themselves. There is no doubt that the Latin tradition has always attributed the effectiveness of the Eucharist to the presence and action of all three Persons of the

---

substantiate the Eastern position, Congar cites Nicholas Cabasilas' and Paul Evdokimov's treatment of it. First of all in Nicholas Cabasilas he finds: «We believe that the Lord's words do indeed accomplish the mystery, but through the medium of the priest, his invocation, and his prayer; here he is referring to the application of the words said by Jesus at the Last Supper, words that the priest uses again in the form of an account in order to apply them to the oblations». Secondly, in Paul Evdokimov Congar notes that «the words of Christ that the priest has memorized may acquire a divine effectiveness, through an invocation of the Holy Spirit. The Holy Spirit makes the words of anamnesis: "Taking bread [...] he gives it to his disciples [...] saying [...] This is my body" an *epiphanic anamnesis*, pointing to the intervention of Christ himself as identifying the words said by the priest with his own words and identifying the eucharist celebrated by the priest with his own Last Supper. This is the miracle of the *metabole*, that is, of the conversion of the gifts». Y. CONGAR, *Le Fleuve de vie*, 312-313 (*The River of Life*, 247-248), as cited from N. Cabasilas, *Commentary on the Divine Liturgy*, 29 and also from P. Evdokimov, *L'Esprit Saint dans la tradition orthodoxe*, 103-104.

29 Y. CONGAR, *Le Fleuve de vie*, 302 (*The River of Life*, 233), as cited from L. Bouyer, *Eucharist*. Theology and Spirituality of the Eucharistic Prayer, 288 and also from S. Salavaille, «Epiclèse eucharistique», 195-196.

30 Y. CONGAR, *Il est Seigneur et Il donne la vie*, 70-71 (*Lord and Giver of Life*, 51).

Holy Trinity. Congar states that most Catholic theologians would hold that «the consecration of the sacred gifts is the act of Christ, the sovereign high priest who is active through his minister and through the Holy Spirit»[31]. However, Congar questions whether what is attributed to the Holy Spirit in connection with the efficacy of the Eucharist is sufficiently articulated in the wording of the liturgy. How can one affirm a certain theological stance without assuring that it is already explicit in the rite itself? For Congar, the principle «*lex orandi, lex credendi*» requires a proper subsequent theologizing[32]. This means that the christological dimension of the Eucharist which is expressed through the narration of the words of institution should be complemented with more extensive reference to the pneumatological dimension:

> The effectiveness of the grace of the sacraments has always been attributed to the effectiveness of the Holy Spirit, the *virtus Spiritus Sancti*, throughout the history of the Church. This means that the sacred action celebrated in the Church's Eucharist calls for the complement of an active coming of the Spirit – though this is a complement that is not in any sense an optional extra[33].

Here Congar states forcefully that a sacrament can exist only when the liturgical commemoration of the saving signs of Christ is animated by the sanctifying activity of the Holy Spirit. This means, in regard to the Eucharist, that the Son and the Spirit effect the consecration through the words of institution and the epiclesis. This solution reflects the salvific plan of the Father, in which the Son and the Spirit have concerted parts. In other words, a well formulated epiclesis in the eucharistic anaphora serves as a profession of faith regarding the active role of the *Pneuma* in the saving mission of the *Logos*. The same should be said with regard to a well formulated narration of the Last Supper; it would be a profession of faith regarding the active role of the *Logos* in the sanctifying mission of the *Pneuma*.

In the light of these reflections, it is understandable that Congar appreciated the official acknowledgement of the importance of the epiclesis in the revised eucharistic texts which were published after Vatican II:

---

[31] Y. CONGAR, *Le Fleuve de vie*, 303 (*The River of Life*, 234).

[32] Cf. Y. CONGAR, «La pneumatologie dans la théologie catholique», 257; see also *Appelés à la vie*, 71-72 (*Called to life*, 62-63).

[33] Y. CONGAR *Le Fleuve de vie*, 320 (*The River of Life*, 250); see also «Pneumatologie ou christomonisme dans la tradition latine?», 396-397, 404.

The most important achievement of the Council in this sphere was undoubtedly the introduction of the epiclesis into the new eucharistic prayers, the second of which is taken almost word for word from the prayer of Hippolytus, which is the earliest liturgical text in existence. [...] The other eucharistic prayers, however, each include two epicleses, one with the consecration or sanctification of the gifts in mind, and the other so that the Spirit will sanctify, fill and unite believers in Christ, within a framework of absolute praise in the communion of saints[34].

With this development of the *lex orandi* in the Western Church, Congar foresees that the long neglected significance of the role of the Holy Spirit in the consecration of the bread and wine would be remedied even in the *lex credendi*. Then it would be possible for Catholic theologians to consider that the consecration of the elements is a gradual event which occurs throughout the entire eucharistic anaphora, rather than an instantaneous one which takes place once the recital of the words of institution has been carried out. Then, too, the epiclesis might be understood not as a gesture subservient to the account of the institution, but as an indispensable calling down of the Holy Spirit who renders the bread and wine a spiritual nourishment (cf. 1 Cor 10, 3-4), as he made the dead Jesus a spiritual body (cf. 1 Cor 15,46).

2. The Constitutive Role of the Post-Consecratory Invocation of the Holy Spirit in the Eucharist as the Foundation of Ecclesial Communion

Congar does not limit his considerations on the relation of the dual divine missions to the issue of the conversion of the elements alone. According to him, the event «*extra nos*» which serves as the basis of the christological dimension of the eucharistic sacrifice is already completed; yet, the event «*in nobis*» which is the purpose of its pneumatological dimension, the on-going sanctification and unity of the faithful, is not yet complete. In other words, the rite of communion in which the eucharistic sacrifice culminates does not properly depend on the «*extra nos*» dimension of this sacrament, but on its «*in nobis*» dimension, that is, the sanctifying and unifying work of the Holy Spirit in the communicants. Congar claimed that since the rise of Scholasticism this insight was not expressed in the Latin Church: «The traditional understanding of the role of the Holy Spirit completing the work of sanctification in the

---

34 Y. CONGAR, *L'expérience de l'Esprit*, 231 (*The Experience of the Spirit*, 170); see also «Pneumatologie ou christomonisme dans la tradition latine?», 406-407; *Le Fleuve de vie*, 313 (*The River of Life*, 241); *Diversités et Communion*, Paris 1982, 73-74; Eng. trans. J. Bowden, *Diversity and Communion*, London 1984, 73.

communicant for whom the body and blood of Christ are given as a nourishment, vanished in the Western countries at the dawn of Scholasticism»[35]. Here Congar points out that the second invocation of the Holy Spirit upon the communicants is meant to bring the economy of salvation to its goal: ecclesial communion and mission. If the previous sub-section focused on how Congar bases the pre-consecratory epiclesis on various ancient eucharistic prayers, this sub-section on the post-consecratory epiclesis points out how he substantiated his arguments by references to tradition.

Congar began with the premise that the purpose of the conversion of the bread and wine into the body and blood of Christ is that they be received by the faithful who are thereby to be joined in ecclesial communion. Since during the messianic time the Spirit completes everything, he is the active agent of ecclesial communion. Congar finds this truth very well expressed in many liturgies in which the Holy Spirit is invoked in order to effect not only the conversion of the gifts into the body and blood of Christ but also the sanctification and unity of the participants. Thus, the pneumatological dimension of the Eucharist:

> does not consist only in attributing to the Holy Spirit, at least by appropriation, the changing of the bread and wine into the body and blood of Christ; it also consists in assuring, through the gifts which have been eucharistified and beyond them, the effect of sanctification and salvation which is aimed at by the Eucharist: this effect is brought about by the operation of the Holy Spirit who dwells in the Church[36].

Therefore, the consecration of the bread and wine reaches its finality only when the Spirit enables the «*extra nos*» self-gift of Christ to become an «*in nobis*» realty for the faithful. Congar notes that many patristic texts and later theological writings examined this topic in great detail, and usually did so by preserving the balance between the christological and pneumatological moments of the economy of salvation. Through his study of the tradition regarding ecclesial communion as the effect of the Eucharist, he designates three quite different approaches: Alexandrian, Augustinian and Syrian[37].

In the Alexandrian approach Congar finds that, because of the Nestorian controversy, theologians such as Athanasius and Cyril

---

35 Y. CONGAR, «Pneumatologie ou christomonisme dans la tradition latine?», 401; see also *L'Église de saint Augustin à l'époque moderne*, 165, 267.

36 Y. CONGAR, «Pneumatologie ou christomonisme dans la tradition latine?», 397; see also *L'expérience de l'Esprit*, 154-155 (*The Experience of the Spirit*, 108).

37 Cf. Y. CONGAR, *Le Fleuve de vie*, 331 (*The River of Life*, 258).

explained the Eucharist in relation to the incarnate Word and the sanctifying and deifying power of his flesh and blood. This does not mean that they associated the deifying power of the Eucharist only with the incarnation and ignored the death and glorification of Christ. Nor, by giving preference to the christological dimension of the Eucharist, did they disregard the pneumatological one. According to the Alexandrians, the heavenly Father causes all things through the Son in the Spirit. Although in their eucharistic theology, they gave prominent place to the Son with regard to the immediate efficacy of the consecrated elements, the lasting effect of communion in the souls of the faithful they attribute to the Spirit. Congar cites many eucharistic texts, in which both these effects are stressed. A terse example is found in the *Commentary on John's Gospel* by Cyril of Alexandria: «Just as the virtue of the sacred flesh makes those who receive it co-corporeal with each other, so too, it seems to me, does the Spirit, who comes to dwell in all of us lead them to spiritual [pneumatic] unity»[38]. This text evidently distinguishes between the christic-corporeal and the pneumatic-spiritual effects of the Eucharist on the members of the Church. This ecclesiological reference is important, since Christ the Head is viewed as feeding the Church with himself, so that all his members might share his glorified corporeal life, or be co-corporeal with him and each other, as Chapter VI of the *Gospel of John* makes quite clear. Yet, the Spirit is also perceived as «feeding» the Church by means of eucharistic grace, which is nothing less than his own in-dwelling in them, so that they be united in mind and heart, as Chapter X of Paul's *First Letter to the Corinthians* attests. Thus, Cyril combines in this text insights from John and Paul which associate the Eucharist with the two main mysteries of Christianity: the incarnation and grace.

Congar synthesizes the Augustinian approach by considering only the *Commentary on the Gospel of John* and the exposition of 1 Cor 10, 3-4. Taking inspiration from the latter text, Augustine argues that, although the sacraments as signs are different, the reality which they indicate is the

---

38 Y. CONGAR, *Le Fleuve de vie*, 332 (*The River of Life*, 258-259); see also «Le Saint-Esprit dans la consecration et la communion selon la tradition occidentale», 385, as cited from Cyril of Alexandria, *Commentarius in evangelium Joannis* XI: 11 [PG 74, 561]. In this connection Congar cites another text from Cyril: «Giving life and uniting himself to a flesh that he made his own, the Word of God made that flesh life-giving. It was suitable for him also to unite himself in a certain fashion to our bodies through his sacred flesh and his precious blood which we receive in the bread and wine of a life-giving blessing». Y. CONGAR, *Le Fleuve de vie*, 332 (*The River of Life*, 265), as cited from Cyril of Aleandria, *Commentarius in evangelium Lucae* XXII [PG 72, 912].

same, Christ the Head: «We all eat and drink the same Christ in the eucharistic bread and wine. The "sacraments" as signs are different, but the reality to which they point is the same - it is Christ. The Jews of the Exodus did not attain to Christ and are therefore *our* fathers only to the extent that they ate and drank *spiritually*»[39]. Congar explains the adverb «spiritually» by noting that Augustine gave prime place to intellectual communion. In other words, for Augustine, in and through eucharistic communion the faithful should come first of all to a personal knowledge of what is meant by the signs of bread and wine. The Jews who ate the manna from heaven and drank the water from the rock did not know Christ as such, but had a prefigurment of him, and thus ate and drank spiritually. Christians, however, have been given the fullness of revelation through faith. This explains his famous phrase: «Believe and you have eaten [Christ]. The man who desires life should approach, believe and be incorporated in order to be given life»[40]. Regarding the identity of Christ, Augustine regards him as the *totus Christus*, the Head joined to all the members of his Body. The divine animator of this Body is the Holy Spirit. Congar thus observes that for Augustine there is always a motion from the sacramental Body to the ecclesial Body of Christ; to be a member of the second, it is necessary to receive the first[41]. Yet, the sacramental Body that one receives through communion does not achieve its ecclesial effect, unless the faithful are illumined and readied by the gift of the Holy Spirit. Therefore, on the one hand, it is necessary to be in the ecclesial Body of Christ in order to have his Spirit, and on the other, the Spirit of Christ enables the faithful to receive the sacramental Body of Christ fruitfully. In short, for Augustine, the principle that animates both the sacrament itself and the ecclesial communion which springs from it is the Holy Spirit. If the members receive the sacrament of the Body with

---

[39] Y. CONGAR, *Le Fleuve de vie*, 333 (*The River of Life*, 259); see also «Pneumatologie ou christomonisme dans la tradition latine?», 405; *L'Église de saint Augustin à l'époque moderne*, 16.

[40] Y. CONGAR, *Le Fleuve de vie*, 333 (*The River of Life*, 259).

[41] Congar finds a certain danger in the Augustinian identity of the real presence and the mystical Body. According to him, while Augustine considers that the consecrated eucharistic gifts symbolize and contain the *totus Christus*, the Scholastics held that, although there is a connection between the real presence and the mystical Body, it is extrinsic to what exits on the altar. Congar prefers to follow the thinking pattern of Thomas Aquinas. Cf. Y. CONGAR, *Le Fleuve de vie*, 339-340 (*The River of Life*, 263-264).

the faith given then by the Holy Spirit, they share in the life of Christ, their Head[42].

In the Syrian approach, Congar finds that the active presence of the Holy Spirit in the consecrated elements is invariably expressed in symbols. The divine *Pneuma* is like fire in the furnace of the bread and wine. Congar cites a sampling of theological writings and liturgical texts:

> *Ephraem Syrus*: "The Fire and the Spirit are in our Baptism; in the bread and the cup are also the Fire and Spirit". *Isaac of Antioch*: "Come and drink, eat the flame which will make you angels of the fire and taste the flavour of the Holy Spirit", or Matins of the Second Sunday after Pentecost: "Here is the body and blood which are the furnace in which the Holy Spirit is the fire"[43].

Reflecting on the specificity of the Syrian tradition as indicated by these texts Congar stated that «what the Holy Spirit has done for Christ in his conception, baptism and resurrection, he causes to function in the Church and the lives of Christians»[44]. Similarly, what the Spirit did for Christ in the Cenacle and on the cross, he does *«in nobis»* in the Eucharist. Therefore, at the Last Supper Jesus himself «filled» the bread and wine with the Holy Spirit who was constantly active in his life. This obviously has implications for the ecclesial rite of the Eucharist, as is illustrated in the *Sermon for Holy Saturday* of Ephraem Syrus: «He called the bread his living body filled it with himself and with the Spirit, stretched out his hand and gave them the bread: "Take and eat with the faith and do not doubt that this is my body". And the one who eats with faith, through it he eats the fire of the Spirit. [...] Eat all of you and eat through it the Holy Spirit»[45]. Since the eucharistic bread and wine are filled with the Holy Spirit, they possess the qualities of the glorified body of Christ, and are thus able to grant the faithful the grace of immortality. The Syrian theologians insisted that the Eucharist is the bread of eternal

---

42 Cf. Y. CONGAR, *Le Fleuve de vie*, 333 (*The River of Life*, 259); see also *L'Église de saint Augustin à l'époque moderne*, 13, 17.

43 Y. CONGAR, *Le Fleuve de vie*, 77 (*The River of Life*, 42), as cited from E.P. Siman, *L'expérience de l'Esprit par l'Église d'aprés la tradition syrienne d'Antioche*, Paris 1971, 105, 223, 107, 224.

44 Y. CONGAR, *Le Fleuve de vie*, 76 (*The River of Life*, 42).

45 Y. CONGAR, *Le Fleuve de vie*, 338 (*The River of Life*, 262), as cited from Ephaem Syrus, *Sermons for Holy Saturday*: vol. IV, in *Hymni et Sermones*: vol. I, ed. T. Lamy, Malines 1882, 415ff. Although Congar has presented many other texts in order to illustrate this aspect, for the sake of brevity this particular one alone is taken into consideration.

life, not because of its relation to Easter alone, but also because of its relation to Pentecost[46].

After pondering on the pneumatological content of these three traditions, Congar comes to the conclusion that the consecrated or «eucharistized» gifts have an effect on the those who receive them, insofar as they make an act of living faith and love which is empowered by the Holy Spirit. Therefore, sacramental communion in itself is not perfect since, if believers are to be transformed the way Christ intends them to be, the sanctifying and unifying action of the Holy Spirit is an essential pre-requisite:

> Rather like a packet placed in a trough and then carried along by a current of living water, my sacramental communion is taken up by the movement and the warmth with which the Spirit, who is invoked and who opens up a channel for himself in me, invests the presence of Jesus. My communion is therefore a cleaving, in abandonment and love, to what Jesus is, wants and brings about in me[47]

Therefore, for Congar, the christological structure of the eucharistic sacrifice is complemented by the pneumatological structure of sanctifying grace. The Holy Spirit opens up a channel for himself in the communicants, so that they might be made holy and animated for their mission. In other words, just as the first epiclesis preceding the consecration of the eucharistic gifts indicates that the Holy Spirit has a part in the salvific mission of the Son, the second epiclesis preceding the communion rite points to the fact, that «the Christ whom the faithful receive in the sacramental communion is the Christ of Easter who has been *"pneumatized"* or penetrated by the Spirit»[48]. Thus, the *Pneuma* is the vital and vitalizing divine principle which sustains the faithful in communion with the body and blood of the glorified Christ.

Congar is thus led to consider the parallel between what the Holy Spirit once did in the life of Christ so that he might become the Head of the ecclesial Body, and what the *Pneuma* does continually in the faithful so that they may become ever more holy and active members of this Body. Hence, for Congar, the epicletic dimension of the Eucharist, both as it effects the consecration of the elements and the communion of the

---

[46] Cf. Y. CONGAR, «Pneumatologie ou christomonisme dans la tradition latine?», 399-400; see also «Le Saint-Esprit dans la consécration et la communion selon la tradition occidentale», 385.

[47] Y. CONGAR, *Le Fleuve de vie*, 339 (*The River of Life*, 263); see also *Essais oecuméniques*: le mouvement, les hommes, les problèmes, 252.

[48] Y. CONGAR, *Le Fleuve de vie*, 340-341 (*The River of Life*, 264).

faithful, explicates that the Spirit is personally active in the three realities that bear the name «Body of Christ»: (1) his natural Body, conceived, put to death and glorified; (2) his sacramental Body on the altar; and (3) his mystical Body, the ecclesial communion. Although these three realities are distinct, and should not be confused, they are intrinsically linked one to the other by the Holy Spirit[49]. In the first reality, from the conception to the resurrection, the Son of God «in the flesh» is permeated by the Holy Spirit. In the second reality, the self-gift of the Son of God «in symbols» of food and drink, is re-actualized for his followers by the invocation of the Holy Spirit on their offerings. In the third reality, the presence of the Son of God «in nobis», is realized by the Spirit who is, as uncreated grace, the common factor which the Head has with the members. According to Congar, the mystical Body is the reality towards which the other two, that is, the glorified Body and the sacramental Body, are directed, and in which they find their fruition as self-gifts of the word «propter nos et nostram salutem». Just as the Spirit constituted the crucified Jesus as Lord, he carries out a parallel role in the eucharistic epiclesis over the bread and wine, and another parallel role in the communion which sanctifies and unites the ecclesial Body[50].

By way of concluding this chapter, and at the same time the entire expository part of this study, it can be said that the fundamental insight from which Congar's sacramental theology springs concerns the collaboration of the Spirit in the salvific mission of the Son not only during his earthly life, but also throughout his glorified state. For, while the Son is physically absent from the followers, the Spirit assures that his saving signs be extended to them, so that they may enjoy the benefits of his life, death and resurrection, and may be united to each other as members of his social Body. Therefore, just as the structure of the economy of salvation is determined by the concerted missions of the *Logos* and the *Pneuma*, so the sacraments derive their fruit both from the Easter-event and the Pentecost-event. Hence, for Congar, in every sacrament there is not only a christological or salvific moment, in which the culmination of the mission of the *Logos* is commemorated at the anamnesis, but also a pneumatological or sanctifying moment, in which the mission of the *Pneuma* serves to render this commemoration efficacious at the epiclesis.

---

49 Cf. Y. CONGAR, *Le Fleuve de vie*, 341 (*The River of Life*, 264); see also *L'expérience de l'Esprit*, 163-164 (*The Experience of the Spirit*, 116-117).

50 Cf. Y. CONGAR, *Le Fleuve de vie*, 341 (*The River of Life*, 264); see also *L'expérience de l'Esprit*, 163-164 (*The Experience of the Spirit*, 116-117).

The epicletic dimension of the sacraments is for Congar a prominent instance of the truth that the whole life of the Church depends on the prayer *Veni, sancte Spiritus*[51]. In other words, the sacraments indicate a broader ecclesiological principle, namely that the sign-character of the Church is made possible, maintained and furthered by the power of the divine *Pneuma*:

> In concrete, this means that the Spirit must actively intervene in the case of any activity that is related to the sacramental or hierarchical institution, whether it has to do with the Word, the pastoral government of the Church or the sacraments in the widest sense of the word, that is, those acts which are concerned with the general sacramentality of the Church[52].

The content of this present chapter on the epicletic dimension of the Eucharist serves quite well to illustrate the centrality of the passage just quoted in Congar's thought. Certainly, the Eucharist is perceived by him as a symbolic act which is constitutive of the sacramentality of the Church. It follows then from the logic of this passage that the Eucharist entails the gratuitous intervention of the divine *Pneuma*. In fact, Congar demonstrates that this is true not only with regard to the consecration of the elements which takes place during the anaphora but also with regard to the communion existing among the faithful who receive the body and blood of Christ. During the anaphora the invocation of the Holy Spirit renders the bread and wine vital and vitalizing by conjoining them to the glorified Christ, thus fulfilling the words which he expressed in the Cenacle and which are pronounced by the presider of the liturgy. Then, as the result of the second invocation of the Holy Spirit on the faithful,

---

[51] Cf. Y. CONGAR, «Actualité renouvelée du Saint-Esprit», 559 («Renewed Actuality of the Spirit», 30); see also *Le Fleuve de vie*, 202 (*The River of Life*, 149); *L'expérience de l'Esprit*, 155 (*The Experience of the Spirit*, 108).

[52] Y. CONGAR, *Il est Seigneur et Il donne la vie*, 65-66 (*Lord and Giver of Life*, 45); see also *Le Fleuve de vie*, 350 (*The River of Life*, 271); *Appelés à la vie*, 90-91 (*Called to Life*, 82-83). For example, Congar regards «the so-called power of the keys» mentioned in the Johannine Pentecost (Jn 20, 19-23) as the root of the Holy Spirit's action in the sacrament of Reconciliation. In the new ritual he finds that a number of times the Holy Spirit is mentioned, and the form of absolution is really an implied model of an epiclesis. In the case of the sacrament of Marriage too the situation is not different. For him, this is very explicit in the Eastern Churches. While the crowns refer to the bestowal of the Holy Spirit on them [crowns placed on the bride and groom], the priest's final prayer is analogous to an invocation of the Holy Spirit. A similar role of the Holy Spirit can be also noted in the case of Anointing of the sick. However, Congar does not limit his epicletic remarks only to the official sacraments of the Church; he extends them to the entire life of the Church. Cf. Y. CONGAR, *Le Fleuve de vie*, 346-350 (*The River of Life*, 269-271); see also *Il est Seigneur et Il donne la vie*, 136-138, 159-161 (*Lord and Giver of Life*, 102-103, 121-122).

the reality of the subsequent ecclesial communion is anticipated, for through operation of grace in them they are unified, sanctified and sent on mission. In effect, the eucharistic epiclesis guarantees the sacramentality of the Church, that is, its character as visible sign of human salvation and sanctification.

PART THREE

**SYNTHESIS AND CONCLUSION
REGARDING CARDINAL YVES CONGAR'S
CONCEPT OF THE EPICLESIS**

CHAPTER VI

A Critical Appraisal of Cardinal Yves Congar's
Understanding of how the Invocation of the Holy Spirit
Constitutes the Sacraments

After having analyzed in the previous four chapters the thought of
Congar concerning the liturgical epiclesis as constitutive of the
sacraments, this final chapter attempts to offer a critical appraisal of it
which is marked by discretion and balance. By discretion, because Congar
is so gifted and prolific a theologian that one could fail to give sufficient
weight to some aspect of a particular theme; and by balance because
Congar is so original that one could err in either praising or criticizing
his ideas excessively[1]. Therefore, after illustrating the valuable and the
limited aspects of his presentation of the topic, attention is given to
indicating some modest means by which its limitations could be
overcome, and its advantages thereby strengthened. In order to attain this
end, instead of the historical and analytical methods, which have been so
far employed, an evaluative-prognostic one is adopted. Thus, the
questions posed in the introduction of this study are now taken up again,
so as to comprehend in a detailed manner what Congar has and has not
achieved in illuminating the constitutive role of the Holy Spirit in the
sacraments.

---

[1] Cf. W. HENN, *The Hierarchy of Truths according to Yves Congar, O. P.*, Roma
1987, 241. A similar observation can be found with regard to an evaluation of Congar's
theology in the writing of M. Winter. For him, «in seeking to analyze Congar's
characteristic ideas one must proceed with caution, since his prodigious literary activity
shows no sign of drying up. Nevertheless a number of clear orientations pervade his
whole outlook». M. WINTER, «Masters in Israel: Yves Congar», *CR* 55 (1970) 281.

The first sub-section of this chapter deals with the positive aspects of the contribution of Congar to the theme of this study. Until recently, the pre-occupation with the institutional aspects of divine revelation dominated Catholic theology; thus Christ, the ministerial priesthood and the liturgical anamnesis were major themes, while the Spirit, the common priesthood and the liturgical epiclesis were minor ones. It seems in retrospect that either christology and pneumatology went their separate ways, or else that the latter was absorbed and neutralized by the former. Recently, however, the situation has begun to change. The identity and mission of the Spirit are receiving more attention, and in the process the basic understanding of the sacraments as the re-actualizations of the paschal mystery of Jesus Christ in which the Holy Spirit has an active share is being enriched[2]. In this regard the writings of Congar have been incomparable. Before Vatican II he consistently maintained that the constitutive role of the Holy Spirit in the sacraments is liturgically expressed in and through the epiclesis. And after the Council he deemed that one of its most important achievements was providing the impetus which made possible the subsequent introduction of the epiclesis in the eucharistic prayers and into the other sacramental rites[3]. Moreover, in the light of post-conciliar trends in sacramental theology the various critical questions which he raised, and the specific answers he offered to them, provide a sound basis for further research on the constitutive character of the invocation of the Holy Spirit at the liturgy. In applying historical as well as systematic methods, Congar endeavored to show that the pneumatological dimension of the sacraments could render Catholics more appreciative of Oriental theology, which explains the liturgy in trinitarian, ecclesiological and eschatological terms.

The second sub-section then highlights some of the deficiencies which are apparent in the manner in which Congar treats the sacramental epiclesis, and which are thus in need of correctives or further clarifications. Although his ecumenical encounters with theologians of the Orthodox Churches caused him to revise the traditional Catholic understanding of the sacraments, he adheres rigidly to the Western preference for the Johannine christology «from above». Very often it

---

[2] Cf. K. McDONNELL, «A Trinitarian Theology of the Holy Spirit?», *TS* 46 (1985) 192; see also E. CLAPSIS, «The Holy Spirit in the Church», in *Come Holy Spirit, Renew the Whole Creation*, ed. G. Limouris, Brookline 1990, 166; E.J. KILMARTIN, «The Catholic Tradition of Eucharistic Theology: Towards the Third Millennium», *TS* 55 (1994) 432-433.

[3] Cf. J.A. KOMONCHAK, «The Return of Yves Congar», *Cow* 110 (1984) 402; see also M. WINTER, «Masters in Israel: Yves Congar», 287.

seems that in his attempts to sketch a pneumatological christology «from below», as is proposed in the *Synoptics*, he simply substitutes the *Pneuma* for the *Logos* in describing the divine nature conjoined to the human nature of Jesus. Moreover, in a world where the majority of people are non-Christians, is it proper to state that the Spirit communicates the universal salvific plan of the Father in the Son only through the sacraments of the Church? The panorama against which to situate a contemporary pneumatology can be more vast than that which Congar offers, because the relevant questions raised by Christians who live with adherents of the world religions challenge many of the presuppositions of the classical theologies of the Church both in the East and in the West. The critique which is articulated here does not mean to imply, however, that the coherent and well-grounded efforts of Congar to include pneumatological insights alongside christological ones in the revised sacramental theology of the Catholic Church have not opened up new perspectives which have enhanced the orthodoxy and animated the orthopraxis of the faithful.

1. The Positive Contribution of Congar to the Topic in the Light of the Major Tensions in Twentieth-Century Sacramental Theology

The extensive influence of Congar on the renewal of various fields of the Catholic theology in the twentieth century has often been publically acknowledged[4]. His ability to combine solid research based on the sources of tradition and his exceptional sensitiveness to the responsibility of theologians to promote the reunion of the Churches led him to adopt a decidedly christic-pneumatic approach to dogmatics. For this reason, it is no exaggeration to say that «of all the theologians alive today, none has

---

4 Cf. F. KRESS, Review of *I Believe in the Holy Spirit* in *Tab* 238 (1984) 42; see also I. CANAVARIS, «The Ecclesiology of Yves Congar: An Orthodox Evaluation», *GOTR* 15 (1970) 85; B. MONDIN, «Yves Congar e la teologia ecclesiologica ed ecumenica», in *I grandi teologi del secolo ventesimo*: vol. 1: I teologi cattolici, Turin 1969, 204-207. A similar observation can be noted in R.P. McBrien too: «Last year Catholic theology lost two of its most distinguished practitioners, Karl Rahner and Bernard Lonergan. For some, it was as if the age of theological giants had finally closed: Karl Barth was gone, and so, too, Bultmann, Tillich, Niebuhr, Buber, and now Rahner and Lonergan. But at least one imposing figure remains, even if wrecked with pain and debilitated by illness. That great theologian is Père Yves Congar, of the Order of Preachers». R. P. McBRIEN, «Church and Ministry: the Achievement of Yves Congar», *TD* 32 (1985) 203; see also G. FINNEGAN, «Ministerial Priesthood in Yves Congar», *RR* 46 (1987) 523.

influenced the Church's thinking as much as Fr. Congar»[5]. With regard to his theological contribution to the theme of this study, it can be said that he consistently viewed each sacramental celebration in terms not only of the institutive role of Christ as indicated in the liturgical anamnesis, but also of the constitutive role of the Holy Spirit as evident in the liturgical epiclesis. On the basis of this study, it can be stated that the questions he posed regarding the act of invoking the Holy Spirit as constitutive of the sacraments directly relate to the various tensions which mark sacramental theology: that between a christocentric and a trinitarian panorama against which to understand the cultic functions of the Church; that between a salvific-commemorative and a sanctifying-charismatic conception of the liturgical action as such; that between a hierarchical-oriented and a communitarain-oriented explanation of sacramental efficacy; and that between an individualistic-interior and an eschatological-prophetic view of sacramental grace. Congar did not seek to alleviate these tensions by stressing one aspect at the expense, or even to the exclusion, of the other. Moreover, his merit consisted in facing them and trying to conjoin them in a greater synthesis. There is no doubt that, given the long-standing prominence of the christological dimension in the sacramental theology in the West, Congar was revolutionary in accentuating the christic-pneumatic dimension of every rite. In the following brief synopsis of the positive aspects of his thought with regard to this topic, the tensions mentioned above can serve as the central categories around which to cluster his many innovative insights.

The epiclesis and the tension between a christocentric and a trinitarian panorama against which to understand the cultic function of the Church. In affirming that the epiclesis is constitutive of the sacraments, Congar consistently held to the conviction that, even in the liturgical actions of the Church, the Spirit is to be equally adored and glorified along with the Father and the Son. Since the three divine Persons are actively involved in the entire economy of salvation, this is true of the sacraments which are its symbolic re-actualization and personalization in human beings. Therefore, the invocation of the Holy Spirit is a topic which did not primarily pertain to sacramental theology, but to the doctrine of Trinity, and then to the accomplishment of human salvation which reflects it[6].

---

[5] A. NICHOLAS, *Yves Congar*, 202; see also M.K. HELLWIG, «Soteriology in the Nuclear Age», *Tho* 48 (1984) 634; R.P. McBRIEN, *Church*: The Continuing Quest, New York 1970, 46.

[6] A similar idea is expressed in R.A. ADAMS, «The Holy Spirit and the Real Presence», 49; see also C.S. SULLIVAN, *Readings in Sacramental Theology*, New Jersey 1965, 65; J.M.R. TILLARD, «L'Eucharistie et le Saint-Esprit», 364, 379, 387; E.J.

Even in his earliest writings, Congar understood that one of the major defects of christocentrism is that it detracts from the trinitarian notion of God by extolling the prominence given to only one of the divine missions, that of the Son. Yet, for Congar everything comes from the Father through the Son, in the Spirit, and everything ascends to the Father in the Spirit through the Son. In other words, no action can be attributed to the Son independently of the Father and the Spirit. Even in the mission or sending of the *Logos* at the incarnation, the *Pater* and the *Pneuma* were essentially involved. Because of the dominance of this theme especially in the later works of Congar, one commentator has observed that «this accentuation on the Spirit is developed within a general theology of the trinitarian missions, which had always been close to the surface of Congar's theology»[7].

From the texts that have been analyzed in this study, it can be said without hesitation that Congar consistently situates the invocation of the Holy Spirit at the sacraments within a trinitarian context. This illumines the truth that the Spirit renders the symbolic re-enactments of salvation through Christ the means by which his followers are sanctified through their union with the Father and with each other. Congar's attempt to ground the invocation of the Holy Spirit in this way helped him to surpass the once prevailing Augustinian emphasis on the immanent divine essence; each of the three divine Persons as such were perceived as having no particular bearing on an aspect of salvation history, such as ecclesial and sacramental life, except by way of appropriation. Viewed apart from their historical missions, the Persons of Trinity were described in terms of a complicated network of processions, relations and properties within the eternity of the Godhead itself[8]. In contrast, Congar held that the

---

KILMARTIN, «The Catholic Tradition of Eucharistic Theology: Towards the Third Millennium», 416, 433.

[7] C. McDONALD, *Church and World in the Plan of God*. Aspects of History and Eschatology in the Thought of Père Congar O. P., 139; see also L.M. NAVARATNE, *The Relationship between Christology and Pneumatology in the Writings of Yves Congar, Karl Rahner and Jacques Dupuis*. Dissertation Abstracts, Roma 1987, 5; P. CZYZ, *Il rapporto tra la dimensione cristologica e pneumatologica dell'ecclesiologia nel pensiero di Yves Congar*. Dissertation Abstracts, Roma 1986, 144; P.G. GIANAZZA, *La teologia dello Spirito Santo in prospectiva ecumenica*. Studio comparativo sulla pneumatologia di Paul Evdokimov (Ortodosso) e Yves Congar (Cattolico). Dissertation Abstracts, Roma 1981, 25, 55.

[8] A similar idea can be found in Karl Rahner too. According to him, Augustine's thought «obscured the connection between the immanent and the economic Trinity, to the detriment of a vitally practical theology of the Trinity, a loss which is not fully compensated for by the lofty speculation on the immanent divine life». K. RAHNER, «Trinity in Theology», in *Sacramentum Mundi*: vol. VI, eds. C. Ernst – K. Smiths –

proper starting point for a theology of the Trinity is a reflection on both the Easter-event and the Pentecost-event. He applied this to the *lex orandi* found in the sacramental rites, since they reveal how the divine Persons of the Trinity communicate their justice, truth and love to humankind through signs. Throughout this study it has been noted that Congar perceived the need to comprehend the sacraments in relation to the salvific mission of the Son and the sanctifying mission of the Spirit, both of which carry out the plan of the Father to bring humankind and creation to ultimate fulfillment. Since Congar insists on the interaction between the *Logos* and the *Pneuma* in the sacraments, he opts neither for a christocentrism nor for a pneumatocentrism, but for a combined christological and pneumatological understanding of the salvific acts of the Church[9]. In view of the almost exclusive emphasis on christology in the sacramental theology of the West, Congar's efforts to complement it by stressing the constitutive role of the Holy Spirit in the liturgical rites are indeed praiseworthy.

From an ecumenical point of view, Congar's accentuation of the importance of the epiclesis for sacramental theology has demonstrated the value of dialogue with the East. From this contact, he learned that the invocation of the Holy Spirit during the liturgy is closely connected to controversial theological issue that has separated East and West, that is, the introduction of the word *filioque*, which seems to subordinate the Spirit to the Son[10]. Consequently, Eastern theologians hold that the epiclesis assures that a proper theology of the Holy Spirit is articulated in the *lex orandi* of the Church. Its neglect in the West demonstrates the inauthenticity of a purely anamnetic view of the sacraments. Congar was sincere in admitting that the *filioque* cannot be justified on the basis of specific Scripture references, and urged that the Roman Church retract it from the creed, on condition that the Eastern Churches would not expect that thereby it was withdrawing from its long-held doctrinal stance

---

K. Rahner, New York 1968-1970, 306; see also ID., *The Trinity*, London 1986, 118-119.

[9] J. DUPUIS, Review of *The Word and the Spirit* in Gre 69 (1988) 153; see also L. M. NAVARATNE, *The Relationship between Christology and Pneumatology in the Writings of Yves Congar, Karl Rahner and Jacques Dupuis*, 6, 55.

[10] For example one of the eminent theologians of the Eastern Churches writes: «It would seem that, in the ecumenical dialogue, the question of the epiclesis is as important at present as that of the *filioque*, since it is above all in the light of the epiclesis that the *filioque* can be correctly restituted within the whole problem». P. EVDOKIMOV, *L'Esprit saint dans la tradition orthodoxe*, 101; see also ID., *L'Orthodoxie*, 250; ID., «Eucharistie mystère de l'Église», *LPO* 2 (1968) 62.

regarding the spiration of the Spirit by the Father and the Son[11]. As an application of the understanding that the Spirit also proceeds, like the Son, from the Father, Congar considers the epiclesis as constitutive of all the sacraments along with the anamnesis. For example, his explicit explanation of the two invocations of the Spirit at the Eucharist, in relation to the conversion of the elements and to ecclesial communion, is an open act of reconciliation with the theology of the Eastern Churches which grants prime place to the epiclesis in all aspects of ecclesial existence. Moreover, Congar was tireless in affirming that the eucharistic prayer as a whole is an act not only of thanking the Father but also of imploring him so that the offerings on the altar be transformed into the body and blood of Christ through the power of the Spirit, and that the partakers of them be joined into the ecclesial Body through the same pneumatic power. Congar thus strives to present the acknowledgment of the activity of the Holy Spirit in the sacraments, along with that of the Father and the Son, as a means of consolidating the traditions of the two Churches[12]. His achievement has in fact already diminished a good deal of disagreement with the East over the trinitarian theology, and thus it is most justified to say that his writings on the epiclesis have favoured a rapprochement not foreseeable for many centuries.

The epiclesis and the tension between a salvific-commemorative and a sanctifying-charismatic conception of the liturgical action as such. Congar's understanding of the constitutive nature of the invocation of the Holy Spirit aids in complementing the one-sided accentuation on the anamnetic conception of the sacraments in the Catholic West by means of an epicletic one. In other words, the sacraments have to be seen both as commemorative acts which render the saving effect of the Pasch operative in Christians throughout history, and as charismatic acts which invoke the Holy Spirit to sanctify the liturgical actions and to create an ecclesial community that is full of joy and zeal. Thus, according to Congar, the epicletic activity of the Holy Spirit at Baptism enables the catechumens to become holy and to make a free response to baptismal

---

[11] Cf. J. KALLARANGATT, *The Holy Spirit, Bond of Communion of the Churches. A Comparative Study of the Ecclesiology of Yves Congar and Nikos Nissiotis.* Dissertation Abstracts, Roma 1990, 36.

[12] Cf. S.P. SCHILLING, «Yves Congar», in *Contemporary Continental Theologians*, London 1966, 200; see also P.G. GIANAZZA, *La teologia dello Spirito Santo in prospectiva ecumenica*. Studio comparativo sulla pneumatologia di Paul Evdokimov (Ortodosso) e Yves Congar (Cattolico), 13; D. TRANOUPOLEOS, «The Holy Spirit in the Church», *Dia* 17 (1982) 45; J.D. ZIZIOULAS, *Being as Communion*. Studies in Personhood and the Church, 127.

grace by taking initiatives by which to express their role in building up the Church. This is the sanctifying effect of the invocation of the Holy Spirit on the water of Baptism and on the catechumens by means of their anointing. They are to become holy and to use their charisms for the good of all[13]. Moreover, Congar similarly stated that these sanctifying effects of the reception of the Spirit by the faithful at Baptism are intensified by the sacrament of Confirmation, which is a symbolic re-actualization of the out-pouring of the divine *Pneuma* on the day of Pentecost. At Confirmation, Christians do not receive «more» of the Spirit, as if his self-communication could be measured and divided into varying degrees of fullness. The Spirit who is already received in fullness at Baptism acts again in Christians at Confirmation, so that they deepen their involvement in the prophetic, cultic and pastoral life of the Church, and thereby grow in holiness and in the exercise of their charisms. Congar certainly maintained even if mostly by implication, that the second initiative invocation of the divine *Pneuma* is enacted at Confirmation. By this seal of the gift of the Spirit, Christians should no longer regard their faith solely in terms of individual holiness, but should venture out into society so as to give witness to their faith, and thus to render public the grace bestowed at the liturgical rite of anointing with chrism[14].

Congar's theology of the two eucharistic epicleses is quite significant, because he shows that the rediscovery of this pneumatological dimension of the sacrament in the West is a matter not of liturgical nicety[15], but of faithfulness to the salvific *oekonomia*. He was convinced that the absence of the epiclesis from the eucharistic liturgy had caused Latin Christians to view the sacrament as a re-presentation of the saving event of Golgotha, but not as a source of sanctification through the use of their charisms for the good of the whole community. When Congar emphasizes the

---

[13] Cf. S.P. SCHILLING, «Yves Congar», 201; see also M.K. HELLWIG, «Soteriology in the Nuclear age», 634; J. AREEPLACKAL, *Spirit and Ministries*. Perspectives of East and West, 237-238.

[14] This insight has been presented in Part II of this thesis, especially Chapter Four, «Baptism and Confirmation: Dual Anointing with the Holy Spirit and Progressive Incorporation into the Body of Christ».

[15] Cf. J.A. JUNGMANN, *The Mass of the Roman Rite*. Its Origins and Development: vol. II, New York 1986, 191-194; see also ID., *The Mass*. An Historical and Pastoral Survey, Minnesota 1976, 134-137; G.C. SMIT, «Epiclèse et théologie des sacrements», *MSR* 15 (1958) 135; E. SCHILLEBEECKX, *Christ the Sacrament of the Encounter with God*, London, 1963, 117; E.G.C.F. ATCHLEY, *On the Epiclesis of the Eucharistic Liturgy and the Consecration of the Font*, Oxford 1935, 179; G. DIX, *The Shape of the Liturgy*, London 1986, 182, 253, 301.

constitutive role of the two epicleses in the Eucharist, he is not thereby disregarding the indispensable importance of the recital of the words of institution. He is simply asserting that the eucharistic liturgy should not be explained only by means of the commemorative act of recalling what Christ once did; it should also be illumined by means of the sanctifying act of calling the Spirit upon the offerings and upon the faithful. For, the anamnesis can be effective only through the epiclesis, since in the divine economy the Holy Spirit makes present the glorified body and blood of Christ, and makes actual his redemptive act for his followers until he returns in glory. For, just as it was necessary that the Holy Spirit «pneumatize» the dead body of Jesus at Easter, so the bread and wine, and the community, need to be «pneumatized», that is, sanctified and sanctifying. Congar's view that not only the words of institution but also the epiclesis are consecratory is based on the insight that the joint efficacy of the Church and of the Spirit build one single and indivisible mystery.

Furthermore, Congar's understanding of the eucharistic epiclesis is sufficiently nuanced since he tries to do justice to the two principal facets of this liturgical act. The relevance of this judgment becomes more forceful when it is pointed out that concern about the exact moment of the eucharistic conversion has resulted in the myopic view that the rest of the anaphora could be deemed as secondary to the recital of the words spoken by Jesus in the Cenacle. Thus, accentuation on the invocation of the Holy Spirit indicates that the whole eucharistic prayer has consecratory significance[16]. For Congar, to ask whether it is the recital of the words of institution or the epiclesis that is more important is to negate that the Eucharist is inseparably an act of the Spirit in the Lord, and of the Lord in the Spirit. The Spirit certainly descends upon the gifts and transforms them into the sacramental body and blood of Christ. And Christ certainly grants the faithful his own self as spiritual food and drink, so that they can be sanctified by the Spirit and inebriated with the fire of divine love. In other words, the two eucharistic epicleses explicate the faith that the Holy Spirit «pneumatizes» the faithful, just as he has first «pneumatized» their gifts[17]. And the anamnesis explicates the faith that Christ becomes present so that the communion of the faithful with him will enable the Spirit to build ecclesial communion among them. This sanctification and

---

[16] Cf. P. CZYZ, *Il rapporto tra la dimensione cristologica e pneumatologica dell'ecclesiologia nel pensiero di Yves Congar*, 118; see also P.G. GIANAZZA, *La teologia dello Spirito Santo in prospectiva ecumenica*. Studio comparativo sulla pneumatologia di Paul Evdokimov (Ortodosso) e Yves Congar (Cattolico), 79.

[17] Cf. Chapter Five, «Eucharistic Consecration as Realized by the Account of the Institutional Words of Jesus and by the Epiclesis of the Spirit».

unification of those who partake of the consecrated bread and wine are meant to increase their commitment to witness to the self-giving love of Christ in their own civil context. Although the faithful take part in the life of the Church through Baptism and Confirmation, their full incorporation into it becomes actual each time they receive the eucharistic Body of the Lord through the power of the Spirit. Congar does not view grace only as an interior strengthening of the faithful by the Spirit, but also as a prophetic empowerment with of his out-going love for the sake of carrying out the mission of Christ and the Church in their social milieu.

The epiclesis and the tension between the hierarchical-oriented and communitarian-oriented explanation of sacramental efficacy. Congar's understanding of the invocation of the Holy Spirit as constitutive of the sacraments is nuanced, also because it brings out clearly that the sacraments are actualized not only through the visible acts of the ordained, who are the instrumental representations of Christ, but also through the invisible empowerment of the Holy Spirit acting with them. According to Congar, each sacramental rite of the Church consists of a «con-celebration» of the Holy Spirit and the ordained ministers. Congar discovered that, although the Scholastics considered the efficacy of the sacraments in relation to their sign-character, subsequent theologians neglected this truth in order to concentrate on more extrinsic notions of causality. The result was that the sacraments were said to achieve their validity from the juridical power of the ordained to pronounce the words of Christ over stipulated matter. By adjoining the pneumatological, or intangible and un-objectified dimension of the sacramental celebration, to its christological, or sensate and structured dimension, as manifested through the instrumental words and gestures of the ordained ministers, Congar attempted to resolve another major tension: that between the role of the ministerial priesthood and the role of the common priesthood in actuating the sacraments. Congar's repeated emphasis on the con-celebration of the Holy Spirit and the ordained ministers at the sacraments is clearly meant to counter the notion that the divine *Pneuma* is monopolized by the members of the hierarchy, as though they dispensed his grace to the faithful, in whom he did not dwell[18]. The epicletic theology of the sacrament of Order which Congar proposes regards the

---

[18] Cf. S.P. SCHILLING, «Yves Congar», 201; see also J. KALLARANGATT, *The Holy Spirit, Bond of Communion of the Churches*. A Comparative Study of the Ecclesiology of Yves Congar and Nikos Nissiotis, 48-49; J. AREEPLACKAL, *Spirit and Ministries*. Perspectives of East and West, 137.

imposition of hands by the bishop on the candidates as the sign that the Holy Spirit is called down on them so that they can function *in persona Christi* and *in persona ecclesiae*. Thus, in concelebrating with them, the Spirit conjoins in them the saving mandate of Christ and the prayer and holiness of the baptized and confirmed.

Even if Congar admits frequently that the apostolic mission of the Twelve and their successors comes from Christ and is an essential part of the hierarchical structure of the Church, he never overlooks the truth that they can carry out their authoritative mission only in the power of the Spirit who is also present in the entire community of the faithful. For example, in all the sacramental celebrations the greeting «The Lord be with you», and the answer «And with your Spirit», indicate that the entire assembly is permeated by the presence of the Spirit, and that the ordained minister is recognized as being Spirit-filled as well. The greeting also demonstrates that in the celebration not only the ordained but also the whole community are to ask the Father to send the Spirit on the catechumens, so that they enjoy the redemption and filiation attained for them by the Son. Similarly, in the sacrament of Reconciliation, the penitents approach the rite through the prompting of the Holy Spirit, and there they accept the gratuitous gift of pardon won for them by Christ and communicated through the instrumentality of the Spirit-filled minister. In fact, at each sacrament the Spirit first quickens the faith of the believers, and then enables them to respond to an aspect of the saving mission of Christ represented by the visible signs, and to receive the grace of holiness and unity. Yet, Congar did not limit the con-celebration of the ordained ministers and the Holy Spirit to the enactment of the sacraments. It is operative also in preaching of the Gospel. Accordingly, the Word of God can penetrate the hearts of the faithful only when the Spirit works both in them and in the preacher[19]. Congar thus describes the «sacramentality of the Church» in terms of the various saving and sanctifying events in which the members both of the hierarchical priesthood and of the common priesthood are led by the Spirit to encounter each other, to render salvation in Christ actual in the Church through word and symbol, and to be sent out on a prophetic mission in society.

---

[19] These insights have been presented in Part II of the thesis, especially in Chapters Two and Three, «The Foundation of the Epicletic Dimension of the Sacraments: Pentecost as the Animating event of the Body of Christ» and «Ordination by the Laying on of Hands as the Solemn Imploration of the Empowerment of the Holy Spirit».

The epiclesis and the tension between an individualistic-interior and an eschatological-prophetic view of sacramental grace. Congar's stress on the constitutive nature of the liturgical epiclesis brought to light an important pneumatological principle: The Spirit is the eschatological gift of the Father, and wherever he acts, there is the presence of the *eschaton*[20]. Thus, when the Spirit is invoked in the liturgical symbols and on the faithful, the advent of the reign of God, its definitive appearance in the risen Lord, is at hand. Not only the anamnesis of Christ, therefore, but also the epiclesis of the Holy Spirit are eschatological moments in the Christian liturgy. The Spirit is the «content» of the risen life of Christ, the harbinger of the last days. The epiclesis therefore comprises the beginning of the *eschaton*, the eruption into history of the life of the world to come. In other words, the community of believers already participates in the end-time through the Spirit acting in each sacramental celebration[21]. According to Congar, the invocation of the Holy Spirit in the sacraments is a reiterated expression of the total dependency of the Church on the triune God, and at the same time an urgent call to labor for the coming Kingdom. Therefore, those who invoke the Spirit at the sacraments respond to his eschatological grace by committing themselves to his promptings to be prophetic. In this way, the faithful are encouraged by the Spirit to have hope in the future, and to deliver others from the distress of the present time caused by human failure, violence and division. The Spirit of the *eschaton* leads Christians neither to despise nor to idealize human institutions and cultures, but to place their trust in the promises of the Father which have been definitively fulfilled in Christ's first coming, and will be completed when he comes again.

Congar grounds the eschatological dimension of the epiclesis in the relation of the Holy Spirit to the parousia of Christ at the end of time, but he does not thereby sever this event from the paschal mystery in which the divine *Logos* had to enter, with the assistance of the divine *Pneuma*, into the darkness of suffering and death. The epiclesis, therefore, is rooted both in the definitive victory of Christ over evil in the paschal stage of his existence, and in the complete fulfillment of this victory at the parousia. In fact, according to Congar, there are two aspects of the mystery of the incarnate Word: the first one being Christ in his Paschal stage, and the second one being Christ in his messianic stage. In the

---

[20] Cf. C. McDONALD, *Church and World in the Plan of God*. History and Eschatology in the Thought of Père Yves Congar O. P., 145; see also T.I. McDONALD, *The Ecclesiology of Yves Congar*. Foundational Themes, 281.

[21] Cf. C. McDONALD, *Church and World in the Plan of God*. History and Eschatology in the Thought of Père Yves Congar O. P., 148.

former, he is the *Alpha* of human salvation and in the latter, he is its *Omega*. This coming of God to humankind forms the basis of the return of humankind to God. The Holy Spirit makes it possible that the two stages of the incarnate Word be present and operative in the Church gathered at sacramental celebrations[22]. Therefore, during the messianic or sacramental time the Spirit enables the past stage of the incarnation to be effective in the here and now, with a view to the absolute future of the incarnation.

Reflecting the modern concern for the future, Congar emphasizes that the Spirit is the eschatological gift of the Father through the Son, and acts so that the whole process of the creation, the salvation and the sanctification of humankind is oriented towards the life of the world to come. In other words, the Spirit's role is to assure that the two divine missions, or the two «hands» of the Father accomplish what they were sent to do. Consequently, at each sacramental celebration the epiclesis represents the movement through which the divine grace passes from the Father through the Son in the Spirit, and returns in the Spirit through the Son to the Father. Thus, the invocation of the Holy Spirit not only explicates his constitutive role in the sacraments, but also reiterates the truth that only in the unity which he provides can humankind glorify the Father and the Son. While in Christ, human beings are re-fashioned to the divine image, in the Holy Spirit they are «pre-fashioned» to the divine glory to be manifested when they return to the Father at the parousia[23]. Thus, the epiclesis is linked to the eschatological dimension both of the anamnesis and of the doxology. The Holy Spirit acting in the Church through the epiclesis is the divine longing that impels the faithful towards God and causes them to attain him as their end.

One of the noteworthy achievements of Congar is that his reflections on the eschatological dimension of the epiclesis do not lead him to concentrate on the interior force of sacramental grace in the souls of individual Christians, but on its prophetic force in their activity in the world. In this respect, Congar offers a challenge to Eastern theology, by linking his eschatological considerations not only to the Church but also

---

[22] Cf. K. JANUS, *Il Cristo e lo Spirito Santo come principi dell'unità della Chiesa. Studio sull'ecclesiologia di Y.M.J. Congar.* Dissertation Abstracts, Roma 1972, 20; see also T.I. McDONALD, *The Ecclesiology of Yves Congar.* Foundational Themes, 298.

[23] Cf. C. McDONALD, *Church and World in the Plan of God.* History and Eschatology in the Thought of Père Yves Congar O. P., 143.

to its mission in the world[24]. For, Congar notes the attitudinal difference between the Eastern and the Western Christians, that is, while the first gives importance to the epiclesis as sanctifying the interior holiness of the Church as a sacramental community [*koinonia*], the second emphasizes the epiclesis as sanctifying the outward-looking service that arises from sacramental grace [*diakonia*]. Yet, Congar insists that it would be a mistake to regard the two as dogmatically incompatible. The entire sacramental celebration by its very nature tends towards the unity of the Church as the presupposition of its going beyond itself in prophetic mission. In other words, the Spirit acts in the liturgical experience of Christians in order that they become prophetic witnesses of grace in the World. The epiclesis represents this convergence of unity and prophecy as the goal of sacramental worship.

As a way of concluding these positive remarks concerning the contribution of Congar to the topic being considered, it must be admitted that he strove in developing this aspect of his theology, as in others, to overcome rather than fan tensions between various tenable, but in the end one-sided positions[25]. By combining the christocentric and the trinitarian, the commemorative and the charismatic, the role of the ordained and that of the baptized, and the interior and prophetic aspects of sacramental theology in general, and of the epiclesis in particular, he intended to reconcile past inter-Church and ideological divisions, and to prepare the way for future collaborative and open-minded research. His christic-pneumatic approach to the sacraments was in itself daring, since it meant parting with Western unilateralism concerning christology, and being accused of conceding too much to what many perceived to be Eastern unilateralism regarding the pneumatology. For example, with his insistence of the need to affirm the unity between the words of institution and the anamnesis on the one hand, and of the pre-consecratory and post-consecratory epiclesis on the other, Congar brought sacramental theology back to its origins in a trinitarian framework. For, at the liturgy the Father, who is divine justice, is glorified by the assembly not only «in,

---

[24] Cf. T.I. McDONALD, *The Ecclesiology of Yves Congar*. Foundational Themes, 302-303, 305-306; see also J. AREEPLACKAL, *Spirit and Ministries*. Perspectives of East and West, 310-311.

[25] Cf. P.G. GIANAZZA, *La teologia dello Spirito Santo in prospectiva ecumenica*. Studio comparativo sulla pneumatologia di Paul Evdokimov (Ortodosso) e Yves Congar (Cattolico), 26; see also L.M. NAVARATNE, *The Relationship between Christology and Pneumatology in the Writings of Yves Congar, Karl Rahner and Jacques Dupuis*, xviii; A. NICHOLAS, *Yves Congar*, 202.

through and with the Son», who is divine truth, but also «in the unity of the Holy Spirit», who is divine love.

Although critical observations are to follow, it can be said declaratively that, by presenting the invocation of the Holy Spirit as a constitutive element of the sacraments in his many writings, Congar has instigated an epochal shift in the Western Catholic theology. Whether many theologians of East and West accept his conclusions or not, almost all would admit that they have benefitted from the research and the writing he has done on the liturgical epiclesis. He is one of the Catholic theologians responsible for the ecumenical openness of all the Churches and for the freedom of mind with which a new generation of scholars can pursue the questions he raised.

2. The Limits of Congar's Achievement Perceived from Biblical, Theological, Ecclesiological and Universal Viewpoints

Because of the competence and the prolixity of Congar as a theologian, a substantial body of secondary literature concerning his thought has already appeared in the form of lengthy reviews of his writings, of monographs dedicated to particular aspects of his thought and of frequent references to his various stances in works by other theologians. Besides the general praise, indicated above, of the topics directly related to this study, a carefully formulated yet seriously intended criticism appears to stem from four major areas of contemporary theology and, when applied to the question of Congar's treatment of the constitutive role of the invocation of the Holy Spirit in effecting the sacraments, leads one to admit that the biblical foundation of the epiclesis, its theological importance, its ecclesiological consequences and its universal implications are not as clearly delineated by him as they could have been[26]. Thus, in the following pages, the criticism arising from each of these areas is succinctly presented, its legitimacy is generally admitted, and some means of rectifying the difficulty in question is briefly indicated. The entire purpose of this procedure is to suggest ways in which the invaluable

---

[26] Although Congar has tried to develop the efficacious role of the Holy Spirit in the sacraments of the Church by depending constantly on Scripture and Tradition, it is doubtful he has fully integrated their many nuances into his theological perception. Cf. L.M. NAVARATNE, *The Relationship between Christology and Pneumatology in the Writings of Yves Congar, Karl Rahner and Jacques Dupuis*, 54; see also A. NICHOLAS, *Yves Congar*, 202.

positive contributions of Congar to the topic at hand can be enhanced in the future.

The biblical basis of the epiclesis is not adequately presented, because the institutive sign-giving of the incarnate Logos is not viewed as intertwined with the constitutive empowerment of the accompanying Pneuma. In order to underline the invocation of the Holy Spirit as constitutive of the sacraments, Congar certainly sought to forge a proper synthesis between christology and pneumatology, that is, he took most seriously the biblical assertions that Christ was conceived of the Spirit, was anointed by him for his ministry, and was accompanied by him in his death and glorification. Furthermore, he grounded each sacrament of the Church not only in the public life of Christ, but also in outpouring of the Holy Spirit at Pentecost. Thus, the re-actualization of salvation in the sacraments is possible both through the institutive sign-giving of the incarnate *Logos* and through the constitutive empowerment of the effused *Pneuma*. Yet, although Congar tried coherently to co-ordinate the distinct roles of Christ and the Spirit in founding of the sacraments, he tended to isolate them one from the other[27]. The sacraments are regarded first as instituted by Jesus during his earthly life and in his paschal mystery, and then as constituted only at the outpouring of the Holy Spirit in the subsequent experience of the early Church. However, in an appropriate synthesis, the constitutive activity of the Holy Spirit in establishing the signs of salvation in history is neither secondary to, nor subsequent to, the institutive activity of Christ, but fully intertwined in it. In other words, a more correct approach to the origin of the signs of salvation would be to state that they were initiated by Christ solely because and insofar as he was filled with the Spirit[28]. Unfortunately, in the way in which Congar presents the biblical basis of the invocation of the Holy Spirit at the sacraments, his role is overclouded by the prominence and priority attributed to that of Christ. Therefore, the constituive activity of the Holy Spirit is reduced to that of giving vitality and efficacy to the forms already instituted by Christ.

This critique concerning the failure of Congar to interweave the institutive role of Christ and the constitutive role of the Holy Spirit, as they are presented in Scripture, is based on the limited pneumatological christology which he proposes. He does indeed conjoin the action of the Holy Spirit with that of the *glorified* Christ and admit their *functional*

---

[27] Cf. S.P. SCHILLING, «Yves Congar», 203; see also J. AREEPLACKAL, *Spirit and Ministries*. Perspectives of East and West, 313.

[28] Cf. J. DUPUIS, *Jesus Christ and His Spirit*. Theological Approaches, 28.

unity (cf. 2 Cor 3,17), but he fails to underscore the part played by the divine *Pneuma* in the actions of the historical Jesus and seems to stress the *functional independence* of what each of the divine Persons accomplished from the Jordan to Calvary[29]. In other words, since the invocation of the Holy Spirit as constitutive of the sacraments is to be based on biblical theology, the inadequate pneumatological christology of Congar hinders his argument. By not fully integrating both christology and pneumatology in his account of the origin of the sacraments, his understanding of the epiclesis as complementing the anamnesis in the liturgical rites of the Church remains less than fully convincing. Had Congar made it more clear that Jesus could become the sender of the eschatological Spirit, since he was already fully permeated by his power throughout his earthly existence, he would have illumined the firm basis of the subject matter of this study in a more sufficient way. It seems, therefore, that his explanation of the invocation of the Holy Spirit as constitutive of the sacraments would have been better grounded by Congar, if his perception of the identity and mission of Jesus had been enriched by the synthetic insights of Spirit-christology, a biblical and patristic mode of thought which had already been revitalized while Congar was writing[30].

In fact, Congar did perceive the need to base the liturgical invocation of the Holy Spirit on the pneumatological or ascending christology of the *Synoptics*, which could combine the uniqueness and the incomparability of Jesus with the universality of his claim and of his Kingdom[31]. Yet, Congar emphasizes the descending christology of the *Gospel of John* to such an extent that he fails to keep in focus the fact that the incarnate *Logos* could fulfil his mission only because he possessed the divine

---

[29] Cf. T.I. McDONALD, *The Ecclesiology of Yves Congar*. Foundational Themes, 292; see also W. REISER, Review of *I Believe in the Holy Spirit* in *Ame* 150 (1984) 155.

[30] Congar is in fact well acquainted with Spirit-christology, as is evidenced by his explicit treatment of this notion in *Le Fleuve de vie*, 219-228 (*The River of Life*, 165-173). However, he has not directly integrated his reflections on Spirit-christology into his presentation of the epicletic dimension of the sacraments. Yet, since in separate writings he presents Jesus as the bearer and at the same time the sender of the Spirit, he would not disagree that the sacraments as the re-actualizations of the Paschal mystery are made efficacious through an invocation of the Spirit of Christ. In this study, it is proposed that these view-points of his could have been consolidated by drawing on the wealth of insights found in Spirit-christology.

[31] Cf. H.Urs von BALTHASAR, *Theologik*. Anlage des Gesamtwerkes: vol. III, Einsiedeln 1985-1987, 52-53; see also N. NISSIOTIS, «Called to Unity. The Significance of the Invocation of the Spirit for Church Unity», 53; ID., «Pneumatological Christology as a Presupposition of Ecclesiology», 235; L. VISCHER, «The Epiclesis, Sign of Unity and Renewal», *SL* 6 (1967) 32; H. BERKHOF, *The Doctrine of the Holy Spirit*, Atlanta 1964, 11-12.

Pneuma without measure (Jn 3, 34-35). Thus, although Congar set out to ground the truth that each sacramental rite entails an epiclesis as well as an anamnesis in a pneumatological christology, his writings accentuate the ontological status of Jesus as the Word made flesh more than his messianic status of being the unique bearer of God's Spirit. It would have been more helpful to Congar's teaching on the epiclesis, had he insisted that the anointing with the Holy Spirit was essential for the sanctification of the human nature of the incarnate Word, for the descending christology needs to be complemented with the ascending one[32]. For example, the ascending christology reveals how the Holy Spirit brought about the sanctification of the humanity of Jesus which had to be elevated to union with the Word who assumes it[33]. It thus seems that the role of the Holy Spirit in the liturgical invocation would have been clarified, if Congar had consistently followed an ascending christology in explaining the saving sign-actions posited by the historical Jesus.

How could the intertwining of the institutive activity of Jesus and the constitutive activity of the Spirit be illustrated in the Gospel narratives which concern the origin of the sacraments? With regard to the biblical basis of the ecclesial sacrament of Confirmation, the account which the *Gospel of Luke* presents of Jesus' actions and words in the synagogue at Nazareth (Lk 4, 16-30) conjoins his role and that of the Spirit in founding a sign of salvation. For, Jesus was filled with the sanctifying and eschatological power of the Father in his decision to choose to read the text «The Spirit of the Lord is upon me, because he has anointed me to preach good news to the poor» (Lk 4,18), to state openly before the gathered assembly that «Today this scripture has been fulfilled in your hearing» (Lk 4,21) and to attest that his prophetic calling entailed a universal rather than a limited scope (Lk 4, 23-24)[34]. If both Jesus and

---

[32] Cf. H. BERKHOF, *The Doctrine of the Holy Spirit*, 10-11, 20-21; see also J.C. HAUGHEY, *The Conspiracy of God. The Holy Spirit in Us*, New York 1976, 10, 27; D. COFFEY, «The "Incarnation" of the Holy Spirit in Christ», *TS* 45 (1984) 475-476.

[33] Cf. P.J . ROSATO, «Spirit Christology: Ambiguity and Promise», *TS* 38 (1977) 424; see also J. O'DONNELL, «Theological Trends. Theology of the Holy Spirit, I: Jesus and the Spirit», *TW* 23 (1983) 48; E.J. KILMARTIN, *Christian Liturgy*: Theology and Practice, Kansas City 1988, 161-162; J. MOLTMANN, *The Way of Jesus Christ*: Christology in Messianic Dimensions, London 1990, 74; R.D. COLLE, *Christ and the Spirit*. Spirit-Christology in Trinitarian Perspective, Oxford 1994, 3.

[34] Cf. H. SCHÜRMANN, *Il vangelo di Luca*. Testo greco e traduzione: vol. I, Brescia 1983, 408; see also F. LAMBIASI, *Lo Spirito Santo: mistero e presenza*. Per una sintesi di pneumatologia, Bologna 1987, 259; P.J. ROSATO, *Introduzione alla teologia dei sacramenti*, Casale Monferrato 1992, 70-73.

the Spirit can be said to be co-institutors of this saving sign, does this mean that Congar's distinction between the christological ground of the sacrament of Confirmation in the paschal mystery and its pneumatological ground in the Pentecost-event is not relevant? No, for the symbolic acts which Christ and the Spirit co-instituted reached their full efficacy, or their definitive culmination, as the divine *Pneuma* raised the divine *Logos* from death, thus validating all the saving signs he had instituted, and as the divine *Logos* collaborates in sending the divine *Pneuma* at Pentecost, thus extending to the Church the very empowerment constitutive of his saving signs.

This Lukan passage seems more convincing as the basis for the prophetic ministry of the Spirit-filled Jesus, and for the eventual ministry of confirmed believers, than does that employed by Congar, namely the baptism of Jesus in the Jordan, at which he received the Spirit, so as to complete and activate his initial messianic anointing at the moment of the incarnation. But apart from the validity of appealing to this particular text to ground the grace of Confirmation as «the seal of the gift of the Spirit», the event described renders it understandable that, as Jesus instituted a saving sign, the Spirit «co-instituted» it with him[35]. In this way the nexus between the christological and the pneumatological dimensions of this sacrament is clear, and there are avoided the nuances of prominence and priority found in Congar's thesis that Jesus, during his public life, and at his death and resurrection, instituted signs of salvation which the Spirit secondarily and subsequently constituted at Pentecost.

The theological importance of the epiclesis is not fully shown, because the specificity of the mission of the Spirit in the sacraments is not clearly differentiated from that of the mission of the Son[36]. This second aspect of the present critique, which is influenced by scholars who have analyzed the thought of Congar on the relationship between christology and pneumatology, explicitly treats the manner in which the mission of the Son is differentiated from that of the Spirit. Since Congar bases the liturgical epiclesis on the latter, the full import of this dimension of sacramental celebrations would not be brought to light, if the sanctifying

---

[35] Cf. J. KALLARANGATT, *The Holy Spirit, Bond of Communion of the Churches. A Comparative Study of the Ecclesiology of Yves Congar and Nikos Nissiotis*, 72; see also J. MEYENDORFF, *The Byzantine Legacy in the Orthodox Church*, New York 1982, 154.

[36] This is evident especially in Chapters Two and Four, «The Foundation of the Epicletic Dimension of the Sacraments: Pentecost as the Animating event of the Body of Christ» and «Baptism and Confirmation: Dual Anointing with the Holy Spirit and Progressive Incorporation into the Body of Christ».

mission of the divine *Pneuma* were not clearly delineated. Although Congar does not consider christology as a complete and self-contained topic apart from the theology of the Father and the Spirit, scholars nevertheless sense that «there is a stress on the christological element. It shows that his synthesis of christology is still imperfect»[37]. In spite of Congar's constant attempts to regard the three Persons of the Trinity as not only sharing the same essence, but also having a proper *hypostasis* and mission, the specific identity and activity of the Holy Spirit in relation to the Son remain somewhat clouded. Consequently, even in his efforts to distance himself from the Western over-emphasis on christology through his pronounced pneumatology, he seems not to have sharply distinguished the *Pneuma* from the *Logos*. Congar rightly declares the principle that the Spirit is the Breath of the Word, and that the Son is the Word of the Breath. Yet, he does not expatiate enough on how the Word is oriented, in the economy of salvation, to a *kenotic* entrance into the darkness of human sin, suffering and death, while the Breath is oriented to an *eschatological* liberation of these very same forms of darkness so that they are permeated with immortal life[38]. In other words, in his explication of the identity and activity of the Holy Spirit, Congar did not show the difference as well as the complementarity between the *kenotic* intention of the Word and the *eschatological* intention of the Breath. For this reason, he did not go beyond the prevailing understanding of the third divine Person.

The failure of Congar to demarcate sharply between the *kenotic*, or descending, mission of the Son and the *eschatological*, or ascending, mission of the Spirit is most evident in his discussion of the Last Supper and the paschal mystery which it initiates. Since the co-ordinated yet distinct activities of the *Logos* and the *Pneuma* in these events ground the consecratory value both of the words of institution and of the epiclesis in the eucharistic celebration, any lack of clarity about the distinct roles of the two divine Persons in the Upper Room and on Calvary invariably renders the understanding of their precise means of involvement in assuring the efficacy of the Eucharist equally unclear. When the «hour» of Jesus arrived as he sat at table in the Cenacle fully aware that his

---

[37] J. KALLARANGATT, *The Holy Spirit, Bond of Communion of the Churches. A Comparative Study of the Ecclesiology of Yves Congar and Nikos Nissiotis*, 74; see also S. P.SCHILLING, «Yves Congar», 202-203.

[38] Cf. I. CANAVARIS, «The Ecclesiology of Yves Congar: An Orthodox Evaluation», 87-88; see also P.G. GIANAZZA, *La teologia dello Spirito Santo in prospectiva ecumenica*. Studio comparativo sulla pneumatologia di Paul Evdokimov (Ortodosso) e Yves Congar (Cattolico), 34; W. REISER, Review of *I Believe in the Holy Spirit*, 155.

kenotic giving of himself was to be completed (cf. Lk 22, 14-30), the Spirit too brought his *eschatological* empowerment of the «descending» intention of the Son to its fulfillment by enabling him to «ascend» all the more as he entered into human sinfulness, suffering and death so as to redeem them from within. In other words, as the Son went deeper into darkness to the point of being overcome by it, the Spirit intensified his intention to render this act a source of immortal life for Jesus and for all his subsequent followers. Had Congar presented the co-ordination of the roles of the Son and the Spirit during the paschal mystery in this or an analogous way, the dominance of the *kenotic* sacrifice of Jesus in his thought would have been attenuated by his equal concern for the *eschatological* liberation of the Spirit which fully directed and permeated it.

This insight has great pertinence in showing the parallel between the activity of the Spirit in the self-offering of Jesus in the Cenacle and on Calvary and his activity in making this unique sacrifice actual and efficacious in the eucharistic celebration. Just as the Holy Spirit brought about the glorification of the dead Jesus, it belongs to him to sanctify the bread and the wine and to give life to the ecclesial community. To put it another way, in the saving economy the activity of Christ is *kenotic* – he gives himself totally, and that of the Holy Spirit is *eschatological* – he sanctifies and gives immortal life[39]. In the Eucharist, the two distinct missions of the Son and the Spirit complement each other. In the anamnesis, the Son renders his self-giving present to the Church and, in the epiclesis, the Spirit guarantees that this generosity be sanctifying and life-giving in the elements and in the faithful. Such insights drawn from a pneumatological christology illumines how the epiclesis in the eucharistic celebration is associated with the gift of life. The epiclesis makes it clear that the self-gift of Jesus in the Eucharist must be accompanied by eschatological power: «it is the Spirit that gives life, the flesh has nothing to offer» (Jn 6,63)[40]. The constitutive dimension of the invocation of the Holy Spirit in the Eucharist is also well expressed in the *Letter to the Hebrews* which speaks of «blood of Christ, who offered himself as the perfect sacrifice to God through the eternal Spirit» (Heb 9,14). The work of the Spirit in the Cenacle, on Golgotha and in the Mass is to enable the

---

[39] Cf. N. HOOK, «A Spirit Christology», *Theo* 75 (1972) 231; see also H. BERKHOF, *The Doctrine of the Holy Spirit*, 26; O. HANSEN, «Spirit Christology: A Way Out of Our Dilemma?» in *The Holy Spirit in the Life of the Church*, ed. P.D. Opsahl, Minneapolis 1978, 183.

[40] Cf. C.K. BARRETT, «The Holy Spirit in the Fourth Gospel», *JTS* 1 (1950) 7; see also W. KASPER, *Theology and Church*, 187.

Son to offer himself without restriction, while he is perfectly assured of the assistance of the eternal *Pneuma*[41].

The distinction between the terms «Son – *kenosis* – anamnesis» and «Spirit – *eschaton* – epiclesis» reflects the christology and the eucharistic theology proposed by the Antiochean tradition which insists less on the divine assumption of a human nature by the *Logos* at the incarnation, than on the transformation operated in him by the *Pneuma* at the moment of his glorification. Thus, the *kenotic* mission of Christ is complemented by the *eschatological* action of the Spirit[42]. This understanding of christology is clearly important for the Eucharist, as is evident in the epiclesis of the *Eucharistic Prayer* of Theodore of Mopsuestia: «And may the grace of your Holy Spirit come upon us and upon this offering and may he dwell in, and descend upon, this bread and chalice and bless and sanctify and sign them in the name of the Father and the Son and the Holy Spirit»[43]. In addition, in his *Catechetical Homilies on the Mass*, Theodore made it clear that the Eucharist is the pneumatic Body of the risen Jesus. Just as the role of the Spirit at the resurrection was to perfect the self-giving mission of the Son, his action at the Eucharist is to effect the sacramental form of his self-giving for the life of the world[44]. The basic pre-supposition here is that the life-giving Spirit, who raised Jesus at Easter, acts in the eucharistic epiclesis to consecrate or «pneumatize» the elements and to sanctify or «pneumatize» the faithful. In other words, Christ, as triumphant *Kyrios*, exercises his saving activity in the Eucharist in unison with the sanctifying, eschatological activity of the *Pneuma*. These missions, and thus their respective functions in actualizing the Eucharist differ, and yet together they effect the bread and wine of immortal life and the vitalized existence of the ecclesial community which consumes them.

Had Congar distinguished between the *kenotic* mission of the Son and the *eschatological* mission of the Spirit, he could have stated more clearly

---

[41] Cf. S. SALAVILLE, «Epiclèse eucharistique», 222; see also R.D. LEE, «Epiclesis and Ecumenical Dialogue», *Dia* 9 (1974) 57.

[42] Cf. P. REGAN, «Pneumatological and Eschatological Aspects of Liturgical Celebration», *Wor* 51 (1977) 332; see also E.J. KILMARTIN, «The Active Role of Christ and the Holy Spirit in the Sanctification of the Eucharistic Elements», *TS* 45 (1984) 238.

[43] J.H. McKENNA, *Eucharist and the Holy Spirit. The Eucharistic Epiclesis in the Twentieth-Century*, London 1975, 38; see also R.A. GREER, *Theodore of Mopsuestia. Exegete and Theologian*, Westminster 1961, 82-82; E. YARNOLDS, *The Awe-Inspiring Rites of Initiation. Baptismal Homilies of the Fourth Century*, London 1972, 245-246.

[44] Cf. E. YARNOLDS, *The Awe-Inspiring Rites of Initiation. Baptismal Homilies of the Fourth Century*, 215-216.

that the saving words of the self-giving Jesus can become efficacious in the Church only through the life-giving action of the sanctifying Spirit. Aided by such an understanding, he could have affirmed that both the words of consecration and the epiclesis of consecration are necessary in the Eucharist, so that there be «a double presence, a double service and mediation, a double action of Christ in the Spirit and the Spirit in Christ serving as the two hands of the Father in drawing man into a new life. [...] In achieving it, however, each Person keeps his own characteristics; the operation comes from the Father, through the Son, and is accomplished in the Holy Spirit»[45]. The reference here is the «new life of human beings» indicates that the epicletic dimension of the Eucharist is considered constitutive, since the transformation of the offerings, which the Spirit effects on the altar, is directed to the spiritual renewal of the community gathered around it[46]. Congar certainly maintained that, without a proper disposition on the part of the faithful, the Eucharist cannot be fully effective in them, for it would simply remain an offer made by the Lord alone, and not shared in by his followers. In other words, the eucharistic epiclesis makes it clear that the Eucharist is there so that the Holy Spirit may «pneumatize» the faithful as he has already pneumatized Christ and the gifts[47]. Yet, Congar did not relate these insights to the *kenotic* mission of the Son and the *eschatological* mission of the Spirit in the Cenacle, on Calvary and in the Eucharist. He should have stated more limpidly that, just as the penetration of the words, gestures and even death of the self-giving Jesus by the Spirit brought about his glorification, so the epiclesis renders the words of institution life-giving in the elements, and communicates the saving effects of the historical and *kenotic* self-giving of the Son to the faithful. Congar intended to differentiate between the missions of the Son and the Spirit, and to apply this reasoning to the epiclesis question. Yet his preference for a descending christology led him to concentrate almost totally on the sanctifying work of the *Pneuma* at the incarnation and anointing of the *Logos*. Had Congar also treated the eschatological work of the Spirit which caused the Son to «ascend» as he entered more and more into the

---

[45] J.H. McKENNA, *Eucharist and the Holy Spirit*. The Eucharistic Epiclesis in the Twentieth-Century, 199-200; see also E.J. KILMARTIN, «The Catholic Tradition of Eucharistic Theology: Towards the Third Millennium», 443-444; R.A. ADAMS, «The Holy Spirit and the Real Presence», 42.

[46] Cf. G. WAINWRIGHT, *Eucharist and Eschatology*, London 1971, 96; see also R.A. ADAMS, «The Holy Spirit and the Real Presence», 50.

[47] Cf. E. CLAPSIS, «The Holy Spirit in the Church», 167; see also J.M.R. TILLARD, «The Eucharist and the Holy Spirit», *TD* 17 (1969) 135.

self-giving act on Calvary, his teaching on the epiclesis would have been more consistent and illuminating.

The ecclesiological consequences of the epiclesis are weakened, because the concelebration of the Spirit with the ordained seems to subordinate rather than affirm his effective collaboration with the baptized and confirmed. This critical observation follows from the previous point concerning the diminishment of the significance of the epiclesis because of the dominance of the salvific mission of the Son in the primarily descending christology of Congar, and the ensuing secondary role attributed to the sanctifying mission of the Spirit. Yet the present observation focuses on the christological moment of the liturgy, on the anamnesis, on the ordained as the successors of the Twelve who act *in persona Christi* and on the «*ex opere operato*» nature of sacramental grace. Surely Congar attempted to complement this perspective by re-introducing the pneumatological moment of the liturgy, the epiclesis, the function of the ordained as acting *in persona ecclesiae*, and thus as collaborating with the baptized and confirmed, and the «*ex opere operantis*» character of the grace received at the sacraments. In his own efforts to formulate a pneumatological christology, Congar intended to do nothing else but to develop a solid and comprehensive theology of the Holy Spirit, so as to counteract the prevailing understanding that the third Person of the Trinity chiefly legitimates the authority of the hierarchy, binds the consciences of the faithful in obedience to ecclesial law, prevents the vicar of Christ from pronouncing error in solemn declarations, and thus guarantees the perennial vigour of the institutional character of the Church[48]. However, in his own systematic reflections Congar does not seem fully to have departed from this idea.

One scholar has put forward the thesis that Congar's approach to ecclesiology, despite his accentuation of pneumatology, is more structure-oriented than life-oriented: «Ever since the first decade of his active theological writing, the Holy Spirit had played a significant role. But, as we have seen, a structure-ecclesiology which is Christ-centered had dominated over a life-ecclesiology, which would be centered on the Holy Spirit. This came as a result of Congar's preference for a christological approach to the Church over a pneumatic approach»[49]. This judgment has obvious connotations for the ecclesiological relevance of the epiclesis in

---

[48] Cf. J. KALLARANGATT, *The Holy Spirit, Bond of Communion of the Churches. A Comparative Study of the Ecclesiology of Yves Congar and Nikos Nissiotis*, 69.

[49] C. McDONALD, *Church and World in the Plan of God.* Aspects of History and Eschatology in the Thought of Père Congar O. P., 124; see also T.I. McDONALD, *The Ecclesiology of Yves Congar*: Foundational Themes, 282-283.

Congar's thought, since the invocation of the Holy Spirit is meant to make the unique and *kenotic* sign-actions of Christ the continuing and life-giving celebrations at the core of ecclesial existence. If, in the end, Congar stresses a structure-ecclesiology rather than a pneumatic one, the force of his teaching on the liturgical epiclesis is attenuated. The focal point of this difficulty seems to be the excessive weight given by Congar to the christological aspect of Ordination. The result is that the baptized and the confirmed, who concelebrate with the Spirit only indirectly, that is, in conjunction with those who act *in persona Christi* and *in persona ecclesiae*, are not granted a constitutive role in building up the life of the mystical Body[50].

Congar clearly desired to emphasize that, since both Baptism and Confirmation entail an anointing with the Holy Spirit, they are similar in dignity to Ordination. All Christians are called by the sacraments of initiation to employ the gifts that are given to them for the construction of the temple of the Holy Spirit. Especially in his later writings, Congar stated that in such a charismatic community all the believers, irrespective of their particular «order», exercise their gifts through various Church-building services as the Spirit inspires them: «There are varieties of service, but the same Lord» (1 Cor 12,4). By stressing the anointings with the Holy Spirit that are bestowed on the faithful through Baptism and Confirmation, Congar intended to situate the hierarchy into the charismatic structure of the whole Church. Yet, in spite of this objective Congar could not avoid granting predominance to the institutional aspect of the Church which is based on the Christ-event and centered on the ordained who stand at the structure-pole of the mystical Body of Christ. Unfortunately, the baptized and confirmed seem to be placed around the life-pole alone, that is, in the area demarcated by holiness of life, reception of the sacraments and witnessing to grace in the world[51]. Orthodox critics of the early work of Congar hold that, although he accepted the Holy Spirit as the divine *Pneuma* through whom all the faithful are brought together and are given a personal calling within the apostolic community, «the interjection of the ministry between God and man obscures the immediacy of Christ and his direct, personal contact through the grace of the resurrection communicated through the Holy

---

[50] Cf. S.P. SCHILLING, «Yves Congar», 203-204; see also A. DULLES, «Catholic Ecclesiology Since Vatican II», *Con* (1985) 10-11; J. AREEPLACKAL, *Spirit and Ministries*. Perspectives of East and West, 253.

[51] Cf. J. KALLARANGATT, *The Holy Spirit, Bond of Communion of the Churches*. A Comparative Study of the Ecclesiology of Yves Congar and Nikos Nissiotis, 45; see also T.I. McDONALD, *The Ecclesiology of Yves Congar*. Foundational Themes, 292.

Spirit to the believing community»[52]. If Congar would have accentuated the constitutive nature of the anointing of the Holy Spirit in the sacraments of Baptism and Confirmation, he could have given the faithful a less subservient place with respect to the ordained, and thus could have situated all members of the Church around both the structural and the life poles of a charismatic community.

From the analysis that has been made in this study[53] it is quite clear that Congar attributes the institution of the sacrament of Order to Jesus of Nazareth who, so as to prolong the messianic mission he had begun, selected the Twelve and sent them to announce the Kingdom to the people through word and deed. They received the vitality and courage to fulfill their mission only when the Holy Spirit descended on them at Pentecost. Throughout the history of the Church this institutive act of Christ and the constitutive act of the Spirit are perpetuated in the sacrament of Order through the anamnesis and the epiclesis. The latter is the ritual action by which the bishop, as the representative of both Christ, the Head, and the members of the community, implores the self-gift of the Holy Spirit upon the candidates, so that they might have the vitality and courage of the Twelve. Although Congar sought in this way to create a balance between the christological and the pneumatological dimensions of the sacrament, he often emphasizes the institutive role of the divine *Logos*, and seems to view the constitutive role of the divine *Pneuma* as that of an agent who authoritatively ratifies a pre-existing and self-contained event of election[54]. For this reason, an Orthodox critic points out that excessive christocentrism renders the Catholic understanding of the epiclesis redundant: «The epiclesis [for Catholics] means ecclesiologically that the Church asks to receive from God what she has already received historically in Christ as if she had not received it at all, i.e., as if history did not count in itself»[55].

---

[52] I. CANAVARIS, *The Ecclesiology of Yves Congar*: An Orthodox Evaluation, Boston 1968, 92.

[53] Cf. Chapter III, «The Foundation of the Epicletic Dimension of the Sacraments: Pentecost as the Animating Event of the Body of Christ».

[54] Cf. J. AREEPLACKAL, *Spirit and Ministries*. Perspectives of East and West, 313; see also J.D. ZIZIOULAS, «Apostolic Continuity and Orthodox Theology: Towards a Synthesis of Two Perspectives», *VTQ* 19 (1975) 81-82.

[55] J.D. ZIZIOULAS, «Apostolic Continuity and Orthodox Theology: Towards a Synthesis of Two Perspectives», 88; see also ID., «Pneumatological Dimension of the Church», 152; N. NISSIOTIS, «Called to Unity. The Significance of Church Unity», 53-54.

However, one of the positive effects of Congar's presentation of the constitutive invocation of the Holy Spirit at Ordination is that he could deviate significantly from the characteristic Western tendency to situate the *in persona ecclesiae* dimension of ordained ministry within its primary *in persona Christi* matrix. Instead, he favours adopting the Eastern predilection of including the *in persona Christi* dimension of Ordination within the over-arching *in persona ecclesiae* framework. Accordingly, Congar proposes that Jesus choose the Twelve from the entire community of his disciples. Furthermore, he stressed the communitarian aspect of Ordination, that is, its relationship to a ecclesial process in which the faithful have a major share both in the selection and formation of the candidates, and in the imparting of the Holy Spirit along with the bishop during the liturgical invocation. Although Congar tries to accentuate this communitarian dimension of Order through his explanation of laying on of hands as a constitutive invocation of the Holy Spirit, he fails to do so adequately. He does not state that the ordained share in the charismatic nature of the members of the entire community which derives from their baptismal incorporation into the paschal mystery of Christ through the anointing with the Holy Spirit, and which entails a part in «the being and ministry of the Spirit-filled Jesus»[56]. In other words, Congar does not properly expose the constitutive invocation of the Holy Spirit as the ground of the service-oriented function of ordained ministry. This can be attributed to the fact that, because of his over-emphasis on the institutive act by which Christ chose the Twelve, the priestly character is perceived as belonging to the realm of power rather than of love[57]. In contrast, if the exercise of authority is comprehended as a charism of the Holy Spirit, it will not be regarded as an obstacle to the freedom which the baptized have to carry out their ministries, but as a means of discerning how these ministries can best meet the needs of the local ecclesial Body and of the most emarginated in society. Had Congar explained the constitutive invocation of the Holy Spirit at Ordination as the principal basis of a communitarian-oriented authority of ministry[58], he would have not given the impression that the baptized and confirmed are subordinated to the ordained. Instead he would have asserted emphatically that the common and the ministerial forms of Christian

---

[56] J. AREEPLACKAL, *Spirit and Ministries. Perspectives of East and West*, 277; G.F. FINNEGAN, «Ministerial Priesthood in Yves Congar», 527.

[57] Cf. I. CANAVARIS *The Ecclesiology of Yves Congar: An Orthodox Evaluation*, 138.

[58] Cf. J. AREEPLACKAL, *Spirit and Ministries. Perspectives of East and West*, 250.

priesthood come from Christ through the Spirit, and are co-ordinated one to the other for the sake of the unity and diversity of the ecclesial mission in the world.

The universal significance of the epiclesis is not taken into consideration, because the activity of the Spirit as Spiritus Filii in the signs of the Church overshadows his concomitant activity as Spiritus Patris in all religious rituals. There is no doubt that Congar has been a pioneer in exploring the ecclesiological status of those outside the Catholic communion, and in giving painstaking attention to the question of the unrecognized presence and activity of the Holy Spirit in the adherents to other religions, and in those who deny God but seek sincerely to live by human values. For, according to him, those who long for God and advocate self-giving rather than egoism are not really strangers to the mystical Body. Or put in pneumatological terms, if they live by the divine Spirit who permeates their existence and moves them toward great moral responsibility, they attain to an encounter with God of which the Church is not corporeally the minister[59]. Yet, at the same time Congar inadvertently manifests a tendency to limit the universal salvific plan of the Father, which is made effective permanently in history through the working of the Holy Spirit, by making the paschal mystery the exclusive focal point of salvation. It follows that the locus of the sanctifying action of the Holy Spirit is to be found in the Church, in its preaching and in its sacraments. Had he adopted a more inclusive understanding of the mission of the Son and the Spirit, he would have been able to insert the anamnesis and the epiclesis in a universal context, so that the rites of other religions could be viewed as related to those of the Church, and thus as valid forms of the saving and sanctifying will of the Creator[60].

Congar should have said more forcefully that the epicletic role of the Holy Spirit is not limited to the sphere of those who explicitly actualize redemption through Christ. Although the eschatological effusion of the Holy Spirit as the *Spiritus Filii* has added an essentially new component to the evolving economy of salvation, the divine *Pneuma* has always been acting as the creative and vivifying power of God the Father, the *Spiritus Patris*. His closeness has been experienced from the very beginning of

---

[59] Cf. K. UNTENER, *The Church-World Relationship according to the Writings of Yves Congar*. Dissertation Abstracts, Roma 1976, 63-64.

[60] Cf. J. MOLTMANN, *God in Creation*. An Ecological Doctrine of Creation, London 1985, 99; see also ID., *The Way of Jesus Christ*: Christology in Messianic Dimensions, London 1990, 276, 278-279; ID., *The Spirit of Life*. A Universal Affirmation, London 1992, 8.

human history, and it still enlivens the entire cosmos, inducing human beings to invoke the Creator to transform all things. How then could Congar have understood the relationship between the universal epicletic activity of the Holy Spirit and its particular form in the Christian community, in its preaching and in its sacraments? It seems that an inclusive christocentrism, which is characterized by confession of the universal presence of the *Spiritus Patris et Filii* represents the only adequate approach to a generally valid Christian theology of religions[61]. In this perspective Jesus Christ is at once the definitive manifestation of the unrestricted presence and recreative activity of the *Spiritus Patris* in the world, and also the starting point for the victorious eschatological mission of the *Spiritus Filii* towards the final consecration of the world. It is his task now to integrate into the reality of Christ, *Alpha* and *Omega*, all human beings and all their efforts to transform the world[62]. The Spirit does this by directing every form of the invocation in the various religions of the globe to the saving signs of Christ, the sacraments, in which the divine *Pneuma* has had from the start a constitutive role. Thus, the multiple expressions of invocation, which are pronounced by adherents to differing religions, are the means by which the *Spiritus Patris* acts to bring humankind to the revealed Son. And in every manifestation of the values of Jesus Christ to be found in those who do not expressly confess the Gospel, the *Spiritus Filii* acts to direct them to the Church where the followers of Jesus gather and where his signs of justice and love are celebrated in anticipation of the Kingdom[63].

In order to systematize what has been said thus far, it is suggested that Congar could have conceived of a large circle within which two other circles are contained in such a way that all three are tending to converge at a single point to the right. The outer circle is the area of activity of the *Spiritus Patris*, that is, of the universal epicletic work of the divine

---

61 Cf. J. DUPUIS, *Jesus Christ at the Encounter of World Religions,* New York 1991, 146-147. Here, Dupuis distinguishes three different approaches: ecclesiocentric, christocentric and theocentric, which respectively correspond to the following positions: exclusivism, inclusivism and pluralism. According to him, with the teaching of Vatican II, the christocentric approach has superseded the others. He finds difficulty with the theocentric approach because of its denial of the uniqueness and universal significance of Christ for the salvation of humankind. Cf. J. DUPUIS, *Jesus Christ at the Encounter of World Religions,* 141-146.

62 Cf. W. KASPER, *Jesus the Christ,* London 1976, 256; see also ID., *The God of Jesus Christ,* London 1984, 211.

63 Cf. F.X. DURRWELL, «Le salut par l'Evangile», *Spi* 32 (1967) 386-387; K. RAHNER, «Anonymous Christians», in *Theological Investigations*: vol. VI, London 1969, 390-398.

Pneuma who leads all individuals and all religious communities from idolatry to sincere invocation of the Creator. The Spirit also inspires them to take responsibility for the material goods which they might incorporate into their rituals. And he fosters in them ever more authentic forms of human solidarity and moral cohesion[64]. Moreover, without ceasing to be the *Spiritus Patris*, the divine *Pneuma* acts in the second circle as the *Spiritus Filii* who first anointed Jesus of Nazareth and accompanied him as he effected the definitive signs of human salvation, and who then raised him to be the Lord and Messiah at the Easter-event and, since Pentecost, enables many to embrace his values of justice and love as their own, thus creating a body of people who may not accept the Gospel or be baptized, but who call upon the name of Jesus in a hidden way and act according to his prophetic lifestyle[65]. Finally the divine *Pneuma* acts in the inner circle in which, without ceasing to labour in the other two as the *Spiritus Patris* or the *Spiritus Filii*, he leads human beings to faith in Christ and to Baptism, and then to Confirmation and the Eucharist – in short, to the ecclesial communion where he is invoked explicitly upon signs and words of the rituals themselves and upon the faithful so that they be sanctified and collaborate with him and the Son in directing all the circles to their convergent point which is the full realization of the Kingdom[66]. It goes without saying that the complete identity of the Holy Spirit is revealed in the inner circle alone, in which he is experienced most directly as the third Person of the Trinity, as *Spiritus dominus et vivificator*. Yet this perfect knowledge of the identity of the Holy Spirit encourages Christians to respect, and point out, his epicletic activity in the other two circles where he is not fully known but

---

[64] The lack of this universal perspective is pointed out in J. FARRELLY, Review of *I Believe in the Holy Spirit*, in *TS* 42 (1981) 675-676; see also C. McDONALD, *Church and World in the Plan of God*. Aspects of History and Eschatology in the Thought of Père Congar O. P., 86, 97; T.I. McDONALD, *The Ecclesiology of Yves Congar*. Foundational Themes, 288, 290.

[65] For example Mahatma Gandhi once wrote: «Jesus Christ was one of the greatest teachers humanity has ever had. To his believers, He was God's only begotten Son. Could the fact that I do not accept this belief make Jesus have any more or less influence in my life? [...] I believe that He belongs not solely to Christianity, but to the entire world, to all races and people». In *The Mind of Mahatma Gandhi*, ed. R.K. PRABHU, Ahmedabad 1967, 98-99.

[66] Cf. P.J ROSATO, *Introduzione alla teologia dei sacramenti*, 125-143; see also J. DUPUIS, *Jesus Christ and His Spirit*. Theological Approaches, 241-244; E. SCHILLEBEECKX, *Church*. The Human Story of God, London 1990, 157-158.

nonetheless obeyed and allowed to be effective in various ways, so that he can speak «through the prophets»[67].

To bring these critical remarks to an end, it must be said, with all respect to Congar, that his intention to incorporate into Western theology the notion of the constitutive role of the epiclesis as it is understood in the Eastern Churches, was not fully realized. Instead of properly integrating the institutive role of Christ and constitutive or «co-institutive» role of the Spirit in effecting the sacraments, which he saw as a needed development of an insight of Vatican II[68], he gives the impression that biblical, theological, ecclesiological and universal viewpoints were not used sufficiently to rectify a pronounced christological bias in his writings on the epiclesis. If one looks critically at the actual results of his endeavour in this respect, one is bound to conclude that, although much light has been thrown on a whole number of individual aspects, an original and coherent paradigm of an epicletic theology has not emerged[69]. This critical judgement is expressed here so as to indicate what Catholic, Orthodox and Protestant scholars who are interested in the pneumatological aspect of revelation find lacking in Congar's approach, even if they laud many particulars of his manner of synthesizing the institutive and the constitutive dimensions of the sacraments. Moreover, by not reflecting more profoundly on the universal epicletic mission of the Holy Spirit, Congar has not provided a link between the transcendental and the categorical aspects of the activity of the divine *Pneuma*. The role of the Holy Spirit in other religions is not interpreted by him as the unrestricted form of epiclesis carried out by the Lord and Giver of life. In this critique, a path that might be taken in the future on the basis of Congar's research has been modestly pointed out as a tribute to his pioneering work in favour of an anamnetic and epicletic sacramental theology.

---

[67] Cf. J. MOLTMANN, Review of *Heiliger Geist in der Geschichte*, in *TL* 108 (1983) 628; see also ID., *The Spirit of Life. A Universal Affirmation*, 9-10.

[68] Cf. Y. CONGAR, «Theology's Task after Vatican II», in *Renewal of Religious Thought*: vol. I, ed. L.K. Shook, New York 1968, 57.

[69] Cf. I. CANAVARIS, *The Ecclesiology of Yves Congar*: An Orthodox Evaluation, 170.

CONCLUSION

It is hoped that through its historical, expository and evaluative parts, this research project has succeeded in systematically exploring the thought of Cardinal Yves Congar on the invocation of the Holy Spirit as a constitutive dimension of the sacraments. In its initial historical part, this study shows how in his early years Congar first witnessed and then contributed to the gradual emergence of a christic-pneumatic approach to sacramental theology, as Catholicism revived its comprehension of the Tradition through biblical, patristic and liturgical studies. The central expository part of this study then offers a detailed analysis of principal texts, selected from Congar's writings spanning approximately fifty years, which deal with the epicletic dimension of the sacraments. In its closing evaluative-prognostic part, this research points out the strengths and weaknesses of Congar's theological explanation of the constitutive part played by the invocation of the Holy Spirit in the sacramental rites of the Church, and suggests some ways in which the short-comings of his reflections on the topic could be corrected, and its value enhanced in the future. Through its structure and its content, this thesis fulfills its intention to examine the thought of a prominent twentieth-century theologian concerning a topic at the center of Catholic and Protestant dialogue with the Orthodox Church.

However, after further reflection, it becomes noticeable that a second thesis runs through the first one, even though it is never explicitly articulated. This second thesis concerns the subtle fashion in which Congar explains that the Holy Spirit is the all-pervasive divine Breath which animates the three essential ways in which the Word is experienced by Christians: the physical, historical form – the glorified, sacramental form – the mystical, ecclesial form. In the first form, from the incarnation to the resurrection, the life, the message and the acts of the Word of God are filled with the power of the Breath of God. The second form, the presence of the glorified Word of God in all the sacred signs of the Church, is effected by the calling down of the transhistorical Breath of God. In the third form, the communal existence of those who abide in the Word of God, announce it and put it into practice continually becomes a community of salvation by means of the sanctifying fire of the Breath of God who makes the eschatological future operative in history. According to Congar, all three of these forms of experiencing the divine *Logos* would be impossible without the divine *Pneuma* who stirs up human desire for salvation and eternal life, and brings it to fruition. The «first» thesis of this study concerns chiefly the glorified, sacramental form of the Word of God brought about by the Holy Spirit through the epiclesis pronounced in the liturgy of the Church. Although the «second» thesis of this study is not much evident, it provides the panorama against which the glorified, sacramental presence of the Word of God through the Breath of God is intelligible.

Because of the ability of Congar to connect the liturgical epiclesis with the three principal experiences which Christians have of the Word of God, this insight can serve as the framework of a succinct summary concerning the manner in which he viewed four sacraments – Order, Baptism, Confirmation and Eucharist as «co-instituted» by the Breath of God. With regard to the sacrament of Order, the Word of God in his physical, historical form chose the Twelve from his many disciples and sent them out to announce the arrival of the Kingdom, assuring them that the Breath of God would teach them what to say and do (cf. Lk 12,12). In his glorified, sacramental form, the Word of God draws candidates to himself, so that they be conformed to his headship and thus love and nourish all his other followers; in the liturgical rite in which the bishop imposes his hands on these candidates, the Breath of God acts, bestowing on them the gifts of power, love and self-control (cf. 2 Tim 1,7). Then in the mystical, ecclesial form of the Word of God, which is the social body of all those who are incorporated into him by faith and Baptism, the ordained continually fashion the Church with the aid of the Breath of God working in their preaching, their sign-giving and their pastoral service. This explanation of Order makes it clear why Congar states that the Holy Spirit concelebrates with the successors of the Twelve: their holiness is not for themselves, but for the people who are to be pneumatized by the power of the Breath of God at work in their variegated ministry to the Word of God.

The sacraments of Baptism and Confirmation should rightly be considered together, since they are for Congar the two anointings with the Spirit – the one initiative and the other prophetic – which respectively conform the catechumens to the messianic being of the Word and to his salvific mission. At the Jordan, the Word of God in his physical, historical form was baptized with water by John the Baptist, and received from on high the Breath of God who would permeate his very being so that it be the definitive presence of divine salvation in history. At the liturgical rite of Baptism the catechumens, who have come to believe in the Word of God and live by him, experience his glorified, sacramental form by being immersed into the bath of regeneration (cf. Tit 3,5) which represents his death and resurrection, and by being anointed by the Breath of God in an initial way, so as to exist in the world as living signs of the divine justification of humankind, and as grateful sons and daughters manifesting in every regard a filial attitude to the Father who has bestowed the *Logos* and the *Pneuma* on them. The adherence to faith and the reception of Baptism enable the newly anointed to abide in the mystical, ecclesial form of the Word of God, the Church, and to attest by a style of life, based on the justice of the Father and sustained by his Breath, that they are a new creation (cf. 2 Cor 5,17). The roles of the Word and of the Breath are the same in rite of Confirmation, the second, prophetic form of anointing which follows the initiative one of Baptism. The distinctive trait of Confirmation, however, is that it seals the gift of the Spirit, and sends Christians on the salvific mission of enabling the justice of God, first manifested in Christ Jesus, to be brought to victory in various social contexts, so that «in his name all the Gentiles will hope» (cf. Mt 12, 20-21).

At the Eucharist, which is the final sacrament of Christian initiation and the one at which the order of the baptized and the confirmed is conjoined to that of the ordained, so as to represent the unity of the members of the Church with their Head, the goal of all the ecclesial signs is attained. This sacrament has its origin in the Last Supper and on Calvary where the Word of God in his physical, historical form was inspired by the Breath of God to enact his most radical of all signs, associating himself with the sacred Lamb of God and giving himself – his flesh and blood – to his followers, first symbolically in the bread and wine on the table of wood, and then corporeally on the wooden cross. Subsequently, Christians experience the glorified, sacramental form of the Word of God at the eucharistic altar, on which bread and wine are placed. Then the very phrases spoken by the Word in the Cenacle are pronounced by the presider, and the transforming Breath of God is called down on the elements, so that they become the real symbols of the pneumatized body and blood of the slain and glorious Lamb and the re-actualization of the paschal mystery. Thus, through the anamnesis and the epiclesis, the Word of the Breath, and the Breath of the Word «conspire» to bestow the merits of divine salvation and sanctification on the members of the worshipping community gathered around the altar. Then at the rite of communion, these members experience the mystical, ecclesial form of the Word of God, that is, union with him and with each other; but this union would remain mute and inert if the Breath of God did not fill them «with spirit and with truth» (cf. Jn 4,24), and send them out into the world to attest through various acts of self-giving that they not only believe in their union with God and others, but are blessed because they put it into practice (cf. Jn 13,17).

The first part of the evaluative section of this study comprises a detailed appreciation of what Congar has achieved by illuminating the constitutive role of the Holy Spirit in actualizing the sacraments. This appreciation is based on the conclusion that with his research on the epiclesis he has been able to face and to mitigate some of the major tensions which have existed in the field of Catholic sacramental theology during the twentieth-century. First there is the tension between a christocentric and trinitarian panorama against which to situate the rites of the Church; by opting for a decidedly christic-pneumatic approach to the sacraments, Congar could present the sacraments as privileged salvific events originating from the Father through the Son and in the Spirit, and as unique eschatological events oriented in the Spirit through the Son towards the Father. Then there is the tension between the christological-commemorative and the pneumatological – charismatic understanding of sacramental efficacy; by proposing that, while the Son has the institutive role and the Spirit the constitutive one in effecting the sacraments, the latter are actually «conspired» at each ritual through the anamnesis and the epiclesis, Congar exposed Western theologians to the thought patterns of their Eastern counterparts, and fostered dialogue and scholarly exchange among them. Then there is the tension between a hierarchical-oriented and a communitarian-oriented view of the liturgical celebration; with his attempt to place the narrower «in persona Christi» role of the ordained within the broader «in persona ecclesiae» one, Congar sought to grant the participation of the baptized and confirmed in the liturgy a reinforced theological basis, insisting that the entire Church is epicletic, and that the prayer of all the orders is indispensable to the efficacy of the sacramental rites. And finally there is the tension between an interior-individualistic and an eschatological-prophetic concept of sacramental grace; with the realization that wherever the Spirit is, there is the eschaton, and with a vital sense that the divine Pneuma still speaks through the prophets, Congar urged that sacramental grace be perceived not as confined solely to the interior depths of individual Christians, but as freeing them in a wholistic sense for forms of mission in society which correspond to the grace given by the various sacraments and which point to the inauguration of the end-time in history.

In the second part of the evaluation, a number of critical observations are offered which set out not to devalue the above-mentioned positive contributions of Congar, but to indicate those aspects of his thought on the epiclesis which contemporary scholars judge in need of reformulation or further research. Some hold that the *biblical basis* of the epiclesis is not adequately presented by Congar because, in stressing the institutive sign-giving of the incarnate *Logos*, he fails to perceive it as intertwined with the constitutive empowerment of the *Pneuma*. Others claim that *theological importance* of the epiclesis is not fully shown in Congar's writings, since he does not clearly differentiate the specificity of the mission of the Spirit in the sacraments from that of the mission of the Son. Especially the Orthodox critics underscore that the *ecclesiological consequences* of the epiclesis are weakened by Congar, since he seems to emphasize the concelebration of the Spirit with the ordained ministers to such an extent that his effective collaboration with the baptized and confirmed is made subordinate to it, rather than affirmed as both independent of and yet co-ordinate to it. The last issue taken up in the critical part is raised by those theologians who are engaged in dialogue with adherents to other world religions and to whom it appears that the *universal significance* of the epiclesis is not taken into consideration by Congar, because his concern with the activity of the Spirit as *Spiritus Filii* in the signs of the Church in effect overshadows his concomitant activity as *Spiritus Patris* in all religious rituals which entail an invocation of the Creator and a commitment to live by the moral norms of justice and love. Credence is given to all these critical observations, and a nuanced personal stance with regard to them is presented, precisely because Congar hoped that his own research would stimulate another generation of scholars to go beyond what he had achieved.

This study can therefore be said to elucidate some important insights of Congar on the sacramental celebration as a whole. He maintains that the constitutive act of invoking the Holy Spirit in the sacraments is not confined to formal epicletic phrases but permeates the entire liturgical event. Similar to the identity of the Spirit, the epicletic dimension of the sacraments is invisible, intangible and un-objectifiable. This justifies the biblical and patristic tendency to express the pneumatological aspect of the sacraments by means of symbols, such as power, breath, fragrance and fire, which point to the indefinable mystery which penetrates every element of the sacramental celebration and which itself is the manifestation of the Lord of glory. Through the Spirit, therefore, the sacramental actions acquire the serenity, transparency and radiance of the risen Christ, and are for this reason prevented from being regarded merely as rites. Through the Spirit, ritual becomes truly revelatory and communicative of divine holiness and love. Hence, the constant liturgical summoning of the Spirit to dwell in water, in oil, in bread and wine, and in persons, so that he might enable their innermost mystery to be disclosed and to be sanctified. In the sacraments, the Spirit neither reveals nor asserts himself, but points «back» to the Father who has been revealed through the Son, and «ahead» to the Son who will hand over all things to the Father (cf. 1 Cor 15,28). In fact, all these graces which the Holy Spirit bestows do not call attention to themselves; rather they efface themselves in order that the Father and the Christ alone may stand revealed. Therefore, there is neither *christomonism* nor *pneumatomonism* involved in the liturgy, for no spoken Word there is without the Breath, and no Breath aspired there is without the spoken Word. In the context of this trinitarian perspective, the liturgical epiclesis reveals two fundamental movements. On the one hand, the Spirit creates a centripetal movement by drawing the recipients of the sacraments towards internal unity. On the other hand, the same Spirit makes the unity of the community that is formed in and through sacramental reception a relational one oriented towards the whole of creation.

Finally it should be said that this thesis has ecumenical bearing, since the question of the invocation of the Holy Spirit as constitutive of the sacraments has been a mainstay of Orthodox theology which Congar along with others has introduced into contemporary Western thought. The epiclesis question does not pertain first and foremost to sacramental theology, but to the economy in which the mystery of the triune God is revealed and communicated to human beings. By attempting to integrate the christological-anamnetic and the pneumatological-epicletic dimensions of the sacraments, Congar has called his Western colleagues to new respect for the tradition of the undivided Church, which is founded on the Apostles, the Fathers and the Councils. He ardently hoped that the two sister Churches, Oriental and Occidental, might be led by the one Spirit, who dwells in them and stimulates them, to recognize that they both confess the same faith, have the same sacraments and are on the same mission. All that has been indicated in this thesis concerning the constitutive role of the Holy Spirit in the sacraments can be summed up: It is in the unity of the Holy Spirit that, in heaven and already here on earth, to the Father, through the Son, is rendered all honor and glory.

ABBREVIATIONS

1. Documents

AG	*Ad Gentes (Decree on the Church's Missionary Activity)*
CD	*Christus Dominus (Decree on the Pastoral Office of Bishops in the Church)*
DH	*Dignitatis Humanae (The Declaration on Human Dignity)*
DV	*Dei Verbum (Dogmatic Constitution on Divine Revelation)*
GS	*Gaudium et Spes (Pastoral Constitution on the Church in the Modern World)*
LG	*Lumen Gentium (Dogmatic Constitution on the Church)*
OT	*Optatam Totius (Decree on the Training of Priests)*
PO	*Presbyterorum Ordnis (The Decree on the Life of*
SC	*Sacrosanctum Concilium (The Constitution on the Sacred Liturgy)*
UR	*Unitatis Redintegratio (The Decree on Ecumenism)*

2. Periodicals

AAS	*Acta Apostolica Sedis*
AER	*American Ecclesiastical Review*
AL	*Archiv für Liturgiewissenschaft*
Ame	*America*
Ang	*Angelicum*
Bij	*Bijdragen*
Bla	*Blackfriars*
CC	*Cross Currents*
Comm	*Communion*
Con	*Concilium*
Cont	*Contacts*
Cow	*Commonweal*
CR	*Clergy Review*
CS	*Chicago Studies*
DA	*Dominican Ashram*

Dia	*Diakonia*
Dial	*Dialogue*
DL	*Doctrine and Life*
DR	*Downwoodie Review*
ECQ	*Eastern Churches Quarterly*
EF	*Ekklesiastikos Faros*
Enc	*Encounter*
ET	*Expository Times*
ETL	*Ephemerides Theologicae Lovanienses*
Étu	*Études*
EV	*Escritos del Vedat*
EVie	*Esprit et Vie*
FZPT	*Freiburger Zeitschrift für Philosophie und Theologie*
GOTR	*The Greek Orthodox Theological Review*
Gre	*Gregorianum*
ICI	*Informations Catholiques Internationales*
ICR	*International Catholic Review*
Int	*Integration*
Iré	*Irénikon*
Ist	*Istina*
ITQ	*Irish Theological Quarterly*
JES	*Journal of Ecumenical Studies*
JLW	*Jahrbuch für Liturgische Wissenschaft*
JR	*Journal of Religion*
JTS	*Journal of Theological Studies*
Kyr	*Kyrios*
Lat	*Lateranum*
LMD	*La Maison-Dieu*
LOS	*L'Orient Syrien*
LPO	*La Pensée Orthodoxe*
LV	*Lumen Vitae*
LVI	*La Vie Intellectuelle*
LVie	*Lumière et Vie*
LW	*Lutheran World*
MC	*Modern Churchman*
MSR	*Mélanges de Science Religieuse*
NBla	*New Blackfriars*
Nic	*Nicolaus*
NRT	*Nouvelle Revue Théologique*
OC	*One in Christ*
OCA	*Orientale Christiane Analetica*
Oec	*Oecumenica*
ÖR	*Ökumenische Rundschau*
OS	*Ostkirchliche Studien*
POC	*Proche-Orient Chrétien*
RR	*Review for Religious*
RSPT	*Revue des Sciences Philosophiques et Théologiques*

RT	*Revue Thomiste*
SA	*Studia Anselmiana*
SD	*Sacra Doctrina*
SE	*Sacris Erudiri*
SE	*Study Encounter*
Sem	*Seminarium*
SL	*Studia Liturgica*
Sob	*Sobornost*
SVS	*Supplément de la Vie Spirituelle*
Tab	*The Tablet*
TD	*Theology Digest*
TER	*The Ecumenical Review*
TG	*Theologie der Gegenwart*
TGl	*Theologie und Glaube*
Theo	*Theology*
THJ	*The Heythrop Journal*
Tho	*The Thomist*
Thou	*Thought*
TJ	*The Jurist*
TL	*Theology and Life*
TQ	*Theologische Quartalschrift*
TS	*Theological Studies*
TT	*Theology Today*
TW	*The Way*
VC	*Verbum Caro*
Voc	*Vocation*
VP	*Vita Pastorale*
VS	*Vie Spirituelle*
VTQ	*St.Vladimir's Theological Quarterly*
VUC	*Vers l'Unité Chrétienne*
WM	*World Mission*
Wor	*Worship*
WW	*Wort und Wahrheit*

3. Other Abbreviations

ed.	*Editor*
eds.	*Editors*
Eng.	*English*
Trans.	*Transilation*
Vers.	*Version*
Vol.	*Volume*
Vols.	*Volumes*

SELECT BIBLIOGRAPHY

1. Works of Yves Congar

A. Books:

Chrétiens désunis. Principles d'un oecuménisme catholique, Paris 1937; Eng. trans. M.A. Bousfield, *Divided Christendom*. A Catholic Study of the Problem of Reunion, London 1939.

Esquisses du mystère de l'Église, Paris 1941; 2nd. ed. 1953; Eng. trans. A.V. Littledale *The Mystery of the Church*, Baltimore, 2nd. rev. ed. 1965.

Vraie et fausse réforme dans l'Église, Paris 1950; rev. ed. 1969.

Le Christ, Marie et l'Église, Paris 1952; Eng. trans. S.J. Henry, *Christ, Our Lady and the Church*, Westminster 1957.

Jalons pour une théologie du laïcat, Paris 1953; rev. ed. 1964; Eng. trans. D. Attwater, *Lay People in the Church*, London 1985.

Neuf cents ans après. Notes sur le schisme oriental, 1054-1954, Belgium 1954; Eng. vers. *After Nine Hundred Years, the Background of the Schism between the Eastern and Western Churches*, New York 1959.

La Pentecôte. Chartres 1956, Paris 1956; Eng. trans. A.V. Littledale, in *The Mystery of the Church*, Baltimore 1965, 146-198.

Le mystère du temple ou l'économie de la présence de Dieu à sa créature de la Genèse à l'Apocalypse, Paris 1958; Eng. trans. R.E. Trevett, *The Mystery of the Temple*, Westminster 1962.

Si vous êtes mes témoins. Trois conférences sur laïcat, Église et monde, Paris 1959; Eng. trans. D. Attwater, *Laity, Church and World*, Baltimore 1960.

La Tradition et les traditions. Essai historique et essai théologique: 2 vols., Paris 1960-1963); Eng. trans. N. Naseby – T. Rainborough, *Tradition and Traditions*. An Historical Essay and a Theological Essay, London 1966.

Les voies du Dieu vivant. Théologie et vie spirituelle, Paris 1962; Eng. trans. A. Manson – L.C. Sheppard, *The Revelation of God*, New York 1968.

Les voies du Dieu vivant. Théologie et vie spirituelle, Paris 1962; Eng. trans. A. Manson – L.C. Sheppard, *The Revelation of God*, New York 1968.

La Foi et la Théologie, Tournai 1962.

Sacerdoce et laïcat devant leurs tâches d'évangelisation et de civilisation, Paris 1962; Eng. trans. A. Hepburne-Scott, *Priest and Layman*, London 1967.

Sainte Église. Études et approches ecclésiologiques, Paris 1963.

La Tradition et la Vie de l'Église, Paris 1963; Eng. trans. A.N. Woodrow, *The Meaning of Tradition*, New York 1964.

Le Concile au jour le jour, Paris 1963; Eng. trans. L. Sheppard, *Report from Rome*. On the First Session of the Vatican Council, Montreal 1963.

Chrétiens en dialogue. Contributions catholiques à l'oecuménisme, Paris 1964; Eng. trans. P. Loretz, *Dialogue between Christians*: Catholic Contributions to Ecumenism, London 1966.

Le Concile au jour le jour. Deuxième session, Paris 1964; Eng. trans. L. Sheppard, *Report from Rome II*. On the Second Session of the Vatican Council, Montreal 1964.

Pour une Église servante et pauvre, Paris 1963; Eng. trans. J. Nicholson, *Power and Poverty in the Church*, Baltimore 1964.

Jésus-Christ, notre médiateur et notre seigneur, Paris 1965; Eng. trans. L. O'Neil, *Jesus Christ*, New York 1966.

Vaste monde ma paroisse. Vérite et dimensions du salut, Paris 1966.

Le Concile au jour le jour. Quatrième session, Paris 1966.

Situations et Tâches présentes de la théologie, Paris 1967; Eng. trans. H. Guthrie, *A History of Theology*, New York 1969.

L'Ecclésiologie du haut moyen âge: de saint Grégoire le Grand à la désunion entre Byzance et Rome, Paris 1968.

A mes frères, Paris 1968.

Cette Église que j'aime, Paris 1969; Eng. trans. L. Delaufente, *The Church That I Love*, New Jersey 1969.

Au milieu des orages. L'Église affronte aujourd'hui son avenir, Paris 1969; Eng. trans. S. Attanassio, *The Church Peaceful*, Dublin 1977.

L'Église de saint Augustin à l'époque moderne, Paris 1970.

L'Église une, sainte, catholique et apostolique in *Mysterium Salutis*: vol. 15, eds. J. Feiner – M. Löhrer, Paris 1970.

Ministères et Communion ecclésiale, Paris 1971.

Die Lehre von der Kirche vom abendländischen Schisma bis zur Gegenwart, Basel 1971.

Une Passion: l'unité. Réflexions et souvenirs 1929-1973, Paris 1974.

Un Peuple messianique. L'Église, sacrement du salut. Salut et libération, Paris 1975.

Église catholique et France moderne, Paris 1978.

Je crois en l'Esprit Saint: 3 vols., Paris 1979-1980; Eng. trans. D. Smith, *I Believe in the Holy Spirit*: 3 vols., London 1983.

Diversités et Communion, Paris 1982; Eng. trans. J. Bowden, *Diversity and Communion*, London 1984.

Martin Luther: sa foi, sa réforme: études de théologie historique, Paris 1983.

Esprit de l'homme, Esprit de Dieu, Paris 1983.

Essais oecuméniques: le mouvement, les hommes, les problèmes, Paris 1984.

Le Concile de Vatican II. Son Église peuple de Dieu et corps du Christ, Paris 1984.

La Parole et le Souffle, Paris 1984; Eng. trans. D. Smith, *The Word and the Spirit*, London 1986.

Appelés à la vie, Paris 1985; Eng. trans. W. Burridge, *Called to Life*, London 1986.

Entretiens d'Automne. Interview ed. by B. Lauret, Paris 1987; Eng. trans. J. Bowden, *Fifty Years of Catholic Theology*. Conversation with Y. Congar, London 1988.

B. Articles:

«Ordre et juridiction dans L'Église», *Iré* 10 (1933) 22-33; 97-110; 243-252; 401-408.

«Pensée orthodoxe sur l'unité de l'Église», *LVI* 13 (1934) 294-314.

«La défication dans la Tradition spirituelle de l'orient d'après une étude récente», *SVS* 43 (1935) 91-107.

«Une Conclusion théologique à l'enquête sur les raisons actuelles de l'incroyance», *LVI* (1935) 214-249.

«Meetings between Catholics and Orthodox: Some Possibilities», *ECQ* 4 (1936) 131-135.

«Ecclesia de Trinitate», *Iré* 14 (1937) 131-146.

«L'Esprit des Pères d'après Möhler», *SVS* 55 (1938) 1-25.

«Note sur l'évolution et l'interprétation de la pensée de Möhler», *RSPT* 27 (1938) 205-212.

«The Idea of the Church in St. Thomas Aquinas», *Tho* 1 (1939) 331-359.

«The Reasons for the Unbelief of our Time», *Int* 1 (1939) 10-26.

«Sacerdoce et Laïcat dans l'Église», *LVI* 14 (1946) 6-39.

«Sainteté et Péché dans l'Église», *LVI* 15 (1947) 6-40.

«Pour une Liturgie et une Prédication réelles», *LMD* 16 (1948) 75-87.

«Pourquoi le Peuple de Dieu doit-il sans cesse réformer?», *Iré* 22 (1948) 365-394.

«Pour une Théologie du Laïcat», *Etu* 256 (1948) 42-54, 194-218.

«L'appel oecuménique et l'oeuvre du Saint Esprit», *VS* 82 (1950) 5-12.

«L'Eucharistie et l'Église de la nouvelle Alliance», *VS* 82 (1950) 347-372.

«Rapprochements entre chrétiens: redécouverte catholique», *VUC* 29 (1951) 2-5.

«Structure du Sacerdoce chrétien», *LMD* 27 (1951) 51-85.

«Ecclesia ab Abel», in *Abhanglungen über Theologie und Kirche*. Festschrift
    für Karl Adam, eds. H. Elfera – F. Hofman, Düsseldorf 1952, 79-108.

«Le Saint-Esprit et le Corps apostolique réalisateurs de l'oeuvre du Christ»,
    RSPT 36 (1952) 613-625; 37 (1953) 25-48.

«L'Esprit Saint dans l'Église», *LVie* 10 (1953) 51-74.

«Le Christ, l'Église et la Grâce dans l'économie de l'espérance chrétienne», *Ist* 1
    (1954) 132-158.

David et Salomon, types du Christ en ses deux avènements», *VS* 91 (1954) 323-
    340.

«Theology of the Apostolate», *WM* 7 (1956) 283-294.

«Salvation and the Non-Catholics», *Bla* 37 (1957) 290-300.

«The Idea of Conversion», *Tho* 33 (1958) 5-20.

«Conscience ecclésiologique en Orient et en Occident du VI au XI siècle», *Ist*
    60 (1959) 187-236.

«Conclusion», in *Le Concile et les conciles*, eds. B. Botte – H. Marot, Paris
    1960, 285-334.

«Le Concile, l'Église, et les autres», *LVie* 45 (1960) 69-92; Eng. vers. «The
    Council, the Church and the Others», *CC* 11 (1961) 241-254.

«The Idea of Reform», *Bla* 41 (1960) 386-391.

«Sainte Ecriture et sainte Église», *RSPT* 44 (1960) 81-88; Eng. vers. «Holy Writ
    and the Holy Church», *Bla* 41 (1960) 11-19.

«Comment l'Église sainte doit se renouveler sans cesse», *Iré* 34 (1961) 322-345;
    Eng. vers. «Constant Self-renewal of the Church», *TD* 10 (1962) 184-
    190.

«The Council in the Age of Dialogue», *CC* 12 (1962) 144-151.

«La Hiérarchie comme service, selon le nouveau Testament et les Documents de
    la Tradition», in *L'épiscopat et l'Église universelle*, eds. B.D. Dupuy
    – Y. Congar, Paris 1962, 67-99.

«Ecumenical Experience and Conversion: A Personal Testimony», in *The
    Sufficiency of God*. Essays in Honour of W. A. Visser't Hooft, eds.
    M.C. Robert – W.C. Charles, London 1963, 71-87.

«La Prière de Jésus», *VS* 110 (1964) 157-174; Eng. vers. «The Prayer of Christ»,
    RR 24 (1965) 221-238.

«L'Église comme Peuple de Dieu», *Con* 1 (1965) 15-32; Eng. vers. «The Church,
    People of God», *Con* 1 (1965) 7-9.

«L'Église, Sacrement universel du Salut», *EV* 17 (1965) 339-355.

«Theology in the Council», *AER* 155 (1966) 217-230.

«The Church Seed of Unity and Hope for the Human Race», *CS* 5 (1966) 25-39.

«La Missione e le Missioni nelle prospettive del Vaticano II», *SD* 11 (1966) 5-45.

«Le Christ dans l'économie salutaire et dans nos traités dogmatiques», *Con* 2
    (1966) 11-16; Eng. vers. «Christ in the Economy of Salvation and in
    our Dogmatic Tracts», *Con* 2 (1966) 4-15.

«Ordinations "invitus, coactus", de l'Église antique au canon 214», *RSPT* 50 (1966) 169-197.

«Le Sacerdoce chrétien», *Voc* 236 (1966) 587-613.

«The People of God», in *Vatican II*. An Interfaith Appraisal, ed. J. Miller, Notre Dame 1966, 197-204.

«Theology's Task after Vatican II», *TL* 1 (1966) 47-65.

«Institutionalized Religion», in The Word in History: *The St. Xavier Symposium*, ed. P. Burke, New York 1966, 133-153.

«Le Diaconat dans la Théologie des Ministères», in *Le Diacre dans l'Église et le Monde d'aujourd'hui*, eds. P. Winninger - Y. Congar, Paris 1966, 121-141.

«Vocation sacerdotale et Vocation chrétienne», *Sem* 19 (1967) 7-16.

«La Pneumatologie dans la théologique catholique», *RSPT* 51 (1967) 250-258.

«Church Reform and Luther's Reformation 1517-1967», *LW* 4 (1967) 351-359.

«L'*ecclesia* ou communauté chrétienne, sujet intégral de l'action liturgique», in *La Liturgie après Vatican II*, eds. J.P. Jossua - Y. Congar, Paris 1967, 241-282.

«La Relation entre Culte ou Sacrement et Prédication de la Parole», *Con* 4 (1968) 53-62; Eng. vers. «Sacramental Worship and Preaching», *Con* 4 (1968) 27-33.

«Theology's Task after Vatican II», in *Renewal of Religious Thought*: vol. I, ed. L.K. Shook, New York 1968, 47-65.

«L'idée de Sacrements majeurs ou principaux», *Con* 4 (1968) 25-34; Eng. vers. «The Idea of "Major" or Principal Sacraments», *Con* 4 (1968) 12-17.

«Le Sacerdoce du nouveau testament. Mission et Culte», in *Les Prêtres*: Formation, Ministère et Vie, eds. J. Frisque - Y. Congar, Paris 1968, 233-256.

«Deux Facteurs de la Sacralisation de la Vie sociale au moyen âge [en Occident]», *Con* 5 (1969) 53-63; Eng. vers. «Two Factors in the Sacralization of Western Society during the Middle Ages», *Con* 5 (1969) 28-35.

«Pneumatologie ou Christomonisme dans la Tradition latine?», *ETL* 45 (1969) 394-416.

«L'histoire de l'Église lieu théologique», *Con* 6 (1970) 75-94; Eng. vers. «Church History as a Branch of Theology», *Con* 6 (1970) 85-97.

«Ministères et Structuration de l'Église», *LMD* 102 (1970) 7-20.

«Pourquoi j'aime l'Église», *Com* 24 (1970) 23-30.

«La personne Église», *RTh* 71 (1971) 613-640.

«Quelques Problèmes touchant des Ministères», *NRT* 93 (1971) 785-800.

«La Réception comme Réalité ecclésiologique», *RSPT* 56 (1972) 369-403; Eng. vers. «Reception as an Ecclesiological Reality», *Con* 8 (1972) 43-68.

«My Path-Findings in the Theology of Laity and Ministries», *TJ* 32 (1972) 169-188.

«Propos en vue d'une Théologie de l'économie dans la Tradition latine», *Iré* 45 (1972) 155-206.

«Actualité renouvelée du Saint-Esprit», *LV* 27 (1972) 543-556; Eng. vers. «Renewed Actuality of the Holy Spirit», *LV* 28 (1973) 13-30.

«Renouvellement de l'esprit et réforme de l'institution», *Con* 8 (1972) 37-45; Eng. vers. «Renewal of the Spirit and Reform of the Institution», *Con* 8 (1972) 39-49.

«Christsein zwischen Vergangenheit und Gegenwart«, *TG* 15 (1972) 187-194.

«Initiatives locales et normes universelles», *LMD* 112 (1972) 54-69; Eng. vers. «The Need for Pluralism in the Church», *DL* 24 (1974) 343-353.

«Actualité d'une Pneumatologie», *POC* 23 (1973) 121-132; Eng. vers. «Pneumatology Today», *AER* 167 (1973) 435-449.

«Norms of Christian Allegiance and Identity in the History of the Church», *Con* 9 (1973) 11-34.

«Une Église vivante», *ICI* 434 (1973) 6-10; Eng. vers. «The Church after the Council», *TD* 23 (1975) 31-37.

«Réflexions et Recherches actuelles sur l'assemblée liturgique», *LMD* 115 (1973) 7-29; Eng. vers. «Reflections on the Liturgical Assembly», *TD* 22 (1974) 150-153.

«Blasphemy against the Holy Spirit», *Con* 10 (1974) 47-57.

«La Tri-unité de Dieu et l'Église», *LVS* 128 (1974) 687-703.

«La Chiesa di Cristo nella storia degli uomini», *SD* 74 (1974) 195-211.

«Church Sructures and Councils in the Relations between East and West», *OC* 11 (1975) 224-263.

«Non-Christian Religions and Christianity», in *Service and Salvation*. Nagapur Theological Conference on Evangelization, ed. J. Pathrapankal, Bangalore 1975, 167-181.

«St. Thomas Aquinas and the Spirit of Ecumenism», *NBla* (1974) 196-208.

«The Church after the Council», *TD* 25 (1975) 31-37.

«Place et Vision du Laïcat dans la Formation des Prêtres après le Concile Vatican II», *Sem* 28 (1976) 59-72.

«The Magisterium and Theologians, a Short History», *TD* 25 (1977) 15-20.

«Fünfzig Jahre der Suche nach Einheit», *ÖR* 26 (1977) 268-286; Eng. vers. «The Search for Unity: 1927-1977», *TD* 27 (1979) 249-254; and also in *Lausanne 77*y. Faith and Order Paper no: 82, Geneva 1977, 48-65.

«Quelle idée s'est-on faite du concile entre Nicée I et Nicée II?», *RSPT* 63 (1979) 429-434.

«Pour une Christologie pneumatologique», *RSPT* 63 (1979) 435-442.

«Méditation théologique sur la troisième Personne», *POC* 29 (1979) 201-211; Eng. vers. «A Meditation on the Holy Spirit», *TD* 31 (1984) 103-105.

«Essai de synthèse», *Con* 17 (1981) 121-137; Eng. vers. «Towards a Catholic Synthesis», *Con* 17 (1981) 68-80.

«Le Monothéisme politique de l'antiquité et le Dieu-Trinité», *Con* 17 (1981) 51-58; Eng. vers. «Classical Political Monotheism and the Trinity», *Con* 17 (1981) 31-36.

«Renouveau charismatique et Théologie du Saint-Esprit», *LVS* 646 (1981) 735-749.

«Unis dans le Baptême, désunis dans l'Eucharistie?», *Nic* 9 (1981) 249-261.

«Reflections on Being a Theologian», *NBla* 62 (1981) 405-409.

«Valeur sacramentale de la Parole», *VS* 644 (1981) 179-189; Eng. vers. «The Sacramental Value of the Word», *DA* 3 (1981) 134-142.

«Le Saint-Esprit dans la Consécration et la Communion selon la tradition occidentale», *Nic* 9 (1981) 383-386.

«Sur la Maternité en Dieu et la Féminité du Saint-Esprit», *EV* 11 (1981) 115-124; Eng. vers. «The Spirit as God's Femininity», *TD* 30 (1982) 129-133.

«Die christologischen und pneumatologischen Implikationen der Ekklesiologie des II. Vatikanums», in *Kirche im Wandel, ed.* G. Alberigo, Düsseldorf 1982, 111-123.

«Actualité de la pneumatologie», in *Credo in Spiritum Sanctum.* Atti del Congresso teologico internazionale di pneumatologia. Roma, 22-26. 3. 1982, Roma 1982, 15-28.

«Structures ou régime conciliaire de l'Église», *Con* 19 (1983) 13-21; Eng. vers. «The Conciliar Structure or Regime of the Church», *Con* 19 (1983) 3-9.

«Où en est l'expression de la Foi?», *Con* 19 (1983) 139-142; Eng. vers. «Where are we in the Expression of the Faith?», *Con* 19 (1983) 85-87.

«Sur la Trilogie: Prophète-Roi-Prêtre», *RSPT* 67 (1983) 97-115.

«Christ – Eucharistie – Église. Cohérence de leurs représentations. Sa validité et ses limites», in *In necessariis unitas.* Mélanges J. L. Leuba, ed. R. Stauffer, Paris 1984, 69-80.

«Letter from Father Yves Congar, O.P.», *TD* 32 (1985) 213-216.

«The Brother I Have Known», *Tho* 112 (1985) 277-296.

«Moving towards a Pilgrim Church», in *Vatican II by Those Who Were There*, ed. A. Stacpoole, London 1986, 129-155.

«Commento di Yves Congar», in *Lasciatevi muovere dallo Spirito.* Lettera enciclica sullo Spirito santo di Giovanni Paolo II. Commento di H.Urs von Balthasar – Y. Congar, Brescia 1986, 131-137.

2. Works on Yves Congar

AREEPLACKAL, J., *Spirit and Ministries.* Perspectives of East and West, Bangalore 1990.

180   INVOCATION OF THE HOLY SPIRIT

AUER, A., «Yves Congar», in *Tendenzen der Theologie in zwanzig Jahrhundert*y: eine Geschichte in Porträts, ed. H.J. Schultz, Stuttgart 1966, 519-523.

CANAVARIA, I., *The Ecclesiology of Yves M. J. Congar*: An Orhtodox Evaluation, Boston, 1968.

————, «The Ecclesiology of Yves Congar: An Orthodox Evaluation», *GOTR* 15 (1970) 85-106.

CONNOLLY, J.M., «Yves Congar. The Church and the Churches», in *Voices of France*, New York 1961, 198-117.

CZYZ, P., *Il rapporto tra la dimensione cristologica e pneumatologica dell'ecclesiologia nel pensiero di Y. Congar*. Dissertation Abstracts, Roma 1986.

DUVAL, A.O., «Yves Congar: A Life for the Truth», *Tho* 48 (1984) 505-511.

FINNEGAN, G.F., «Ministerial Priesthood in Yves Congar», *RR* 46 (1987) 523-532.

GIANAZZA, P.G., *La teologia dello Spirito Santo in prospettiva ecumenica*Y. Studio comparativo sulla pneumatologia di Paul Evdokimov (Ortodosso) e Yves Congar O.P (Cattolico). Dissertation Abstracts, Rome 1981.

HENN, W., *The Hierarchy of Truths according to Yves Congar*, Roma 1987.

HELLWIG, M.K., «Soteriology in the Nuclear Age», *Tho* 48 (1984) 634-644.

JANUS, K., *Il Cristo e lo Spirito Santo come principi dell'unità della Chiesa*. Studio sull'ecclesiologia di Y. M. J. Congar. Dissertation Abstracts, Roma 1972.

JOSSUA, J.P., *Yves Congar*. Theology in the Service of God's People Chicago 1968.

————, «L'oeuvre oecuménique du Père Congar», *Etu* 357 (1982) 543-555.

KALLARANGATT, J., *The Holy Spirit, Bond of Communion of the Churches*. A Comparative Study of the Ecclesiology of Yves Congar and Nikos Nissiotis. Dissertation Abstracts, Roma 1989.

KEMBE, K., *Conciliarité et Unité à la lumière de l'Ecclesiologie de Yves Congar*. Dissertation Abstracts, Roma 1989.

KOMONCHAK, J.A., «The Return of Yves Congar», *Cow*, 110 (1984) 402-405.

LAUBACH, J., «Yves Congar», in *Theologians of our Time*, ed. L. Hreinisch, Notre Dame 1964.

LE GUILLOU, M.J., «Yves M. J. Congar», in *Bilancio della teologia del XX secolo*: vol. IV, ed. H. Vorgrimler, Roma 1972, 189-205.

McDONALD, C., *Church and World in the Plan of God*. Aspects of History and Eschatology in the Thought of Père Yves Congar O. P., Bern 1981.

McDONALD, T.I., *The Ecclesiology of Yves Congar*. Foundational Themes, Milwaukee 1984.

MARCHESI, G., «Yves Congar, passione per la Chiesa», *VP* 72 (1982) 34-36.

McBRIEN, R., «Church and Ministry: The Achievement of Yves Congar», *TD* 32 (1985) 203-211.

MEINI, M., *Lo Spirito Santo nell'ecclesiologia di Yves Congar*. Dissertation Abstracts, Siena 1988.

MONDIN, B., «Yves Congar e la teologia ecclesiologica ed ecumenica», in *I grandi teologi del secolo ventesimo*, vol. I: I teologi cattolici, Turin 1969.

NAVARATNE, L.M., *The Relationship between Christology and Pneumatology in the Writings of Yves Congar, Karl Rahner and Jacques Dupuis*. Dissertation Abstracts, Roma 1987.

NICHOLAS, N., «T. S. Eliot and Yves Congar on the Nature of Tradition», *Ang* 61 (1984) 473-485.

———, *Yves Congar*, London 1989.

OSNER, M., *L'Action du Saint-Esprit dans la communion ecclésiale*. Etude sur l'oeuvre d'Yves *Congar*, Strassbourg 1980.

PUYO, J., *Yves Congar*. Une vie pour la vérité, Paris 1975.

SCHILLING, S.P., «Yves Congar», in *Contemporary Continental Theologians*, London 1966, 185-205.

STACPOLLE, A., «Early Ecumenism, Early Yves Congar, 1904-1940. Commemoration of the Half-Century of the Beginnings of the World Council of Churches, 1937-1987», *TM* 21 (1988) 502-510.

UNTENER, K., *The Church-World Relationship according to the Writings of Yves Congar*. Dissertation Abstracts, Roma 1976).

WINTER, M., «Masters in Israel VI: Yves Congar», *CR* 55 (1970) 275-288.

3. Other Sources

ADAMS, R.A., «The Holy Spirit and the Real Presence», *TS* 29 (1968) 37-51.

ALLCHIN, A.M., «The Holy Spirit in Christian Life», *Sob* 1 (1965) 170-180.

ALLMEN, J.J. von., «Worship and the Holy Spirit», *SL* 2 (1963) 124-135.

———, *Worship*: Its Theology and Practice, New York 1965.

ANDERSON, J.B., *A Vatican II Pneumatology of the Paschal Mystery*: The Historical – Doctrinal Genesis 1, 2-5, Roma 1988.

ASHANIN, C.B., «The Holy Spirit in the Liturgy», *Enc* 34 (1973) 351-360.

ATCHLEY, E.G.C.E., «The Epiclesis», *The* 3 (1921) 90-98.

———, «The Epiclesis: A Criticism», *The* 29 (1934) 28-35.

———, *On the Epiclesis of the Eucharistic Liturgy and in the Consecration of the Font*, Oxford 1935.

BALTHASAR, H.Urs von., *Theologik Anlage des Gesamtwerkes*: vol. III, Einsiedeln 1985-1987.

BARRET, C.K., «The Holy Spirit in the Fourth Gospel», *JTS* 1 (1950) 1-15.

BARRET, C.K., *The Holy Spirit and the Gospel Tradition*, London 1970.

———, *The Second Epistle to the Corinthians*, New York 1973.

———, *Church, Ministry and Sacraments in the New Testament*, Exeter 1985.

BAVAND, G., «Note sur la mission du Saint Esprit», *FZPT* 86 (1972) 120-126.

BERKOHF, H., *The Doctrine of the Holy Spirit*, Atlanta 1964.

BERMEJO, L., *The Spirit of Life*. The Holy Spirit in the Life of the Christian, Gujarat 1987.

BERNADOT, M.V., *De l'Eucharistie à la Trinité*, Paris 1978.

BERTETTO, D., «Lo Spirito Santo santificatore: Il compito proprio dello Spirito Santo nel dinamismo soprannaturale», in *Credo in Spiritum sanctum.* Atti del congresso teologico internationale di pneumatologia: vol. II., Roma 1982, 563-570.

BILANIUK, P.B.T., *Theology and Economy of the Holy* Spirit. An Eastern Approach, Bangalore 1980.

BOBRINSKOY, B., «Worship and the Ascension of Christ», *SL* 2 (1963) 108-135.

———, «Présence réelle et communion eucharistique», *RSPT* 53 (1969) 402-420.

———, «The Holy Spirit, Life of the Church», *Dia* 6 (1972) 303-320.

———, «The Indwelling of the Spirit in Christ: Pneumatic Christology in the Cappadocian Fathers», *VTQ* 28 (1984) 49-65.

BOISMARD, M.-E., «La révélation de l'Esprit-Saint», *RT* 55 (1953) 5-21.

BORDONI, M., «Cristologia e Pneumatologia: L'evento Pasquale come atto del Cristo e dello Spirito», *Lat* 47 (1981) 432-492.

BOSC, J., «Le Saint-Esprit et l'Église», *LVie* 74 (1965) 29-39.

BOTTE, B., «L'épiclèse dans les liturgies syriennes orientales», *SE* 6 (1954) 48-72.

BOUHOT, J.P., *La confirmation sacrement de la communion ecclésiale*, Lyons 1972.

BOUYER, L., *Le Consolateur*. Esprit-Saint et vie de grâce, Paris 1980.

———, *Eucharist*. Theology and Spirituality of the Eucharistic Prayer, Notre Dame 1968.

BRACKEN, J.A., «The Holy Trinity as Community of Divine Persons», *THJ* 15 (1974) 257-270.

BRADSHAW, P.F., *Ordination Rites of the Ancient Churches of East and West*, New York 1990.

BRETCHER, S., «Decree on the Church's Missionary Activity: Origin and History of the Decree; Doctrinal Principles», in *Commentary on the Documents of Vatican II*: vol. IV, ed. H. Vorgrimler, London 1989, 87-124.

BREUNING, W., «Pneumatologie», in *Bilan de la théologie du XXe siécle*: vol. II, eds. R.V. Gucht – H. Vorgrimler, Paris 1970, 345-350.

BRIGHTMAN, F.E., *Liturgies*: Eastern and Western, Oxford 1896.

——, «Invocation in the Holy Eucharist», *Theo* 9 (1924) 33-40.

BROCK, S.P., «Studies in the Early History of the Syrian Orthodox Baptismal Liturgy», *JTS* 23 (1972) 16-64.

——, «The Epiclesis in the Antiochene Baptismal Ordines», *OCA* 58 (1974) 183-218.

——, «World and Sacrament in the Writings of the Syrian Fathers», *Sob* 6 (1974) 685-696.

——, «Mary and the Eucharist: An Oriental Perspective», *Sob* 1 (1979) 50-59.

——, *The Holy Spirit in the Syrian Baptismal Tradition*, Poona 1979.

BURGESS, S.M., *The Spirit and the Church*: Antiquity, Peabody 1984.

——, *The Holy Spirit*: Eastern Christian Traditions, Peabody 1989.

BURGHARDT, W.J., «What is a Priest?», in *The Sacraments*. Readings in Contemporary Sacramental Theology, ed. M. J. Taylor, New York 1981, 155-170.

BUTLER, C., *The Theology of Vatican II*, London 1967.

BUX, N., «L'olio, simbolo dello Spirito Santo», *SA* 87 (1983) 123-135.

CANTALAMESSA, R., *The Holy Spirit in the Life of Jesus*, Minnesota 1994.

CASEL, O., «Zur Epiclese», *JLW* 3 (1923) 100-102.

——, *The Mystery of Christian Worship*, London 1962.

CHADWICK, H., «Eucharist and Christology in the Nestorian Controversy», *TS* 11 (1950) 145-164.

CHAVASSE, A., «L'épiclèse eucharistique dans les anciennes liturgies orientales. Une hypothèse d'interprétation», *MSR* (1946) 197-206.

CHENU, M.D., «The New Awareness of the Trinitarian Basis of the Church», *Con* 17 (1981) 14-21.

CLAPSIS, E., «The Holy Spirit in the Church», in *Come Holy Spirit, Renew the Whole Creation*, ed. G. Limouris, Brookline 1990, 158-170.

CLÉMENT, O., «Quelques approches pneumatologiques de l'Église», *Cont* 39 (1987) 17-30.

CODRINGTON, H.W., «Epiclesis», *ECQ* 9 (1952) 200-205.

COFFEY, D., «The Incarnation of the Holy Spirit in Christ», *TS* 45 (1984) 466-480.

COLLE, R.D., *Christ and the Spirit*. Spirit-Christology in Trinitarian Perspective, Oxford 1994.

CONNOLLY, R.H., «The Meaning of Epiclesis», *JTS* 25 (1923) 337-364.

CORCORAN, P., «Christ's Action in the Mass», *TS* 27 (1966) 89-96.

——, «Theology of the Eucharistic Consecration: Role of the Priest in Celtic Liturgy», *TS* 40 (1979) 334-343.

CORCORAN, P., «Eucharistic Epiclesis: New Evidence and New Theory», *TS* 41 (1980) 698-712.

CREHAN, J.H., «The Typology of Episcopal Consecration», *TS* 21 (1960) 250-255.

————, «The Theology of Eucharistic Consecration: Role of the Priest in Celtic Liturgy», *TS* 40 (1979) 334-343.

CUNLIFFE, J.H., «Two Questions concerning the Holy Spirit», *Theo* 75 (1972) 298-300.

DANIÉLOU, J., «L'Esprit-Saint et l'histoire du salut», *VS* 84 (1950) 127-140.

DELCUVE, G., «Becoming Christians in Christ. The Dynamics of the Sacraments of Baptism, Confirmation and the Eucharist», *LV* 28 (1973) 77-96.

DIX, G., *Theology of Confirmation in relation to Baptism*, Westminister 1946.

————, *The Shape of the Liturgy*, London 1986.

DULLES, A., «Vatican II and the American Experience of Church», in *Vatican II. Open Questions and New Horizions*, ed. G.M. Fagin, Wilmington 1984, 38-57.

————, *The Reshaping of Catholicism. Current Challenges in the Theology of Church*, New York 1988.

DUMITRU, S., «The Role of the Holy Spirit in the Theology and the Life of the Orthododx Church», *Dia* 9 (1974) 343-359.

DUNN, J.D.G., *Baptism in the Holy Spirit*. A Re-examination of the New Testament Teaching on the Gift of the Spirit in Relation to Pentecostalism Today, Philadelphia 1970.

————, «Rediscovering the Spirit», *ET* 84 (1972) 40-44.

————, *Jesus and the Spirit*: A Study of the Religious and Charismatic Experience of Jesus and the First Christians as Reflected in the New Testament, Philadelphia 1975.

DUPUIS, J., *Jesus Christ and His Spirit*. Theological Approaches, Bangalore 1977.

————, *Jesus Christ at the Encounter of World Religions*, New York 1991.

DURRWELL, F.X., *L'Eucharistie, présence du Christ*, Paris 1971.

DURRWELL, *L'Eucharistie, sacrement pascal*, Paris 1980.

————, *Holy Spirit of God. An Essay in Biblical Theology*, London 1986.

————, *The Resurrection*, London 1986.

————, *The Spirit of the Father and of the Son*, Trowbridge 1989.

EVDOKIMOV, P., *L'Orthodoxie*, Paris 1959.

————, «Eucharistie mystère de l'Église», *LPO* 2 (1968) 57-78.

————, *L'Esprit saint dans la tradition orthodoxe*, Paris 1969.

————, *La preghiera della Chiesa orientale*, Brescia 1970.

FLANNERY, A., ed. *Vatican Council II*. The Conciliar and Post-Conciliar Documents, Minnesota 1975.

FORTE, B., *The Trinity as History*, New York 1989.

GASSMANN, A., «The Holy Spirit and Church Ministry», *Dial* 13 (1974) 40-44.

GAYBBA, B., *The Spirit of Love*. Theology of the Holy Spirit, London 1987.

GELPI, D.L., *The Divine Mother*. A Trinitarian Theology of the Holy Spirit, New York 1984.

GERARDI, R., *Rinati nell'acqua e nello Spirito*. Studio sui sacramenti del battesimo e della confermazione, Napoli 1982.

GREER, R.A., *Theodore of Mopsuestia*. Exegete and Theologian, Westminster 1961.

GRISBROOKE, W.J., «Recent Reforms of Ordination Rites in the Churches», in *Ordination Rites*. Papers Read at the 1979 Congress of Societas Liturgica, eds. W. Vos – G. Wainwright, Rotterdam 1980, 108-124.

GUILLET, J., «The Holy Spirit in Christ's Life», *LV* 28 (1973) 31-40.

HAAS, L., *Personal Pentecost*. The Meaning of Confirmation, St. Meinrad 1973.

HAMMAN, A., ed. *The Mass*. Ancient Liturgies and Patristic Texts, New York 1967.

HANSEN, O., «Spirit Christology: A Way Out of Our Dilemma?», in *The Holy Spirit in the Life of the Church*. From Biblical Times to the Present, ed. P.D. Opsahl, Minneapolis 1978, 172-203.

HARRISON, C., «The Ministry of the Spirit», *MC* 15 (1972) 191-195.

HOOK, N., «Spirit Christology», *Theo* 75 (1972) 226-232.

HRYNIEWIEZ, W., «The Centrality of Christ in Orthodox Theology», *CT* 46 (1976) 153-168.

JUNGMANN, J.A., *The Mass*. An Historical, Theological and Pastoral Survey, Minnesota 1975.

————, *The Mass of the Roman Rite*. Its Origins and Development: 2 vols., New York 1986.

KASPER, W., «A New Dogmatic Outlook on the Priestly Ministry», *Con* 5 (1969) 21-33.

————, ed. *Kirche, Ort des Geistes*, Frieburg 1976.

————, *Jesus the Christ*, London 1977.

————, *God's Time for Mankind*. Reflections on the Church Year, Chicago 1978.

————, «The Spirit Acting in the World to Demolish Frontiers and Create the Future», *LV* 34 (1979) 86-99.

————, ed. *Gegenwart des Geistes*. Aspekte der Pneumatologie, Freiburg 1979.

————, *The God of Jesus Christ*, New York 1984.

————, «Unity and Diversity in the Eucharist», *TD* 33 (1987) 133-136.

————, *Theology and Church*, London 1989.

KAVANAGH, A., «Initiation: Baptism and Confirmation», in *The Sacraments*. Readings in Contemporary Sacramental *Theology*, ed. M.J. Taylor, Now York 1981, 81-94.

KENNETH, S., «Anaphoral Offering: Some Observations on Eastern Eucharistic Prayers», *EL* 94 (1980) 209-228.

KERN, C., «En marge de l'épiclèse», *Iré* 24 (1951) 166-194.

KILMARTIN, E.J., «Ministry and Ordination in Early Christianity aganist a Jewish Background», in *Ordination Rites*. Papers Read at the 1979 Congress of Societas Liturgica, eds. W. Vos – G. Wainwright, Rotterdam 1980, 42-69.

———, *Church, Eucharist and Priesthood*. Theological Commentary on "The Mystery of and Worship of the Most Holy Eucharist", New York 1981.

———, «The Active Role of Christ and the Spirit in the Divine Liturgy», *Dia* 17 (1982) 95-108.

———, «The Active Role of Christ and the Holy Spirit in the Sanctification of the Eucharistic Elements», *TS* 45 (1984) 225-253.

———, *Particular Liturgy of the Individual Church*. The Theological Basis and Practical Consequences, Bangalore 1987.*Christian Liturgy*: Theology and Practice, Kansas City 1988).«Sacraments as Liturgy of the Church», *TS* 50 (1989) 527-547.

———, «The Catholic Tradition of Eucharistic Theology: Towards the Third Millennium», *TS* 55 (1994) 405-457.

KRESS, R., «The Church as a Communion. Trinity and Incarnation as the Foundation of Ecclesiology», *TJ* 36 (1976) 127-157.

KÜNG, H., «The Word and the Spirit», *CR* 55 (1970) 338-341.

———, «Die Firmung als Vollendung der Taufe. Edward Schillebeeckx zum 60. Geburstag», *TQ* 154 (1974) 26-47.

LAMBERTS, J., «Eucharist and the Holy Spirit», *TD* 34 (1987) 51-55.

LAMBIASI, F., *Lo Spirito Santo*: mistero e presenza. Per una sintesi di pneumatologia, Bologna 1987.

LAMPE, G.W., *The Seal of the Spirit*: A Study in the Doctrine of Baptism and Confirmation in the New Testament and the Fathers, London 1951.

———, *God as Spirit*, Oxford 1977.

LANNE, E., «The Liturgical and Spiritual Tradition among the Orthodox», *Dia* 3 (1969) 342-351.

———, ed. *Lo Spirito Santo e la Chiesa*, Roma 1970.

———, «L'acqua e l'unzione nelle chiese orientali», *SA* 87 (1983) 137-156.

LAWLER, A.G., *Symbol and Sacrament*. A Contemporary Sacramental Theology, New York 1987.

LÉCUYER, J., «Le sacerdoce des fidèles chez les Pères», *LMD* 27 (1951) 7-50.

———, «La grâce de la consécration épiscopale», *RSPT* 36 (1952) 389-417.

LÉCUYER, J., *Le sacerdoce dans le mystère du Christ*, Paris 1957.

———, «La confirmation et la Pentecôte chez les Pères», *LMD* 54 (1958) 23-51.

———, «La théologie de l'anaphore», *LOS* 5 (1961) 385-412.

LEE, R.D., «Epiclesis and Ecumenical Dialogue», *Dia* 9 (1974) 56-62.

LEEMING, B., *Principles of Sacramental Theology*, London 1960.

LEFEBVRE, G., *The Spirit of Worship*, New York 1959.

LEGRAND, H.M., «The "Indelible" Character and the Theology of Ministry», *Con* 8 (1972) 54-62.

———, «Theology and the Election of Bishops in the Early Church», *Con* 8 (1972) 31-42.

LENGELING, E., «Blessing of Baptismal Water in the Roman Rite», *Con* 3 (1967) 35-37.

L'HUILLIER, P., «Théologie de l'épiclèse», *VC* 14 (1960) 306-327.

LIESAL, N., *The Eucharistic Liturgies of the Eastern Churches*, Minnesota 1963.

LODI, E., *Infondi lo Spirito degli Apostoli*. Teologia liturgico-ecumenica del ministero ordinato, Padova 1987.

LONERGAN, B., «Mission and the Spirit», *Con* 10 (1974) 69-78.

LOSSKY, V., *Orthodox Theology*. An Introduction, New York 1978.

———, *In the Image and Likeness of God*, New York 1985.

———, *The Mystical Theology of the Eastern Church*, Cambridge 1991.

LUFTI, L., «Der pneumatologische Aspekt der Sakramente der christlichen Mystagogie», *Kyr* (1972) 97-106.

MACKEY, J.P., «The Holy Spirit: Relativizing the Divergent Approaches of East and West», *ITQ* 48 (1981) 256-267.

———, *Christian Experience of God as Trinity*, London 1983.

MARSH, T., «The Theology of Confirmation», in *The Sacraments*. Readings in *Contemporary Sacramental Theology*, ed. M.J. Taylor, New York 1981, 105-115.

MARTELET, G., «On a Definition of the Holy Spirit through the Multiform Generation of Christ», *LV* 28 (1973) 54-76.

MAZZA, E., *The Eucharistic Prayers of the Roman Rite*, New York 1986.

McBRIEN, R.P., *Church*. The Continuing Quest, New York 1970.

McDONNELL, K., «A Trinitarian Theology of the Holy Spirit?», *TS* 46 (1985) 193-220.

McKENNA, J.H., *Eucharist and the Holy Spirit*. The Eucharistic Epiclesis in the Twentieth Century Theology, London 1977.

———, «Eucharistic Epiclesis: Myopia or Microcosm?», *TS* 35 (1975) 265-284.

MEYENDORFF, J., *The Orthodox Church*, London 1962.

MEYENDORFF, J., «Notes on the Orthodox Understanding of the Eucharist», *Con* 3 (1967) 51-58.

———, *Catholicity and the Church*, New York 1983.

MITCHELL, L., *Baptismal Anointing*, Notre Dame 1978.

MÖHLER, J.A., *Die Einheit in der Kirche oder das Prinzip des Katholizismus*, Darmstadt 1957.

MOLTMANN, J., *God in Creation*. An Ecological Doctrine of Creation, London 1985.

———, *The Church in the Power of the Spirit*, London 1989.

———, *The Way of Jesus Christ*: Christology in Messianic Dimensions, London 1990.

———, *The Spirit of Life*. A Universal Affirmation, London 1992.

MÜHLEN, H., «Die Firmung als sakramentales Zeichen der heilsgeschichtlichen Selbstüberlieferung des Geistes Christi», *TG* 57 (1967) 263-286.

NEUNHEUSER, B., «Der Heilige Geist der Liturgie», *TG* 35 (1943) 11-24.

———, *Baptism and Confirmation*, New York 1963.

———, «Taufe im Geist. Der heilige Geist in den Riten der Taufsliturgie», *AL* 12 (1970) 268-284.

NICHOLAS, A., *Theology in the Russian Diaspora*. Church, Fathers, Eucharist in Nikolai Afanas'ev (1893-1966), Cambridge 1989.

NISSIOTIS, N., «Spirit, Church and Ministry», *TTo* 19 (1962) 484-500.

———, «Pneumatologie orthodoxe», in *Le Saint Esprit*, ed. F.J. Leenhardt, Geneva 1963, 85-107.

———, «Importance of the Doctrine of the Trinity for Church Life and Theology», in *The Orthodox Ethos*: vol. I, ed. A.J. Philippou, Oxford 1964, 32-70

———, «La pneumatologie ecclésiologique au service de l'unité», *Ist* 12 (1967) 323-340.

———, «Pneumatological Christology as a Presupposition of Ecclesiology», *Oec* 2 (1967) 235-252.

———, *Die Theologie der Östkirche in ökumenischen Dialog*: Kirche und Welt in Orthodoxer Sicht, Stuttgart 1968.

———, «Called to Unity. The Significance of the Invocation of the Spirit for Church Unity», in *Lausanne 77*. Faith and Order Paper no: 82, Geneva 1977, 48-64.

———, «The Church as a Sacramental Vision and the Challenge of Christian Witness», in *Church, Kingdom, World*. The Church as Mystery and Prophetic Sign, ed. G. Limouris, Geneva 1986, 99-126.

O'DONNELL, J., *The Mystery of the Triune God*, London 1988.

———, «In Him and Over Him: The Holy Spirit in the Life of Jesus», *Gre* 70 (1989) 25-45.

OESTERLEY, W.O.E., *The Jewish Background of the Christian Liturgy*, London 1965.

O'LEARY, P., «The Holy Spirit in the Church in Orthodox Theology», *ITQ* 46 (1979) 177-184.

OSBORNE, K.B., *Sacramental Theology*. A General Introduction, New York 1985.

————, *Priesthood*. A History of the Ordained Ministry in the Roman Catholic Church, New York 1989.

PARKER, T.D., «The Political Meaning of the Doctrine of the Trinity», *JR* 60 (1980) 165-184.

POURRATT, P., *Theology of the Sacraments*: A Study in Positive Theology, London 1930.

RAHNER, K., «The Theology of Symbol», in *Theological Investigations* vol. IV, New York 1966, 221-252.

————, «Priestly Existence», in *Theological Investigation*: vol. III, London 1967, 239-262.

————, «Experience of the Spirit and Existential Decision», *Con* 10 (1974) 38-46.

————, «Introductory Observations on Thomas Aquinas' Theology of the Sacraments in General», in *Theological Investigations*: vol. XV, New York 1976, 149-160.

————, *Foundations of Christian Faith*: An Introduction to the Idea of Christianity, New York 1978.

————, *The Church and the Sacraments*, London 1986.

RICHARD, D.S., «Problem of the [double] Epiclesis in the New Roman Eucharistic Prayers», *EL* 91 (1977) 193-202.

RICHARD, L., «The Witness and Mission of the Eastern Catholic Churches», *Dia* 15 (1980) 159-167.

RINAUDO, S., *La nuova Pentecoste della Chiesa*. Ciò che hanno detto in Concilio Vatican II e Paolo VI sullo Spirito Santo, Torino 1977.

ROBERTS, W.P., *Encouters with Christ*. Introduction to the Sacraments, New York 1985.

ROSATO, P.J., «Spirit Christology: Ambiguity and Promise», *TS* 38 (1977) 423-449.

————, «Called by God in the Holy Spirit. Pneumatological Insights into Ecumenism», *TER* 30 (1978) 110-126.

————, «Priesthood of the Baptized and the Priesthood of the Ordained», *Gre* 68 (1987) 215-266.

————, *Introduzione alla teologia dei Sacramenti*, Casale Monferrato 1992.

RYK, M., «The Holy Spirit's Role in the Deification of Man according to Contemporary Orthodox Theology», *Dia* 10 (1975) 24-39; 109-130.

SALAVILLE, S., *An Introduction to the Study of Eastern Liturgies*, London 1938.

————, «Epiclèse eucharistique» in *Dictionnaire de théologie catholique*: vol. V, eds. A. Vacant – E. Mangenot, Paris 1939, 194-299.

SCHILLEBEECKX, E., *De Sacramentele Heilseconomie*, Antwerp 1963.

————, *Christ the Sacrament of the Encounter with God*, London 1989.

————, *Church*. The Human Story of God, London 1990.

SCHLIER, H., «Über den Heiligen Geist. Eine neutestamentliche Untersuchung», *WW* 28 (1973) 24-33.

SCHMEMANN, A., *Of Water and the Spirit*, New York 1974.

————, *Church, World and Mission*. Reflections on Orthodoxy in the West, New York 1979.

————, *Introduction to Liturgical Theology*, New York 1986.

————, *For the Life of the World*, New York 1988.

————, *The Eucharist*, New York 1988.

SCHNACKENBURG, R., *The Church in the New Testament*, London 1968.

SCHOONENBERG, P., «Baptism with the Holy Spirit», *Con* 10 (1974) 20-37.

————, «Spirit Christology and Logos Christology», *Bij* 38 (1977) 350-375.

SCHULTZE, B., «Die dreifache Herabkunft des Heiligen Geistes in den östlichen Hochgebeten», *OS* 26 (1977) 105-143.

SCHÜRMANN, H., *Il vangelo di Luca*. Testo greco e traduzione: vol. I, Brescia 1983.

SERRA, D., «The Eschatological Role of the Spirit in the Lord's Supper», *DR* 11 (1973) 185-202.

SIMAN, E.P., *L'expérience de l'Esprit par l'Église d'après la tradition Syrienne d'Antioche*, Paris 1971.

SMIT, G.C., «Epiclèse et théologie des sacrements», *MSR* 15 (1958) 95-136.

STOMMEL, E., *Studien zur Epiklese der römischen Taufwasserweihe*, Bonn 1950.

SUENES, L., «The Charismatic Dimension of the Church», in *Council Speeches of Vatican II*, eds. H. Küng – Y. Congar, London 1964, 18-21.

SULLIVAN, S., *Readings in Sacramental Theology*, New Jersey 1965.

TAFT, R., «The Spirit of Eastern Christian Worship», *Dia* 12 (1977) 103-120.

TERANANT, P., «L'Esprit du Christ et l'intervention humaine dans l'envoi en mission. A l'époque Neo-Testamentaire», *NRT* 95 (1973) 367-392.

THOMPSON, J., «The Holy Spirit and the Trinity in Ecumenical Perspective», *ITQ* 47 (1980) 272-285.

THRONTON, L.S., «The Holy Spirit in Christian Initiation», *ECQ* 7 (1948) 53-69.

————, *Confirmation*. Its Place in the Baptismal Mystery, Westminster 1954.

TILLARD, J.M.R., *L'Eucharistie, pâque de l'Église*, Paris 1964.

TILLARD, J.M.R., «L'Eucharistie et le Saint-Esprit», *NRT* 90 (1968) 363-387; Eng. vers. «The Eucharist and the Holy Spirit», *TD* 17 (1969) 133-138.

————— «The Ordained "Ministry" and the Priesthood of Christ», *OC* 14 (1978) 231-246.

—————, «Blessing, Sacramentality, and Epiclesis», *Con* 21 (1985) 70-86.

TONY, P.K., «A Study of Thematic Differences Between Eastern and Western Religious Thought», *JES* 10 (1973) 337-360.

TORRANCE, T.F., «Come Creator Spirit, for the Renewal of Worship and Witness», in *Theological Foundations for Ministry*, ed. R.S. Anderson, Edinburgh 1979, 370-389.

—————, *Trinitarian Perspectives*. Towards Doctrinal Agreement, Edinburgh 1994.

VAGAGGINI, C., *Theological Dimensions of the Liturgy*. A General Treatise on the Theology of the Liturgy, Minnesota 1977.

VANDENBROUCKE, F., «Esprit Saint et structure ecclésiale selon la liturgie», *QLP* 39 (1958) 115-131.

VERHEUL, A., *Introduction to the Liturgy*. Towards a Theology of Worship, Westminster 1987.

VISCHER, L., *La confirmation au cours des siècles*. Contribution au débat sur le problème de la confirmation, Neuchatel 1959.

—————, «The Epiclesis, Sign of Unity and Renewal», *SL* 6 (1967) 30-39.

—————, ed. *Spirit of God, Spirit of Christ*: Ecumenical Reflections on the Filioque Controversy. Faith and Order Paper no: 103, London 1981.

VOGEL, C., «An Alienated Liturgy», *Con* 8 (1972) 11-25.

WAINWRIGHT, G., *Eucharist and Eschatology*, London 1971.

—————, «Some Theological Aspects of Ordination», *SL* 13 (1979).

WONG, J.H.P., «The Holy Spirit in the Life of Jesus and of the Christian», *Gre* 73 (1992) 57-95.

WRIGHT, J.H., «The Church: Community of the Holy Spirit», *TS* 48 (1987) 25-44.

WYBREW, H., *The Orthodox Liturgy*: The Development of the Eucharistic Liturgy in the Byzantine Rite, London 1990.

YARNOLDS, E., *The Awe-Inspiring Rites of Initiation*. Baptismal Homilies of the Fourth Century, London 1972.

ZEIDLER, J.C., «Anointing», in *The New Dictionary of Sacramental Worship*, ed. P.E. Fink, Dublin 1990, 56-57.

ZIZIOULAS, J., «Some Reflections on Baptism, Confirmation and Eucharist», *Sob* 5 (1969) 644-652.

—————, «Ordination and Communion», *SE* 6 (1970) 187-192.

—————, «The Eucharistic Community and the Catholicity of the Church», *OC* 6 (1970) 314-337.

ZIZIOULAS, J., «Ordination - A Sacrament?», *Con* 8 (1972) 33-40.

———, «The Pneumatological Dimension of the Church», *ICR* 1 (1974) 142-158.

———, «Apostolic Continuity and Orthodox Theology: Towards a Synthesis of Two Perspectives», *VTQ* 19 (1975) 75-108.

———, *Being as Communion*: Studies in Personhood and the Church, New York 1985.

INDEX OF AUTHORS

TABLE OF CONTENTS

PART THREE
SYNTHESIS AND CONCLUSION
REGARDING CARDINAL YVES CONGAR'S CONCEPT
OF THE EPICLESIS

Riproduzione anastatica: 3 novembre 1995
Tipografia Poliglotta della Pontificia Università Gregoriana
Piazza della Pilotta, 4 – 00187 Roma